FALLING FAMILIES
FALLEN CHILDREN

2E

OTHER BOOKS
by
Raymond Lloyd Richmond, Ph.D.

ANGER AND FORGIVENESS
HEALING
PSYCHOLOGY FROM THE HEART
PRAYING THE LITURGY OF THE HOURS
DISASTERS AND TRAUMA
THOUGH DEMONS GLOAT
BEYOND THE VEIL OF LUST
BOUNDARIES
WEIGHT REDUCTION

FALLING FAMILIES
FALLEN CHILDREN

2E

Second Edition

Raymond Lloyd Richmond, Ph.D.

ISBN-13: 978-1981123681

ISBN-10: 1981123687

CONTENTS

Part Two
Questions and Answers

PREFACE

Christianity is astonishingly simple. If only we loved God with all our hearts, all our souls, all our strength, and all our minds, we would refuse to commit sin. If only we took up the Cross and followed Christ, we would refuse to hate. But many of our family experiences during childhood fill us with anger and hatred. Mistreatment, manipulation, a lack of emotional awareness, and hypocrisy make us vulnerable to the influence of evil, and they become impediments to love.

In the early years of the Church—indeed, during the first few centuries of Christianity—Christians lived in the midst of pagan and heathen societies. Consequently, Christians survived by strengthening their Christian identity. That is, the focus of their lives became the definition and preservation of true Christian doctrine.

This focus on doctrine, however, was not just a matter of abstract theology. It applied directly to practical matters of everyday life. Just look at the epistles of Saint Paul, who was among the first to put this doctrine into writing so as to defend and preserve true Christian conduct in the early Christian communities.

Consider also two early Christian documents: the *Didache* and the *Letter Attributed to Barnabus*. Both of these documents provide detailed descriptions of Christian behavior, in regards both to the practice of virtue and also to the avoidance of immoral conduct.

In all of this, though, notice to whom the writers speak: to Christians.

So where have all the Christians gone? Where is faith?

The Politicization of Christianity

In her early years, the Church lived in a hostile, anti-Christian environment. Although she tried to convert the pagans and heathens to Christianity, her primary appeal was to her own children.

Once the emperor Constantine made Christianity the formal religion of the Roman Empire, however, everything began to change. Christians lost their inner mystical sense of alertness to the hostility of the world. After all, once the world was declared to be Christian, Christians could let their guard down—or so they thought. In so far as they could define society itself as Christian, they did not need to be concerned with maintaining a personal spiritual battle against evil, especially as it manifested in pagan society. Thus a profound sense of the Christian mystical battle with evil ultimately gave way to a complacent conformity to superficially "Christian" laws and social conventions. Christian faith gradually became a mere social identity—a requirement, as it were—for social status and acceptance. Essentially, this politicization of Christianity has been the governing identity of Western society for centuries.

But now, in the world today, we are experiencing the unraveling of this complacency. We are witnessing the disintegration of the illusion of a "Christian" society. We watch in horror as baptized Christians, right along with their non-Christian neighbors, work subversively to shake off the "burdensome yoke" of Christian morality.

The Christian Task: To Become Christian

No one can stop the slow disintegration of our once "Christian" society by stepping in front of it. It's a losing battle because the underlying spiritual battle against evil was lost by "Christian" society centuries ago through its own arrogance, complacency, and neglect.

So what can we do? We need to convert ourselves back to real Christianity.

We need to stop telling secular society how to live, and we need to start telling ourselves how Christians are supposed to live. We need to start living genuine Christian lifestyles so that we can witness our faith to those who have lost faith. And perhaps in doing this we will rediscover, as Saint Ignatius of Antioch wrote in his letter to the Romans (3:3), that Christianity's quiet witness of eternal truth manifests its greatness when it, like Christ Himself, triumphs over the world's hatred.

Rediscovering Christian Identity

Imagine if all Christians today had the identity witnessed by the *Didache*, an anonymous early Christian treatise (also known as *The Teaching of the Twelve Apostles*) from the first century that detailed some core elements of the Christian lifestyle. Imagine if today we could say things such as these with the same unified conviction as the early Christians:

- Christians' lives are ordered by chastity.

- Christians respect the sanctity of Holy Matrimony and do not divorce and remarry.

- Christians do not kill an unborn child through abortion, nor destroy it after birth.

- Christians respect their bodies as temples of the Holy Spirit and clothe themselves with dignity by dressing modestly.

- Christians live sober lives and do not smoke cigarettes, abuse alcohol, or use marijuana or other drugs.

• Christians resist cultural brainwashing by not concerning themselves with glamor, lust, competition, or popular entertainment.

Yes, imagine if all Christians had a common Christian identity and refused to engage in the wickedness of the world around them. What if all Christians refused to support the fundamentally anti-Christian arts, entertainment, and advertising industries? What if all Christians refused to spend money on movies and popular magazines? What if all Christians refused to wear immodest clothes? What if all Christians refused to allow their minds to be corrupted by social media, movies, and television? What if all Christians refused to waste time with video games and sports? Think of the power that Christian behavior could have in witnessing a genuine love for God in a world grown cold with pride, lust and hatred.

But now, sadly, Christian behavior has no more power than the filth it wallows in. That's why we are in the mess we're in today.

That's why so many families are falling into psychological and spiritual dysfunction. Contemporary family life has been corrupted and impaired with liberal, anti-Christian ideology; traditional Christian values of integrity, personal responsibility, and honesty have been expunged from secular society, leaving children in a desolate moral wasteland. And that's why so many children have forsaken the Way of Perfection and have fallen into the anti-

Christian social wasteland of the Way of Doom.

Deliverance

Most people today who call themselves *Christian* are too much under the influence of evil spirits (see Chapter 27) to have a common Christian identity. Nevertheless, all Christian individuals can make a personal vow to seek deliverance from the evil in the world around them that has infected their hearts. Thereafter, a confident personal Christian identity will serve as a noble indicator of their freedom from demonic influence.

So, if you have committed your life to chastity and have renounced all sexual activity outside Holy Matrimony and all lustful sexual activity within it, and if you have committed your life to modesty and have renounced immodest clothing, foul language, and competition, and if you have committed your life to respecting your body and have renounced all drugs, addictions, and sloth, and if you have committed your life to forgiveness, patience, and kindness and can renounce all temptations to hatred, lust, and anger when they arise, then you have the confident Christian identity necessary to working out your salvation with the fear and trembling of which Saint Paul spoke (see Philippians 2:12b).

But realize that once you choose to live a devout spiritual life you step onto a path that leads out of the city and right to your own crucifixion. You have to walk out knowing you will never come back. If you turn back, there is nothing but hell. And if you begin to doubt and hesitate and look to the world to entertain you along the way, rest assured that the Cross won't come to get you—but the devil himself will soon show up, wearing a nice tuxedo, holding the door to his limousine, just for you. Which is why you now see so many "Christians" happily waving to you from their limos as they ride by.

Lord, how shall the young remain sinless?
By obeying Your word.
　　　　　　　　　　— *Psalm* 119:9

Part One

FALLING FAMILIES

FALLEN CHILDREN

Do not provoke your children to anger, but bring them up with the training and instruction of the Lord.

Ephesians 6:4

1 BACKGROUND

No one is an island, according to the old saying, and so it should be recognized that no psychological problem is ever a purely individual problem. Therefore, any psychological distress felt by an individual has roots in society at large.

Contemporary American society certainly offers ample opportunity for psychological distress. In a permissive, self-indulgent society, there is little use for self-discipline and self-restraint. Lacking traditional values of integrity, personal responsibility, and honesty, culture loses any sense of moral direction, and anything goes. When anything goes, nothing means anything, and all paths lead nowhere. And right in the middle of nowhere you are sure to find distress, anxiety, and depression.

This does not mean, however, that all psychological problems can be solved by changing society. Although political activists work to spread this ideology through social media, for the sake of mental and spiritual health the individual must be responsible for recognizing and transcending—or "seeing through"—all the social illusions that can lead a person astray. Many persons have been brought to psychological and spiritual disaster by believing that they can change, control, or be responsible for anyone else.

In fact, any attempt to control the behavior of another person is just an unconscious attempt to control—that is, keep hidden, rather than face up to and heal—your own inner life, a life that to some persons is so embarrassing and shameful that they are terrified of anyone catching a glimpse of it. Nevertheless, until you have made peace with yourself you will never be able to live in peace with anyone else. So, as much as you might like to change others, you can't change anyone but yourself. Then, it can be hoped, your example might influence others to change themselves.

This is how it works in life, and this is how it works in a family.

2   FAMILY SYSTEMS

In the early part of the 20th century, the psychologist Carl Jung noted that children tend to live out the unconscious conflicts of their parents. Furthermore, as a branch of psychotherapy called *Family Systems Theory* teaches, all too often a child will be marked as a "problem" or the "black sheep" of the family—the *Identified Patient*, in Family Systems language—when really the entire family is locked into some dysfunctional pattern of interaction.

A stunning example of a child "acting out" a family dysfunction can be seen in the 1964 movie, *The Chalk Garden*. The movie dramatizes a basic problem: that parents often have children because of their own desires; perhaps they need to feel loved, and they believe that a child's helplessness will be a source of love; or perhaps they have in mind a particular role for the child to fulfill. As a result, they end up expecting that the child will grow up to be totally obedient to them as a sign of love. But the child feels suffocated by the parents' desire and tries to find his or her own destiny. This search for independence only marks the child, in the parents' minds, as disobedient, ungrateful, and unloving. Parental "love" quickly turns to hate and disaster follows.

> Note carefully, however, that parents must insist that the children be obedient to the teachings of the Church and to its obligations, such as Mass attendance (on Sundays and Holy Days of Obligation) and Confession. In asserting such discipline, parents are not saying, "Be obedient to me" but are saying, "Be obedient to God"—and then parents must set an example by their own obedience to God.

Many of the clinical disorders of infancy, childhood, and adolescence, such as the Communication Disorders (e.g., stuttering), Learning Disorders, Attention-Deficit and Disruptive Behavior Disorders, Conduct Disorders, Elimination Disorders (e.g., bedwetting), and Sleep Disorders (e.g., nightmares) can all have origins within the overall family system, whereby the child acts out through his or her psychological symptoms the hidden anxiety and conflicts of the parents (and siblings).

In such cases, it's always easiest to medicate the "Identified Patient" and then ignore the rest of the family. It would be far better, and more clinically appropriate, to ask some specific—and painful—questions about how the child's symptoms may be reflecting parental conflicts and family anxiety.

Failed Communication

The family process can be relatively easy and smooth if parents learn how to communicate effectively with their children. If parents are sufficiently committed to their own moral beliefs—if they have any—they can encourage their children to learn about and discuss those beliefs as they grow up, and there won't be anything for the children to challenge as they get older.

But if parents are authoritarian, do not seek to have a caring emotional awareness of their children, and impose their beliefs on their children, that only gives the children a reason to question and resent their parents.

> So what is an authoritarian parent? It is someone who, when questioned, responds defensively and says, "Because I say so, that's why!"

Also, if parents are lukewarm or lacking in heartfelt moral and spiritual convictions, their children will grow up without any sense of honest, compassionate discipline. Most children are smart enough to realize that when parents give them too much freedom it really means that the parents don't care—or don't know any better themselves. So the children can end up with such profound emptiness and guilt about the meaningless pursuit of self-gratification that they question—or even defy—everything out of pure frustration. And where does that lead? It leads right to bitter identity confusion, anger, and depression.

Consequently, children can grow up feeling worthless because their parents' lives are valueless—that is, lacking in meaningful, spiritual values. Communication fails because the family is governed by a fear of mutual cooperation in the task of living a holy life.

Hence, much of childhood "acting out" (which technically means communicating behaviorally rather than verbally) is the children's unconscious attempt to prove to the parents that they are full of you-know-what.

Lack of "Normality"

Many persons think that if someone looks ordinary then he or she must be "normal." Well, those who have some psychological insight know what a dysfunctional family is, and they know very well that above all else dysfunctional families do their very best to always look ordinary and "nice." Broken by adultery, alcoholism, contradictions, divorce, drug use, emotional abuse, hidden agendas, physical abuse, sexual abuse, violence—take your pick—the whole family devotes a tremendous effort to keeping family "secrets," and each family member adopts a discrete role to play in the deception held up to the outside world.

The problem for children in such families is that they have to live a lie. In fact, some of these children can become quite skilled in passing themselves off as nice, likable, normal children with wonderful futures and no problems. Other children can become quite skilled in developing images as risk-taking rebels; but that image, too, is just a lie, created as a flash of adrenaline-charged excitement to ward off dull feelings of despair. So, too, cigarettes, alcohol, marijuana, tattoos, occult practices, and deafening music played with hellish theatrical effects are all attempts to flirt with death because a person has no sense of real life.

Therefore, outward appearances don't really count for much. They can easily hide a boiling pot of shame, fear, anger, cynicism, frustration, and loneliness.

Wealth

People are always looking at outward signs of wealth and saying, "What a shame. She had everything a child could want. How could she have done that?" Well, she had everything, all right—except love.

We are especially prone to thinking that material success brings "happiness." We are so indoctrinated with this belief that if someone has material success we just assume that he or she must be "happy." We rarely stop to ask ourselves if there might be something else to life, something missing in the anti-Christian social media, advertisements, television, sports, music, and movies that surround us.

Yes, a child can grow up in a wealthy family with a million-dollar house and for all outward appearances look normal and happy. So what's the problem? Maybe the problem has to do with parents

- who do not bother to ask their children what they are thinking or feeling;

- who do not try to understand their children's emotional experiences but rather control and manipulate the children to serve the parents' desires;

- who do not touch their children in kindness and affection;

- who do not sit down to eat with their children;

- who are so busy accumulating social status and wealth that they do not have time to talk to their children;

- who trample on their neighbors and colleagues in order to get a few steps ahead of anyone else;

- who have shattered their family's security with adultery and divorce;

- who are so much a product of our permissive anti-Christian society that they have forsaken self-restraint and self-discipline and cannot even correct their children when they do something wrong.

So imagine: some children seem to have everything. They

should be normal and happy. What's the problem? How could they be dysfunctional?

3   MARRIAGE

Consider the *holy* meaning of marriage.

Christian marriage has its origin in the concept of a man and a woman giving themselves to each other for life in order to bring new life into the world: to create a family that honors such values as faith, hope, and love, and, in so doing, encourages the salvation of all individuals in the family. Both spouses must help each other through mutual cooperation to overcome any emotional deficits from childhood and to ensure that the children are raised in an atmosphere of kindness, wise guidance, and protection from evil. There is no place in a Christian marriage for manipulation, cynicism, sarcasm, and hostility—or lust. The sacrament of marriage guarantees a commitment to a holy life. Marriage, therefore, is an act of service to God, not a psychological "right" to use a sex "partner" to soothe a fear of emptiness with erotic pleasure.

Across cultures and through the ages, however, the concept of marriage has been perverted into a mere economic contract that simply guarantees the closed transmission of wealth, status, and power, all the while giving free rein to lust. Even the concept of "family" is irrelevant to this kind of marriage, except in so far as children serve as necessary and vital agents of hereditary transmission. Keep in mind that none of these economic concerns have anything to do with romance—or real love.

When most people today think of marriage, however, they think of "love." Yet even though they might talk about committed relationships, to what is their "commitment"? Free sex? Financial security? Self-gratification? What sort of commitments are these? Where is love?

When marriage is just a commitment to economics or lust there is no place in it for the spiritual welfare of the husband, wife, and children. The real commitment of an indissoluble marriage between a man and a woman for the sake of their natural children is the glue that has held Christian society together for ages. Altering this concept is like someone remodeling a house who decides that removing a load-bearing wall will give the house more openness—but as soon as the wall is removed, the whole house collapses.

Over the last several decades, though, even Christians themselves have so defiled the sanctity of marriage with lust, contraception, cohabitation, in vitro fertilization, surrogacy, adultery, abortion, divorce, remarriage after divorce, blended families—and a general indifference to-ward the liturgical celebration of Holy Matrimony—that marriage has been turned into a social cesspool. Is this love?

Love

Love. It's a word often used and just as often misused—and here is precisely where the psychological problems begin. The philosopher Aristotle said that "to love is to wish good to someone."[1] Therefore, all the moral decisions about marriage and family actually derive psychologically from love—real love, not the "love" of popular fantasy. Lust, adultery, divorce, abortion, contraception, in vitro fertilization, surrogacy, and euthanasia, for example, all defile love through a focus on personal pleasure and convenience, at the expense of the dignity—and even the life—of another human being.

Sadly, contemporary culture tends to think of "love" as a way to find personal fulfillment in life. That is, each "partner" (i.e., sex partner) expects the other "partner" to fill up the existential void in his or her life. Ultimately, this is *impossible*. It's impossible to heal your own emotional brokenness through the body of another person—a mere sex object—as mortal and broken as you are.[2]

This concept of the *impossible* can be approximated by the question, "What is the sound of one hand clapping?"

For example, I have seen both men and women who have

tried to seduce a woman to get from her the nurturing and attention they never received from their mothers. And I have seen both women and men who have tried to seduce a man to get from him the protection and attention they never received from their fathers. In the end it's all an impossibility. The moral is simple, and cuts across the board, male and female, heterosexual and homosexual: *you can never seduce your despair, and you can never find real love through any form of sexual activity.*

Thus, no one needs a "partner" to have a meaningful life. Notice, though, that having a *meaningful life* is not the same as being a *good citizen*. A good citizen is a spiritually empty, insatiable consumer, and because of the efforts of the advertising and entertainment industries lust has become a prime consumer activity. So let's give a round of applause to the advertising and entertainment industries that are driving our culture away from real love and into the insanity of perversion and spiritual doom. Ah, can you hear it?—the pathetic sound of one hand clapping.

4   DIVORCE

In 1997, a prominent psychologist wrote an article which appeared in an American psychological journal. The author reviewed several commonly held beliefs about psychology, and one of his claims was that the brain is quite resilient to the effects of trauma. He noted that rats which had been subjected to trauma as infants developed into apparently well-adjusted adults.

I wrote a response[1] to his claim in which I noted that, unlike animals, we humans have language—along with a memory system with which to process it—and that trauma has a unique linguistic way of lingering in our unconscious minds. Humans, just like rats, may give the appearance of being well-adjusted, but, as any experienced mental health clinician has seen over and over, many of the seemingly "well-adjusted" individuals walking around in our society are tormented by inner lives of emptiness and self-destructive despair.

Professor, physician, lawyer—they all say the same thing to me in the consulting room: "I feel like mush inside."

Why? Well, most of them, as children, saw their families shattered by divorce.

We take divorce so much for granted today that it is hard *not* to find someone who has been divorced or who has married someone who has been divorced or who has parents or relatives who have divorced. Yet, like that prominent psychologist, we brush it off and say, "It doesn't matter."

But it does matter.

Children need to have both a mother and a father who will protect them, care for them, teach them, and guide them through darkness into the way of peace. Even the trauma of losing a parent to death is less a trauma than losing a parent to divorce, for in divorce a parent essentially says to a child—and to a spouse—"My personal desires are more important to me than is your welfare. This family is nothing to me, and you are just objects to be moved around like pawns in my self-indulgent search for happiness."

Laboratory rats have only cheese and mazes. What can they say about trauma? Children, however, have phobias, eating disorders, alcohol, cigarettes, drugs, unwanted pregnancies, sexual diseases, abortion—and suicide, and guns—to "speak" about their traumas.

Our anti-Christian culture of insanity, however, continues to look at divorce and say, "It doesn't matter." Sadly, many Catholics follow along, right in step with the culture around them, believing that if everyone else does it, what's wrong with it?

> Neither shall you allege the example of the many as an excuse for doing wrong.
>
> — Exodus 23:2

5   THE FATHER

We all need mothers—just as almost every animal in this world needs a mother. A mother's role, right from the child's conception, is to nurture the child so that the child can develop strength and inner security. To do this, the mother must provide comfort and tactile security so that the child can experience the bliss of resting peacefully in total surrender to the mother's gentle love. Then, as the child gets older, the mother must provide the child with hope and encouragement as the child explores and encounters the world.

> The Blessed Virgin did this perfectly for the child Jesus. The Bible witnesses to it: "Blessed is the womb that carried you and the breasts at which you nursed," we hear from Luke 11:27.
>
> Look at the icon of *Our Mother of Perpetual Help*. At the sight of the Cross, the child Jesus leaps into His mother's arms, one sandal dangling from His foot as testimony to His haste in seeking out His mother's protection. Notice this well: a mother's protection, until the time is ripe for the real Cross. Jesus didn't run to His

mother to hide from the Cross; He ran to His mother
to get comfort to face the Cross. Thus a mother must
be a solid core of faith in the family so as to teach her
children how to pray, to prepare them for the journey
to their own crosses.

If the mother fails in her task by being emotionally cold
or distant, or by being critical rather than supportive, or
by being manipulative rather than understanding, the
child will be crippled, at the least, with a terrifying sense
of emotional emptiness and, at the worst, with a terrifying
sense of being hated. Still, all is not lost, because the father,
if he does his job,[1] can "fill in" the lack left by the mother.

So here we come to the role of a father. A father must
"come between" a mother and the child to sever the child's
natural bond of dependence on the mother and to lead the
child out into the world so that the child can develop his
or her talents and take up a meaningful, productive life
of honesty and integrity. In doing this, though, the father
does not destroy the child's need for a mother; instead, the
father redefines the child's experience of a mother.

In this regard, consider that most children experience the
delight of being fed and protected by a mother when they
are helpless infants. In fact, if they don't experience it, they
die. The delight of this early infantile experience, which
makes no demands on us and leaves us free simply to enjoy
it, is at the root of our adult yearnings for a "utopia" in
which all of our needs are taken care of effortlessly.

But to function responsibly as an adult, a child must pass beyond this care-free infantile state of dependence on a mother. This psychological passage depends on the guidance of a strong and dependable father. If this task fails because of a missing father, the child will remain neurotically dependent on maternal care and will be afflicted with doubts and anxieties about assuming personal responsibility in the world. Moreover, the child's talents will either remain buried in fear or will be expressed largely through an unconscious grandiosity. Also, alcoholism and drug addictions can develop in adolescence and adulthood, because all addictions have their roots in a desire to escape the demands of personal responsibilities and return to an idyllic feeling of care-free bliss.

A child, therefore, has three essential tasks which must be accomplished under the guidance of a father.

1. To learn how the world works.

The father must teach the child not only about the abstract—and often dangerous—dynamics of social relationships beyond the family itself but also about practical rules governing the physical world, including honest, productive work in the world.

> Imagine a primitive society of forest dwellers. To teach the child how the world "works," the father must take the child out into the depths of the forest and show

the child how to survive and eat by using weapons, building fires, and making shelters. Now, the modern world may not be a forest anymore—though it is often enough called a jungle—yet the forest metaphor aptly describes the process by which a father must teach a child "how the world works" and how to survive in it.

2. To learn to trust.

A child will trust a nurturing mother. This sort of trust is a necessary part of mother-infant bonding for the sake of the infant's physical survival.

A deeper trust, though, requires that the child grow to depend on and respect the father, a person *different* from the mother from whom the child originated; that is, the father is a *different body* and a *different gender* from the mother. The father—and only a father—can therefore teach the child to enter the world and encounter *difference* confidently.

But, to be a successful teacher, the father must teach from the place of his own faith and obedience. In other words, the father must live from his heart the rules he teaches to his children. In witnessing their father's faith and obedience, the children can learn to trust him through his own integrity. Otherwise, the children will see him for a hypocrite and will disavow—openly or secretly—everything he represents.

3. *To learn to trust oneself.*

As a child receives instruction from a trustworthy father and develops a sense of confidence under the father's compassionate guidance, the child will then be able to function more and more independently, assimilating the father's external guidance into an internal, psychological confidence.

> First the father builds a fire, saying to the child, "Watch me." Then the father encourages the child to build the fire. Finally the child goes off into the forest alone, and builds a fire on his own, confident in what he learned from his father.

True Love is Hard Work

Living a genuine Christian life is hard work. It doesn't just occur by itself. It requires discipline. It's tedious. It's often frightening. It requires constant effort to monitor our feelings and the impulses that arise with our feelings, and to override those impulses—those signs of what we want personally—with a firm decision to live a holy lifestyle by subordinating our wills to doing God's will.

Consequently, for a child to learn how to live a Christian life the child needs parents who can teach the child both through words and through actions that they are willing to do the hard work themselves. So it's worth repeating:

living a genuine Christian life is hard work. It's all far easier to serve the devil by doing whatever we want. *Do what thou wilt.* That's the pernicious motto of Satanism.

Lack

Now, considering all of this about the role of a father, look about you and see how many fathers fail miserably in their responsibilities. How many fathers are absent from the family because they are emotionally insensitive to their children's needs? How many fathers are absent from the family because they are preoccupied with work or sports? How many fathers are absent from the family because of divorce? How many fathers are absent from the family because their adultery draws them away to another woman—or, sad to say, to another man? How many fathers are absent from the family because they are preoccupied with their own pride and arrogance? How many fathers are absent from the family because of alcoholism? How many fathers are absent from the family because they were nothing more than sperm donors in a moment of lust? How many fathers are absent from the family because a woman decided she didn't need a man to have a child? It can go on and on. And it does.

> Consider communities in which single mothers are the norm, rather than the exception. What do you see there? A male disrespect for women, low educational performance, social disobedience, violence, drug use,

child abuse, prostitution, and a general lack of social opportunity.

The sad thing is that when a father is absent—whether physically or emotionally—his lack causes a psychological lack in the children. Lacking understanding of how the world works, lacking trust in others, and lacking trust in themselves, children—whether they be boys or girls— become lost, insecure, and confused. They lack confidence. They lack real faith. They lack a spiritually meaningful future. They lack life. All because their fathers were lacking.

Unconscious Distortion

Please note, though, that all of this lack resulting from the lack of a father is, in many cases, largely unconscious.

Yes, some persons are truly crippled—both emotionally and socially—by the lack of a father, and their lives become dysfunctional and stuck. Sadly, some of them die in childhood from abuse.[2]

But other persons are able to keep up a surface appearance of functionality; they hold jobs, they get married, and they have children. Yet under the surface of normality a deep secret of anger and victimization is buried. Here are the dark roots of symptom after symptom of secret resentment for the father.

In the unconscious, however, the anger gets distorted because it is difficult for children to accept being angry with a father from whom they still desire a sign of love. To protect themselves from the threat of their own anger, then, the children distort that anger by turning it against themselves to ensure that they do *nothing*.

- Addictions (alcoholism, drug addiction, obesity, smoking, marijuana use, video games, casinos, etc.) allow them to feel filled when they are really empty; thus they *feel nothing*.

- Argumentativeness prevents them from accepting truth, which includes the truth that the father has failed them; thus they *accept nothing*.

- Being late for appointments and meetings prevents them from having to wait; thus they *wait for nothing*.

- Immodesty (revealing clothing, tattoos, gaudy make-up, piercings, etc.) prevents them from respecting their own bodies; thus they *respect nothing*.

- Learning disorders prevent them from discovering a world that seems hidden from them; thus they *discover nothing*.

- Mental confusion (often expressed by forgetting things, getting lost, or as difficulty with math) prevents them from engaging with the signs and symbols of life; thus they *engage with nothing.*

- Procrastination prevents them from stepping out into the world that they don't know how to negotiate in the first place; thus they *accomplish nothing.*

- Sexual preoccupation, whether as self-created mental fantasies, pornography, lust, or sexual acts (masturbation, fornication, adultery), prevents them from experiencing emotional intimacy; thus they are *intimate with nothing.*

- Suspiciousness prevents them from having to trust a world they fear; thus they *trust nothing.*

In the end, all these *nothings*, taken together, lead to the nothingness of death: both *symbolic death*, which keeps a child emotionally disabled as punishment for his or her anger, and *real death* through slow self-sabotage or through outright suicide by which the child, in making herself or himself the "missing one," draws attention away from the truth that the father has been missing from the child's life all along.

There is no current psychiatric diagnosis for this collection of symptoms, so I have named a psychoanalytic diagnosis: *Ira Patrem Latebrosa* (hidden anger at the father). This is an anger at the father that so cloaks itself in invisibility that a person afflicted with it will deny that it even exists. Yet it does exist, and the evidence above proves it, like tracks in the snow that reveal the presence of an animal lurking nearby.

EMOTIONAL ENMESHMENT WITH A MOTHER

When fathers are weak and lacking in compassionate command authority, mothers will often step in to take control of the family. More often than not this control will take the form of manipulation, using sulking, withdrawal, and anger to make others bend to the mothers' will.

Consequently, children in such families can become enmeshed with their mothers, seeking always to please the mothers, and always terrified of slipping up and drawing down on themselves the wrath of a slighted mother. As a result of always trying to do what their mothers want, such children, when they become adults, will be preoccupied with the thought of, "What would my mother want me to do?" Thus they will be lacking in a confident ability to think independently.

Many of these persons can fall into stifled, dysfunctional lives and suicidal tendencies. Nevertheless, some of these persons can function fairly well, and they can even give the impression of being good workers. But when faced with any stressful, trying situation that requires decisive action, these persons will be unable to assert a clear and confident command authority to cope with the situation; instead they will tend either to withdraw into fear or into sulking depression or to get angry and fly into a rage, essentially doing to others what their mothers did to them.

So, is there a cure for this? Yes, but as in many things psychological, it can be difficult to go there, because it means facing the truth. To overcome their enmeshment with their mothers, such individuals must admit something very true, but very repugnant: "I hate my father and mother." Yes, deep in their unconscious they hate their fathers for being weak, and they hate their mothers for being manipulative and controlling—but in defensive denial they will insist, "My father is (or was) a good man. And my mother is (or was) a long-suffering saint." Still, if only they can admit the truth about their hatred, then they can proceed along the path of psychotherapeutic healing. On that path they can face the childhood emotional pain of lacking fatherly guidance and protection and of being controlled and manipulated by a domineering mother. Once they face the truth of that pain, they can face—and overcome—the hatred they have long denied but that has long crippled their lives with indecision, withdrawal, and anger.

6   ANGER

We all feel hurt or irritated when someone or something obstructs our needs or desires. The obstruction can be something ordinary, such as what a child experiences when told that he or she cannot eat ice cream before dinner; it can be something more serious, such as someone being late for a meeting; or it can be something that might bring us to the boiling point, such as a rude driver who suddenly cuts in front of us.

Unlike the feeling of irritation, though, anger is not an emotion; instead, it's a *desire* to cause harm.[1] For many persons, this statement is counter-intuitive and confusing because it contradicts popularly held, but psychologically incorrect, cultural beliefs.

Consider here that emotions serve to inform us about our spontaneous reaction to the reality around us; we are not morally responsible for our emotions, and therefore they are not sins. In its true psychological sense, though, *anger* refers to **the desire to hurt the cause of an injury;** and *revenge* refers to accomplishing that hurt. Therefore, unlike emotions, anger and revenge are both acts of free will for which we are morally culpable.

Because anger is not a feeling, it is possible to "be" angry even though you do not feel anything. This is the problem with unconscious anger (see Chapter 34): you don't feel angry, so, even as the anger works its poison in you, you believe it isn't even there.

Revenge, too, has its way of being hidden from direct awareness. Although it can be enacted openly and actively through hostility, cursing, sarcasm, sexuality (pornography, promiscuity, adultery, masturbation, etc.), or disobedience to authority, it can also be enacted secretly and passively through passive-aggression as well as through self-sabotage—for example, drug use, alcohol abuse, gluttony, obesity, smoking, suicidality, or the inability to achieve goals (i.e., fear of success).

Anger has no fitting place in a family because, to be healthy, a family should be oriented toward love, growth, and mutual support, not revenge and hostility. But when parents fail to understand and guide their children's emotional experiences, the children will be fearful of the unknown, and they will be overwhelmed with negative beliefs about themselves:
    I don't matter.
    I have no right to succeed.
    I am worthless.
    I am bad.

Without my father's [or mother's] love I am doomed.
God hates me.

And resentment and anger will stain their lives.

In contrast to all the dysfunction of anger, then, we have
another option. That is, when we are hurt, we don't have
to fight back, trying to hurt others as they have hurt us.[2] If
we trust in God's perfect justice and providence to protect
us (see Chapter 25), then we can accept all injury quietly,
peacefully, and without grumbling or protest. Therefore,
despite our injuries, we can give patience, understanding,
compassion, forbearance, mercy, and forgiveness to those
who hurt us, all the while praying that ultimately they will
repent the injury they have done to us.

To do this, though, it is necessary that you admit openly
to yourself the truth of how you have been injured; furthermore, it is necessary that you then endeavor to feel
the entirety of the emotional pain caused by the injuries.
Many persons unwittingly block this healing process
because they cling to a false belief that they are responsible for and therefore must protect those—such as their
parents—who injured them. Sadly, rather than protecting
anyone, this unwillingness to admit the truth only drives
the hurt into the unconscious where it stews in hidden
resentment that causes psychological complications of
anxiety and depression, family enmeshment and loss of
personal autonomy, and physiological illnesses.

7   DOMESTIC VIOLENCE

As sure as there are marital problems, there are many couples who resort to violent confrontation. Those who seek to console, to understand, and to love are strong in wisdom; violence, however, has been said to be the last resort of the weak.

Although some people claim differently, domestic violence is not so much a political problem rooted in "male domination of women" as it is a psychological problem rooted in an unwillingness to take responsibility for one's own life. Granted, there are some persons—male and female— who are so filled with frustration and anger that they will attack anyone—including children, and pets—without provocation. But just as often there is provocation, and violence becomes a sly family dance. There are even some individuals so good at subtle provocation that they always come off looking like innocent victims. It's a dirty business overall.

The psychiatric[1] diagnosis called *Intermittent Explosive Disorder* is characterized by several discrete episodes of failure to resist aggressive impulses that result in serious assaultive acts or destruction of property, and it describes a sort of aggressiveness that is way out of proportion to anything that could have precipitated it. For example, a family member might go into a rage because the mashed potatoes at dinner have lumps in them. Or someone might throw a punch and start a fight after he accidentally bumps into another person who then says, "Watch where you're going!"

Nevertheless, this diagnosis, like any other psychological diagnosis, tells us little, if anything, about the underlying reasons for the behavior. It really amounts to nothing more than a fancy way of describing a bad temper in a person who cannot manage emotional hurt, forgive others, or live with true peace of mind.

Even in a case that seems "political"—say, for example, the wife wants to work outside the home and the husband does not want to allow her—the real problem derives from a lack of loving communication. The woman harbors anger and frustration toward her husband and criticizes him at every opportunity; the husband feels threatened, rejected, and humiliated, often triggering traumatic memories of abuse he suffered as a child. Violence erupts because real communication has degenerated into a power struggle. Neither person has approached the problem from a position of empathy and unconditional acceptance of the needs of the other. When empathy is lacking, everyone, including the children, suffers.

California law mandates that when a psychotherapist or any other mandated reporter has knowledge or suspicion of it, the "unjustifiable mental suffering" of a child witnessing family violence is to be reported as child abuse.

Offenders

Many persons who get violent have been abused in some way as children. When children are abused, they feel very helpless and vulnerable, and so unconscious defenses work very hard to keep this feeling under "control" by pushing it out of conscious awareness. When those children grow up, they may feel the unconsciously motivated urge to control and manipulate everyone in their home; whenever they feel insulted, all the old vulnerability "leaks out," and they can resort to anger and violence out of pure frustration for not being able to do anything else. (Remember: violence is the last resort of the weak and powerless.) In the end, those who "lose control" never really had any control in the first place; that is, they are under the control of their unconscious fears.

So, if you are prone to violence, the real "cure" in all this has three steps.

1. Admitting your old emotional wounds;

2. Recognizing when those wounds are being triggered by

an external provocation;

3. Mustering the self-discipline to walk away from the situation before the tension builds to violence.

This is an emotional process, not an intellectual process, so you don't learn it by reading about it; you learn it from dedicated practice.

The most effective treatment for men who are prone to domestic violence is group education and treatment in a men's group, rather than individual psychotherapy. Many domestic violence programs offer such treatment for men, whether they come voluntarily or whether they are mandated into treatment by the court after being arrested for violence.

> Note that in California, for example, domestic violence is illegal, period. It's considered a crime against the state, regardless of whether the abused person presses charges or not.

Non-offenders

As for those who are abused by violent offenders, there can be many reasons why a person gets involved with someone prone to violence. Sometimes it's a matter of having been abused as a child and unconsciously seeking out abusive patterns of behavior that seem "familiar." Sometimes it's a matter of being attracted to the illusions of control and power in another person that on the surface seem protective but that only mask the underlying aggression and violence. Sometimes it's a matter of having a rebellious and argumentative nature of one's own that "plays off" the hostility of another.

In any event, once subjected to violence, victims can begin to perceive the violence from the perspective of an external locus of control[2] and can then make the tragic mistake of blaming themselves for the abuse and trying to appease the offender. Regrettably, this only makes the victim all the more susceptible to further manipulation by the offender.

The only healthy way to cope with violence is to (a) seek physical safety; (b) encourage the offender to seek healing through proper treatment; and (c) for the sake of forgiveness, endeavor to set aside hatred and, if possible, work for reconciliation[3] with the offender.

8   CHILD ABUSE

Whenever parents are violent, with or without provocation, there is always the possibility of child abuse—and even animal abuse. Families can be very good at hiding their "secrets," so it might take an alert physician who notices a child's injuries, a teacher who notices a child's neglect, a veterinarian or animal control officer who notices a pet's neglect or injuries, or a dentist who notices facial injuries, to uncover the hidden violence in the family.

Moreover, with or without violence, child sexual abuse can be another hidden secret of even the most apparently upstanding families. The psychiatric diagnosis called *Pedophilia* is characterized by recurrent, intense sexually arousing fantasies, sexual urges, or behaviors involving sexual activity with a child or children generally less than 13 years old. Technically, though, this diagnosis cannot be made unless the fantasies, sexual urges, or behaviors cause clinically significant distress or impairment in social, occupational, or other important areas of functioning. One might wonder, though, how much most child molesters are distressed by their behavior—unless it be the distress of worrying about getting arrested for their crimes.

In its unconscious dimension, pedophilia is really a sort of sexual vampirism in which the adult seeks to cheat his or her own emotional death by preying on the vitality of young innocence.

Through my clinical work I have seen that fantasies related to pedophilia are "fueled" at the core by feelings of unconscious anger. The pedophile, lacking an innocent childhood himself, craves to devour the innocence of his victim child, and, in devouring it, to defile it. To his conscious mind, all the pedophile sees is desire, and he might even interpret this desire as "love," as the name *pedophilia* (from the Greek *paidos*, a child, and *philos*, loving) suggests. But, ironically, in its deep unconscious reality pedophilia is nothing but envious hatred for the good and the innocent.

Furthermore, when priests, rabbis, and ministers molest children, it only goes to show how much they are caught in the grip of false spirituality. Instead of seeking divine sustenance through spiritual denial of self, they choose to deny the good in order to glorify their own perverted emptiness.

Types of Child Abuse

- *Physical Abuse* is characterized by physical injuries such as bruises; burns; internal injuries; fractures; etc.

- *Physical Neglect* is characterized by deficiencies such as a lack of medical or dental care; a lack of food; a lack of sleep; inadequate hygiene; unsanitary living conditions; etc.

- *Emotional Maltreatment* is characterized by emotional injuries such as belittling; bullying; irrational parental hostility; screaming; threats; family violence; etc.

    Note that even dog bites can be a sign of emotional maltreatment. Why? Well, remember that dogs are pack animals and are very sensitive to each other's status within the pack. A dog that bites a child may perceive the child as being lower in status than itself because it has witnessed the child being maltreated by other family members.

- *Sexual Abuse* is characterized by sexual contact between adults and minors; sexual contact between minors; sexual exploitation such as pornography or prostitution; etc.

    Sexual contact can refer to penetration (genital, anal, oral); fondling; kissing and/or hugging in a sexual way; and "showing" the genitals.

    Note that the above definitions apply even if a child says the experience was pleasurable or non-threatening. On the purely physical level, some aspects of coercive sexual contact can feel pleasurable to a child.

Moreover, men who have been abused as children are particularly apt to deny that the experience was abusive because many cultures socialize boys with the false belief that males should be always eager for sexual activity.

But abuse is abuse, simply because using a child for erotic pleasure strips the child's vulnerable ego of its dignity and humanity and makes the child's body into a mere object; this experience leaves the child with the life-long psychological scars of shame, guilt, and anger and of feeling unconsciously like a piece of garbage.

Repressed Memories of Abuse

Sigmund Freud more-or-less started the issue about repressed memories when his clinical case studies in the late nineteenth century and early twentieth century inspired him to develop his psychological theories about the nature of unconscious mental processes. He used the term *repression* to describe the way emotionally painful events could be blocked out of conscious awareness so that their painful effects would not have to be experienced consciously.

Note that this repression process is a completely automatic psychological defense against emotional trauma and does not involve conscious intent. In contrast, deliberately pushing something out of awareness because you want to avoid any responsibility for it is called *suppression*.

Freud's theories all came together in his technique and philosophy of psychoanalysis, and repression has been a key concept within that philosophy ever since.

Freud's speculative theories have today been taken up in the context of allegations of childhood sexual abuse when an older child or adult suddenly "remembers" having been abused in childhood by some particular person, usually a parent. Opinions are clearly divided here, some groups saying that these things occur all the time and that the recovered memories reflect historically real events, while others say that recovered memories are false. Some groups even argue about the definition and reality of the mechanism of repression.

As a clinician, I certainly know about the reality of child abuse, and I know about the danger of false memories and self-justification by clinicians. I have also treated clients who remembered "forgotten" traumas. I have even seen improvement in physiological symptoms apparently because of previously forgotten events that were recalled and discussed in psychotherapy. But I always approach such occurrences as "personal revelations" whose historical truth is irrelevant, because, after all, the point of psychotherapy is to help the client cope with dysfunction in the present. I don't go looking for "repressed traumas," but if "remembered" events give clinical relief, so be it.

It would require intense scientific scrutiny to allow the personal revelations of a client to take on any legal or cultural significance, or to use them to substantiate any theoretical claims. All objective details would have to be meticulously verified by outside sources. In the end, I'm not willing to be a private investigator—I'll focus on helping people reclaim their human dignity, even though we might never know what "really" occurred in the past.

Furthermore, I myself have had to come to terms with ordinary remembered experiences in my own life that were later shown to be seriously distorted. As a result, I know how tenuous and fragile a "memory" can be, and I realize that the only thing we can be sure of in life, besides doubt, is what we believe in and value.

The Clinical Issue of Being Believed

While a child is being abused, the child's greatest desire is that someone with power and authority will recognize the abuse and put a stop to it. If this doesn't occur, and if the child simply endures years of pain into adulthood without ever being believed, there will always be a childlike part of the adult that desires desperately—and repetitively—to make others recognize any sort of injustice. This frustration can even be one of the underlying psychological factors motivating terrorism.

If such a person enters psychotherapy for the treatment

of trauma, the issue of "Do you believe me?" can quickly emerge as a therapeutic problem. If the psychotherapist says, "Oh, it's all in your head. Why don't you just get over it?" then all of the client's inner experiences surrounding the traumatic "memory" are invalidated.

Here is precisely where the real damage is done. Mind you, the damage has nothing to do with accepting or denying the past. It doesn't matter whether the psychotherapist believes that the event in question actually occurred exactly as the client remembers it. But it does matter that the psychotherapist *believe the client's pain* because the real therapeutic issue is whether the psychotherapist can help the client believe his or her own pain enough to sit and listen to it without running from it.

In the end, psychotherapy is all about the adult part of a personality finally listening to the frightened child part of a personality tell its story—and taking adult responsibility for the healing process that the child part cannot manage on its own. For the psychotherapy, then, "Do you believe me?" is not a *question* about facts but a *yearning* for emotional respect and comfort.

> Worrying about whether any abuse actually occurred won't help you. Nor will it help you to try to get the suspected person(s) to admit the truth. The best thing you can do is vow that, regardless of what others around you might do, you will endeavor to purge dishonesty from your life.

Repression as Protection from Anger

Although it should be no surprise to a clinician well-trained in the psychology of the unconscious that psychological disorders tend to originate for self-protective reasons, the average person can be shocked by—and even skeptical of—this clinical truth. For example, imagine a psychologist explaining to a client that "you got depressed to keep yourself from going crazy." The client would be astonished to hear such a thing.

Yet when children grow up in dysfunctional families in which the parents are emotionally unavailable, manipulative, and critical, it can be so emotionally traumatic for the children to admit the truth about their parents' lack of caring that, to protect themselves from being torn apart by the cognitive dissonance of fear and anger toward parents whose protection is needed, the children will turn the anger against themselves, blaming themselves for their parents' failures. The children will construct negative beliefs such as "I'm to blame," or "I'm bad," or "I'm disgusting," or "I'm just damaged goods." Under the pressure of this self-imposed judgment, the children will become depressed, because, as every skilled clinician knows, depression is anger turned inwards.

In a similar way, memories of sexual, physical, and emotional abuse in childhood can be repressed as a self-protective mechanism. Because some part of the child's personality knows that the abuse could provoke intense and damaging anger—both toward the perpetrator and toward the self—the memory of the abuse can be repressed to protect everyone from the risk of the child's own violent rage.

> In a family, parents who have experienced a trauma in their past but have kept it secret and have not spoken about it therapeutically will inflict trauma through their unconscious on their children. It's psychologically inevitable—until someone says, "Enough. This has to stop."

Consequently, for real emotional healing—not just containment—to be possible, it is necessary for adults who have been abused as children to understand and make peace with their fear of their own anger. This is a deep psychotherapeutic process, but, in its essence, it begins with the understanding that anger is not an *emotion* but a *desire for revenge*—that is, a desire to hurt someone or something because you have been hurt. Then comes the understanding that *impulses to anger*—that is, fantasies of harm to others and of harm to the self—are not shameful but are natural products of the human mind. Finally comes the understanding that when these impulses are *recognized*—rather than suppressed in fear and shame— they can be psychological cues for rejecting aggressive responses to emotional hurt and for consciously choosing spiritually healthy and assertive emotional boundaries.

Once this process has been mastered, then it can be safe

for full memory of the past to be recalled without the danger of wild rage overwhelming you.

Detachment from the Abuse

Keep in mind that a family system is like a living organism that will do anything to maintain its equilibrium. If family members sense that one member is trying to alter the system's equilibrium by detaching from its abusive patterns, that member will be perceived as a threat, labeled as a "black sheep," and much pressure, such as manipulation with shame and guilt, will be applied to draw that member back into the family dysfunction.

Consequently, if you seek to detach yourself psychologically from your family's abuse, the retaliatory threat from other family members may be so great that you will also need to disengage from the family physically, so that you will have some "space" for your own growth. It's critical, though, that this physical separation be done for the sake of your healing and growth, not out of anger or hatred for your family. When you leave your family because of anger or hatred you are really hiding from emotional pain, not growing emotionally.

Note also that if you disengage yourself from your family physically but falter in the work of psychological detachment from your need for their acceptance and approval, you will fear to speak the truth. Hence you will always be in danger of sabotaging your own freedom because of your fear of being left alone if you hurt someone's feelings. The irony is that in your fear of speaking the truth you really are hurting someone: yourself.

Cognitive Impairment from Abuse

Whether the abuse was physical, sexual, or emotional, it can cause cognitive impairments that impede a person's growth. In childhood, the sheer terror of what is occurring at home can prevent a child from sitting still and learning in school, and then from doing homework outside of class. Moreover, in adulthood, negative beliefs that were developed in childhood—such as "I don't matter," "I don't deserve it," "I will never succeed," "I'm not good enough"—can have a self-sabotaging effect on a person's academic progress. Such beliefs can also impede a person's ability to make use of psychotherapy unless the inhibiting beliefs can be identified and overcome in the psychotherapy itself.

Consequently, it is very important that persons who were abused in childhood pray diligently to be able to stretch themselves past the cognitive obstacles that obstruct their progress.

9   DENIAL AND LIES

Adolescence is a time for children to transition from being more-or-less dependent on adults to taking personal responsibility for their own lives. Consider, though, how difficult this task of an adolescent taking personal responsibility can be when most adults deny responsibility for almost everything and lie about their motives for almost anything.

- The whole point of smoking cigarettes is to pollute the body with noxious, addictive chemicals. So, even though most adults deny this reality, is it any surprise when smokers die of cancer? Is it any wonder that so many children express their self-hatred by smoking cigarettes?

- The whole point of drinking alcohol is to impair judgment so that painful facts aren't seen for what they really are. So, even though most adults deny this reality, is it any surprise when adults get drunk and do stupid things? Is it any wonder that so many children drink alcohol?

- The whole point of using street drugs is to deaden emotional pain, distort mental processes, and thumb your nose at the painful facts of life. So, even though most adults deny this reality, is it any surprise when addicts become criminals? Is it any wonder that so many children use drugs?

- The whole biological point of having sexual intercourse is for a woman to get pregnant. So, when most adults deny this reality, is it any surprise that there are so many unloved and abused children in this world? Is it any wonder that so many teenage girls get pregnant?

- The whole point of dressing immodestly is to incite lust in others. So, when most adults deny this reality, is it any surprise that so many women are sexually harassed by persons obsessed with lust? Is it any wonder that so many children are enslaved to pornography, masturbation, and sexual perversions?

- The whole point of having an abortion is to kill an unwanted child. So, when most adults deny this reality, is it any surprise that so many people have a contempt for life? Is it any wonder that so many children commit suicide?

- The whole point of keeping loaded guns in a house is to kill someone. So, even though most adults deny this reality, is it any surprise that so many people get killed with guns? Is it any wonder that children can find unsecured loaded guns in their homes and then kill someone?

• The whole point of rejecting moral values is to say that anything goes. So, when most adults deny this reality, is it any surprise that violence and murder are such a large part of our cultural reality? Is it any wonder that so many children will do anything—even kill their parents or teachers or classmates?

10   LUST AND VIOLENCE

In order to develop a stable sense of identity, children need a relatively long period of innocence when they are able to play and learn in emotional safety from the harsh realities of life.

In times past, the greatest violation of this safety was sexual abuse. Childhood innocence was shattered when the cruel and manipulative aspects of sexuality were forced on a child emotionally unprepared for the realities of adulthood.

But other things today have arisen that equal the emotionally dangerous effects of molestation by another person: violent and pornographic entertainment. Today, when all the manipulative aspects of sexuality are imposed on them through public education, entertainment and social media, children have no opportunity to develop a stable identity other than that of slaves to lust and violence. Consequently, the loss of innocence caused by violent and pornographic entertainment, especially through its easy access on the Internet, is having profoundly dangerous effects on our culture.

Such forms of entertainment are popular because they allow children to experience an outward expression of the very same anger and frustration they are already feeling inwardly because of their dysfunctional lives. Keep in mind here that the expression of hostile feelings and impulses in entertainment has no healing function; instead, it only "fans the flames" of inner confusion and discontent.

Moreover, such forms of entertainment have a tendency to "infect" us with their destructive values of lust, vulgarity, hostility, and revenge. When this occurs, all the moral values supporting real love are undermined, and human dignity falls into contempt—and the door to evil is thrown wide open.

> In a pathetic denial of reality, we crave to be entertained with imaginary violence and death, but there will come times—just as we are telling ourselves that we are having fun—that real violence and death will take us by surprise. And we will have no one to blame but ourselves.

In 1962, Rachel Carson's book *Silent Spring* gave solemn warning about the dangerous effects of the indiscriminate use of pesticides. Thankfully, the book had profound effects on governments around the world in changing their environmental policies. Today, however, lust and violence are far too ingrained in our culture for us to reverse course, no matter what warning we might receive. We are on a slow march into ever deepening evil.

The Enemy Is Us

Through his comic strip character Pogo, Walt Kelly said, in 1971, ". . . the enemy . . . is us."[1] Well, we have come a long way since then, but we don't seem to have learned much at all.

Our culture is wounded by a lack of love: the lack of parental values that are grounded in love, and the ultimate fraud of all authority that is based in nothing but lust and spiritual emptiness. Sadly, there is no cultural fix for a culture headed to disaster. The only hope is in individuals willing to commit themselves to fighting the great spiritual battle against evil—and, in many cases, it's an evil hidden in our own hearts as much as in the culture around us.

11 SHAME AND GUILT

Shame and guilt result from the childhood psychological wounds of family dysfunction. Parents all too often fear real love and shrink from the time and the hard work it takes to teach their children real love. So the parents resort to using shame and guilt to control their children, constantly telling the children that they are "bad" (which causes *shame* in the children) and constantly threatening the children with fear of punishment in hell (which causes the children to feel *guilt* for their behavior).

If this occurred in your family, then, because of your inability to understand why your parents were so hurtful, you most likely came to believe that something must really be wrong with you and that you really deserved everything inflicted on you. Thus you cultivated a secret shame that yearned to be punished for being defective. Furthermore, you would have become angry at your parents because of their dysfunction, and then you would have become so terrified of your anger that you felt guilty about it, thus secretly desiring to be punished for your anger. Call it a sort of double masochistic whammy: shame and guilt.

Thus whenever you do (or think about doing) something "bad," you don't want to admit it or seek help because you are terrified of the scorn that might be inflicted on you if anyone were to discover your secret. So you do anything to hide from discovery, while your secret festers in the dark depths of your heart. Moreover, in this forlorn state, you are far removed from real love because all the good you do for others is motivated unconsciously by the desire to appease others to keep them from abandoning you if they should discover your real thoughts and feelings.

Self-sabotage and Fear of Dreams

In speaking about dreams here I am not referring to the dreams that occur in your sleep. I am speaking about your profound inner ambitions for your future. For example, some children have simple dreams about a birthday present, a social event at school, or a family vacation. Some children have profound dreams about their professional careers, about Holy Matrimony and family, or about acts of service to humanity.

Yet some individuals have no dreams at all. Or, to be more correct, it *seems* as if some persons have no dreams when really they squash their dreams as soon as one gets started.

Why? Well, children who suffer emotional pain in childhood because they are mistreated by parents, family, peers, teachers, or others learn from experience that if they express any of their needs, they will be punished or rejected by others. Caught in this mess, then, children will learn to fear rejection and criticism and will conclude that denying their needs—holding their needs back, as it were, like an animal on a leash—will prevent their being rejected. So, as soon as a dream materializes, BANG! they shoot it down before it has a chance to get off the ground.

These are the persons who say, "I don't know" when asked what they want. These are the persons who say, "I don't know" when asked what they feel. These are the persons who say, "Whenever I try to do anything, it never works out. This is how it will always be. There's no point in trying." These are the persons who will say, "It isn't fair! God hates me!"

But God doesn't hate them. They don't believe that God loves them because they are unconsciously angry at their parents. They hate themselves—they condemn themselves, they punish themselves, they sabotage themselves—because of their guilt for being angry at their parents.

The Path Out of Guilt

It's bad enough for a family to be burdened with guilt over all the mistakes and injuries that have occurred in it over time—even across generations. But the narrow psychological path out of guilt is more painful than the guilt itself. It's a classic situation in which the cure is more painful than the symptom. That's why alcoholics and addicts, for example, remain stuck in their addictions. The cure is too painful compared to the relative ease of denial and self-destruction, because the dreaded cure for guilt is nothing other than love: a complete surrender to God's mercy through your repentance, penance, and forgiveness.

To understand this, it is important to realize that any damage that was ever done to you has in turn led you to damage others. Those who are hated learn to hate; those who are abused learn, if not to abuse, at least to hold on to anger, a lack of trust, and an unconscious desire for revenge.

But if you allow yourself to feel sorrow for the pain that you and others have inflicted on each other because of hate and abuse, and if you acknowledge all of your shame that you have hidden from God, and if you trust that God will not scorn you but will have mercy on you, then you will be ready to find healing from the damage that was done to you in the first place. In other words, it's the sorrow for sin itself—out of real love for God—that makes it possible to accept that terrible, painful "cure" for your guilt.

12 DISOBEDIENCE

Through my clinical work, I have looked deep into the hearts and souls of many persons, not just lay persons but also those in religious life and those contemplating entering religious life. And I have consistently seen there a certain "ugliness"—a stain, so to speak—resulting from childhood emotional wounds.

The "Stain"

Sometimes a child is stained by blatant family dysfunction, such as alcoholism, adultery, divorce, physical abuse, emotional abuse, or sexual abuse. These children grow up with deep psychological wounds, sometimes with a bitter inner attitude of social defiance, even to the point of criminal activity.

Yet, more often than not, children suffer only from the wounds of more "normal" families in which parents fail to understand the children's emotional experiences and rather try to control and manipulate the children to serve the parents' desires. The children then become frustrated and fearful, and grow to resent the parents.

Furthermore, parents can also be spiritually hypocritical. That is, it's rare in today's world to find any families who teach children to love God with all their hearts and souls and strength and minds, and who don't indoctrinate their children right after baptism with all the impiety of the anti-Christian world around them. Because most parents do not live out in their actions whatever religious faith they profess with their lips, normal family life is more often than not characterized by self-gratification, resentment, defensiveness, manipulation, hidden alliances, and a general lack of honest communication.

This lack of communication can take either of two courses. On the one hand, authority in some families can be all a fraud, just an excuse for manipulation or intimidation, whereby the parents become domineering, defensive, and controlling and thereby deprive the children of the emotional autonomy that is necessary to love God with the free will of a pure heart. This deprivation leaves the children emotionally crippled, exasperated, and prone to anger and depression—and even suicide.

On the other hand, if parents give children too much freedom, the children will grow up without any sense of compassionate discipline and guidance. Most kids are smart enough to realize that when parents give them too much freedom it really means that the parents don't care—or don't know any better themselves. So the children can end up with such profound emptiness and guilt about the meaningless pursuit of self-gratification that they challenge everything out of pure frustration. And where does that lead? To bitter identity confusion, fear, anger, and depression.

In either case, then, many children tend to develop an unconscious resistance to authority.

Resistance to Authority

When children aren't taught the "language" of honest emotional encounter within their families, children tend to seek out "natural" ways—that is, physical, bodily ways—to derive attention and satisfaction from the world, such as through food, drugs, or sexuality. And so we have a world filled with addictions, eating disorders (anorexia, bulimia, and obesity), and perversions (immodesty, pornography, prostitution, piercings and tattoos, and, in general, lifestyles defiant of chastity).

This unconscious resistance to authority more often than not leads to defiant behavior that focuses on immediate physical satisfaction and a need to "be in control" to ward off feelings of vulnerability and helplessness. This unconscious attitude not only disrupts social harmony, but it can also cause spiritual problems in regard to one's religious faith. Rather than make the personal sacrifices necessary to respect and defend the tradition of the Church, many persons seek out nothing but the self-gratification of their own personal desires: "We don't care what you want—or what's legal or moral. We want what we want, and we will get it, one way or another." That's the rallying cry of the disgruntled, stemming from the motto of Satanism: *Do what thou wilt.*

It's a very sad thing. Family emotional wounds can leave children believing that God is cruel, that God is unfair, that God plays games with us, and that they have no other recourse than to take matters into their own hands to get what they think is right. But God is not unfair. It's families who have lost their grounding in faith that are cruel and unfair, and it's all because they have turned interpersonal relationships into game playing.

I have often seen how some persons struggling with inner emotional confusion try to hide this confusion by putting on a religious habit or by taking up excessive religious devotions. They use an outward show of religious practices as a psychological defense to make themselves seem holy and to appear as if they were being obedient. And therein they miss the point about real holiness. Genuine Christianity requires a deep, humble commitment of the heart; it's not like some sort of computer software application that you conveniently run on your existing—and confused—operating system. True Christianity is an entirely new "operating system" that completely replaces the old one.

Some individuals from dysfunctional families are often drawn to religious life—or quasi-religious life (i.e., secular religious orders)—because they think that obedience is easy. But, really, obedience for them is not an act of love, it's an act of spite, a mere psychological defense against their unconscious anger. "All right. So you're going to treat me miserably? Well, I'll show you! I'll take everything you can dish out and I'll take it without a murmur. So there!" But, oh! Just wait. Slowly the frustration builds, and then the anger erupts! It all goes to prove the point that you can't carry your cross if you are carrying resentment.[1] In fact, the most common impediment to spiritual progress is the grudge that chains you to the past.

Sooner or later, then, persons with a confused emotional life will go astray simply because their unconscious resistance to authority prevents them from clinging to the rock of true faith.

The Way of Dysfunction

When children grow up in an environment of family dysfunction, they are essentially being trained to develop psychologically unhealthy habits. Oppressed by their parents' general lack of emotional awareness, and their defensiveness, manipulation, criticism, and abuse, children learn to hide the truth, to keep secrets, to not talk about their own inner experiences, to doubt God, to fear rejection and abandonment by others, and to crave acceptance from anyone—even the devil. Comparing themselves to others who appear to be well-functioning, they carry the secret shame of thinking of themselves as defective, inadequate and unworthy of love.

But then, as a psychological compensation for these stifling and self-defeating beliefs, an unconscious urge to resist the authority that has oppressed the children leads them into disobedience. A pervasive resistance to cooperation with any spiritual morality develops, and an attitude of relativism emerges to oppose anything representative of absolute truth. Hearing about the teachings of the Church, for example, they say, "That doesn't fit my experience. The Church must be wrong." Sadly, it's the dysfunction of the children's parents that is wrong. But dysfunction is blind; children trained in the way of dysfunction carry out that dysfunction, even against their trainers, just as they have been trained to do.

13 A LESSON FROM DOG TRAINING

Families are often taken by surprise at how easily and quickly attempts at honest communication can fall into misconceptions and angry rebuttals. Actually, this is a common problem, and it occurs to one extent or another in most families. Despite the parents' best attempts to protect and discipline a child, there can be elements in the parents' words and behavior that leave the child feeling misunderstood and criticized. With no one to correct the miscommunication, the parents will become more and more frustrated, the child will become more and more hurt and angry, and a huge emotional rift will separate the family.

The child, in feeling hurt, alone, and frightened, will do and say things to express disappointment, but the parents, believing that the child's behavior is willfully disrespectful, will get offended, and will say, "This deserves the belt!"

Parents, however, can be of greatest help just by not taking their children's behavior personally. Rather than respond with indignation at what children say or do, it is very important for parents to think, "This is the way my child is expressing hurt and fear. It's a plea for help. This child needs comfort, encouragement, and protection, not criticism or punishment."

But if the parent takes the children's behavior as a personal offense and reacts defensively and critically, it will only provoke the children into more hostility.

When children act or speak disobediently, a parent can non-threateningly remind them that their communication has gotten off track and that the parent is willing to help them express themselves more honestly.

"That was a rude thing to say. That's unacceptable behavior. Try saying it again, but this time say it without anger." Then, until the child does speak politely, keep repeating, "That was still said with anger. Try saying it again, from your heart, politely." Wear the child down with gentle teaching.

Although I do not watch television, several of my clients have told me about a TV program that was about a Mexican dog trainer. It all begins with a family whose dog is out of control. Everyone grumbles and says, "This dog is bad news. It needs medication or something!" Then the dog trainer comes in, works with the dog using appropriate techniques of discipline and punishment, and in a short time the dog is gentle and obedient. It all proves the point that the dog's behavior was the result of the family's misguided attempts to control it! It wasn't really a "bad" dog and it didn't need medication. The dog trainer simply knew how to understand the dog's issues.

Similarly, understanding, rather than blame, is the critical issue in parenting. *Understanding*, although it requires real love, does not mean *unconditional acceptance of anything*.

> As a megalomaniac expresses his social-political views about the need for him to take control of the world, a man listens patiently, and then says, "Yes, I understand."
>
> The megalomaniac smiles as he says, "I'm glad to hear that you agree with me!"
>
> The man replies, "I said I *understood* what you were saying; I didn't say I *agreed* with you."

True healing involves two things. First, we must see clearly what is wrong; second, we must have the compassion to call it to change. This means that unconditional acceptance of anything gets you nowhere. If you take no responsibility for the world around you, and if you're unwilling to call error for what it is—that is, if you're always missing the point—then you contribute nothing of any healing value to the world. That's not love. On the other hand, if you forsake understanding and treat error with hatred, condemning it to hell, the bitter poison in your own heart will end up condemning you to hell. And that's not love either.

Now, resolving family conflicts takes as much patience as

dog training. But with love and patience you might find that the most difficult of children can turn around for the love of love.

14   PHYSICAL AFFECTION

Many years before he started psychotherapy, a nurse in his physician's office suffered the sudden death of her father. Just out of kindness, this man sent the nurse a sympathy card. The next time he saw her, not too long after she received the card, she ran up to him, threw her arms around him, and gave him a big hug. He almost fainted. The fact that a woman he hardly even knew was putting her arms around him was one thing, but the real surprise—as odd as it sounds—was that no one had ever given him such an innocent, spontaneous hug before. That hug initiated a radical change in his life.

> In the late 1950s, H. F. Harlow's experiments with monkeys [1] showed that when physical contact was withheld from infant monkeys, they became fearful, withdrawn, and apathetic.
>
> We know now that the same is true for human infants. Without physical affection, infants cease to thrive.

This man was raised with all the basic care an infant

needs. His family, however, was not an emotionally open family. Yes, they were close, and they did everything together. But, beyond infancy and early childhood, aside from a handshake or a kiss on the cheek, he never learned to touch or be touched.

Once he saw the deficits of his childhood through the perspective of his psychotherapy, he took up the hard work of remedying the problem. When he discovered that bodily awareness relates to emotional awareness, he practiced psychological techniques of bodily awareness, and he became attentive to his inner emotional experiences. He developed social confidence. And he learned how to hug.

Emotional Intimacy

In order to develop emotional intimacy, children need to be touched and caressed. A lack of physical affection and the resulting lack of emotional intimacy in childhood can cause great psychological pain. Lacking touch and emotional spontaneity in their families, individuals won't even know how to recognize their own emotional experiences. They repress their emotions, they suffer psychosomatic illnesses, they become socially insecure, and they confuse a need for simple physical affection with sexual desire.

These emotional wounds can be healed, but the healing doesn't occur by receiving hugs from a psychotherapist; the healing occurs through the hard work of your overcoming the fear that you are blaming your parents by speaking the truth about their failures,[2] then by putting into language the emotional pain you felt because of not having received physical affection from your parents, and finally by accepting from Christ the love you have wanted, but haven't received, from your parents. It's hard work to do this, but it can be done, if only you try. It's all He asks.

15   EDUCATING CHILDREN

During the post-WWII years, at the time Communism was a threat throughout Latin America, the dictator of a Caribbean island made an astute decision. He realized that to ensure his success in imposing a Communist government on a predominantly Catholic culture he had to undermine the authority of the Church. Yes, he could—and did—persecute the Church, but he devised a cunning, long-term plan as well: he attacked the minds of the children.

His henchmen went into the schools and, with feigned concern for the children, said to them, "Wouldn't you like some ice cream right now? Well, why don't you pray to your God for ice cream?"

The children, like innocent lambs, closed their eyes and obediently prayed for ice cream.

The henchmen told the children to open their eyes. With a self-satisfied sneer in their voices, they asked the children, "Well, did your God give you any ice cream?"

"No," the children sadly replied.

"Well, then, children," the dictator's henchmen said with a sly smile, "pray now to Mr. [dictator]. Ask him for ice cream."

Again, the children closed their eyes and prayed—not to God, but to Mr. [dictator].

Meanwhile, the dictator's henchmen wheeled ice cream carts into the classroom. They told the children to open their eyes, and they gave out the ice cream, telling the children, "You see? Your God can do nothing for you, but Mr. [dictator] knows how to take care of you!"

The above story is a perfect illustration of how the devil gets his way. The procedure is simple. To undermine resistance to his nefarious desires, he attacks the very root of the resistance: the children. By bypassing the adults and brainwashing their children, he creates a host of new, pliant converts to his anti-Catholic ideology.

The same thing is occurring throughout the world today. In order to propagate their liberal, atheistic hedonism, and to undermine Christian values, political activists are brainwashing children through television (and the subversive commercial advertising that goes with it), movies, popular music, social media, sports, video games, and—even more brazenly—through advocacy and indoctrination programs in public schools.

But do not be surprised. This is all occurring for a reason. Once the Roman Empire made Christianity a state religion, Christians came to believe that they could resort to politics to enforce Christian values rather than personally witness the faith. Throughout subsequent ages, they have grown morally lax, and now they have grown lax in teaching their children. They have become lukewarm. Furthermore, Christ knew it would occur. Now we are paying the price.

> In the book of Revelation (3:15-19), Christ warned that He knows our works; He knows that many Christians are neither cold nor hot. Because they are lukewarm, neither hot nor cold, He threatened to spit them out of His mouth. They say that they are rich and affluent and have no need of anything, and yet they do not realize that they are wretched, pitiable, poor, blind, and naked. Christ advised them to buy from Him gold refined by fire so that they may be rich, and white garments to put on so that their shameful nakedness may not be exposed, and buy ointment to smear on their eyes so that they might see. Those whom He loves, He reproves and chastises. So He warned them to be earnest, therefore, and repent.

Will we repent? The devil is brainwashing our children right under our noses because, in our lukewarm laziness, we have carelessly opened the door to him. Will we close the door?

Yes, will we close the door? That's a providential question, because to "close the door" on the devil requires a huge spiritual battle against evil and tremendous work. To close the door means that Christian parents must be involved in the education of their children. The parents must rely on home schooling or they must send their children to trusted private schools or they must spend hours every night at home with their children teaching the truth and correcting the lies that were planted in the children's minds during the day in public schools.

> To send children to the average public school is like condemning them to hell. They will be brainwashed into the ways of evil, their morals will be corrupted, and their faith will be poisoned.

But note this well: children will not listen to their parents unless their parents live the faith in sincerity from their hearts, as a true holy lifestyle. If the parents spend their evenings passively entertaining themselves with the insidious influence of television, movies, social media, popular music, sports, and video games, the children will smell the stench of this hypocrisy and will say to themselves, "Why listen to these losers? Mr. [dictator] can do more for me than they can!"

How can those who reject the mandate of Christianity[1]

teach their children to love and to fear God and to keep His commandments? Well, they can't. They can't give their children a proper education in anything but sin. Such is the chastisement inflicted on the lukewarm. "I will spit you out of My mouth" (see Revelation 3:16).

Whoever causes one of these little ones who believe in Me to sin, it would be better for him to have a great millstone hung around his neck and to be drowned in the depths of the sea.

— Matthew 18:6

16   DISCIPLINE: AN OVERVIEW

Techniques of behavioral psychology offer many different ways to shape a child's behavior so that it conforms to the values the parents want to teach. This shaping can occur through psychological procedures to *increase* selected behaviors or through psychological procedures to *decrease* selected behaviors.

Increasing Behaviors

There are two ways to increase a particular behavior; one is called *positive reinforcement* and the other is called *negative reinforcement*.

Positive Reinforcement occurs when you *give* something to increase a specific behavior. What you give can be pleasant, such as a reward of money, food, or privileges, or unpleasant, such as a verbal correction. For positive reinforcement to be effective it must

• *follow* the child's behavior,

- be *delivered immediately* after the child's behavior,

- be large enough to be *significant* to the child,

- be *consistently* applied, and

- have *verbal clarification*; that is, it should be made clear to the child what the child did, why it was right or wrong, the nature of and reason for your action, and what the outcome is expected to be.

Negative Reinforcement occurs when you *take away* something to increase a specific behavior. This can be a hard concept to understand, so consider the example of relieving a child from washing the dinner dishes after you have noticed that he or she just completed a special report for school. The idea here is that in being relieved of an undesirable task the child will be motivated to keep doing well in school. Even though taking away the task may seem like a reward, it technically involves removing something, so it is a "negative" reinforcement.

Decreasing Behaviors

Several psychological methods can be used to decrease a particular behavior.

Overcorrection is a two-step process which involves first making restitution for the undesired behavior, and then performing correct behaviors. For example, a child might be required to pick up all the clothes from the floor of her bedroom and then to clean the floors of several other rooms in the house.

Time Out involves removing positive reinforcement for a brief, specified time. For example, each time a child has a temper tantrum, he or she can be sent away from pleasant family activity to a specified place (such as a chair across the room) and ignored for a short time (such as 30 seconds). [For more details, see the next chapter.] Note that locking the child in a closet, for example, is traumatic abuse, not a healthy form of psychological correction. Furthermore, sending a child to his or her room as a so-called "time out" can, ironically, be perceived by many children as a form of reward if the room has a computer, video games, television, and other entertainment to occupy the child.

Extinction is a technique to decrease a previously reinforced behavior by removing the reinforcement for it. A parent probably won't have much use for this technique—unless in reading this section you find out that you have been unwittingly reinforcing a bad behavior and now want to remedy it. For example, you might stop giving attention to a child when he or she performs the undesirable behavior.

Differential Reinforcement involves positively reinforcing all behaviors except the unwanted behavior. Like extinction, this technique is not likely to be used by a parent. Unlike extinction, this technique requires you to actually give something to a child for all behaviors except the undesired behavior during a certain time period.

Punishment occurs when you do something (which the child finds to be unpleasant) to decrease a specific behavior. An example would be removing driving privileges or adding extra tasks for a child to perform in response to a speeding ticket—all with the goal of decreasing unsafe driving habits.

For punishment to be effective, it must

- *follow* the child's behavior,

- be *delivered immediately* after the child's behavior,

- hurt enough to be *significant* to the child,

- be *consistently* applied, and

- have *verbal clarification*; that is, it should be made clear to the child what the child did, why it was wrong, the nature of and reason for your action, and what the outcome is expected to be.

The average person, untrained in psychology, often misunderstands the simplicity and benefits of punishment, so this leads to the next chapter.

17 PUNISHMENT

Because children are not born with moral perfection, children need to be punished when they have done something wrong. After all, punishment is a part of the reconciliation process, and unpunished guilt can impair the relationship between parents and children.

As I said in the previous chapter, punishment is just a simple psychological technique to decrease a specific behavior. To be effective, however, punishment must be used properly. That is, the punishment must be *just*: it must be consistent, fair, and adequate to the transgression. And it must be tempered with mercy.

In its psychological sense, *mercy* means to withhold some—or all—of the punishment demanded by justice if the guilty person shows deep sorrow for his or her behavior.

But merciful punishment is just the beginning. A parent can't expect to administer punishment by remaining uninvolved. In fact, to administer punishment is to get involved. For example, don't expect to take away a child's driving privileges and then say, "Well, you need to drive to school, so you can use the car for that. Just come home right after school." What child couldn't see through that nonsense—and learn to abuse it immediately? So wake up. You will have to drive your child to and from school, no matter what the inconvenience to you.

As another example, don't expect to confine a child to the house and then expect that you can come and go as you please, leaving the child alone in the house, while saying "Don't go anywhere." Wake up again. You will have to stay home and monitor your child, never letting him or her leave your sight. Homework must be done under your supervision, not alone in a bedroom. Meals must be eaten together. Entertainment must be in your presence. Everything must be done in your presence, and, as a result—like it or not—you will be drawn closer to your child.

Does this sound difficult? Well, that's why so many families have so many family problems: the parents are always too busy to really get involved in the children's punishment. In the end, it must be accepted that the punishment will hurt the parent as much as the child. If it doesn't, it will not be effective.

Finally, parents cannot provide healthy punishment unless they themselves live by healthy values—courage, integrity, and responsibility, for example—that they can pass on to their children through teaching and action.

Sadly enough, most adolescent "acting out" derives from the fact that many parents' values aren't grounded in religious faith and a deep devotion to the holy. So the behavior of the adolescent in effect says, "Your values are all a fraud. They're arbitrary. Why should I do what you say? It's not fair. I'll do what I want because my desires are just as valid as any of yours."

Furthermore, a permissive parent who fails to administer punishment consistently and mercifully actually causes a child to perceive punishment as arbitrary and irrational. Then the child can actually engage in violence as an unconscious plea to be punished for an unspoken, aching sense of guilt for other acts that were never justly punished.

Guidelines for Punishment

1. For a young child, an excellent form of punishment (removing something to decrease a specific behavior) is **time out**. But, for this to work, there has to be in place both a system of positive *recognition of the child's good behavior* and a clear set of *family rules*. With these in place, "time out" then becomes the response of choice when the child breaks a rule: the child is removed from pleasant family activity in such a way that he or she can still witness it while being excluded from it. For example, if a child curses, the parent responds—in a neutral tone, not angrily—"That's a time out." The child then goes to the time-out location (previously established according to family rules), such as

a chair on the other side of the room, and is ignored by everyone else. Then, after about 30 seconds, the parent says "Okay" and calls the child back. Then the parent must offer positive recognition to the child, such as by giving a hug and saying, "I like the way you accepted the time out so willingly and how, even though you felt upset, you handled your frustration very well."

2. Any infliction of punishment can easily become abuse, in which the punisher takes pleasure in the punishment. In terms of parental-child discipline, this is clearly not acceptable. Period. Many adults use the excuse that the abuse they inflict on children is "punishment," but this is just a smoke-screen to hide the adult's unconscious sadism—or sado-eroticism, for sadly enough many adults derive a sort of perverse erotic pleasure in inflicting pain on children.

3. Physical punishment can also be an "easy way out" for a parent who has botched up the whole job of parental discipline all along and tries to "save face" sporadically by viciously lashing out at the child. I feel sorry for any children in these circumstances because they will be wounded for life. Some will seek psychotherapy as adults, but others will end up in prison—or in their own private hell of drugs and alcohol or sexual perversions.

4. As for "just" punishment, there cannot be any legitimate reason for punishment that involves a series of repeated blows, as in caning (whether with a cane or a belt) or in

humiliating spanking. So for older children the punishment should be focused on the removal of privileges or perhaps the assignment of extra tasks. For younger children in circumstances involving obstinate behavior, rather than simple childish desires, a gentle whack on the butt, along with a strong "No!" can be quite effective. But even this has to be done in compassion. And it needs to be done only once. If the child doesn't get the idea with one whack, then something else is going on, and the parent needs to re-evaluate the whole situation to determine whether hidden parental conflicts are causing family distress and affecting the child's behavior.

> For example, according to California law, striking a child anywhere other than on the butt, or with an instrument (such as a belt, cane, or paddle), constitutes child abuse.

18   SHAPING POSITIVE BEHAVIOR

He was a "latchkey kid." That is, he came home from school to an empty house while both his parents were still working. He spent his time watching TV, and he neglected his homework. When his parents came home, his mother was too tired to do anything with him, and his father blew up at him in anger. The child became disruptive in his classes; he began to set fires and to shoplift. He was given medication for ADHD (Attention Deficit Hyperactivity Disorder). It seemed there was nothing he could do right. Nothing, that is, except play video games.

Maybe he couldn't sit still in school, but he could focus his attention for hours on the games, achieving advanced levels of play. He was one of the best.

So how do we understand this? Well, the video games offered three things that were sadly missing in his family:

1. *Clear Rules.* He knew exactly what he had to do to get points and exactly what would occur if he made any mistakes.

2. *Rewards for good behavior.* As long as he followed the rules, he earned his points immediately.

3. *Punishment for breaking the rules.* If he did make a mistake, the game punished him for it. But the punishment was never critical or belittling. It was just a fact: "You did this, so this is the cost." And then the game resumed.

Therefore, we can learn from this that families need several things to ensure healthy functioning.

Rules of Conduct. Families need rules of conduct that are clearly stated. This includes the *no's* (no cussing, no hitting, no lying, etc.) and the *do's* (do your homework, come to dinner clean and on time, go to bed at the appointed time, etc.).

> Needless to say—although in today's world it may be necessary to say it anyway—the parents must abide by the same rules as the children. Period.

Positive Recognition. Families need to give children positive recognition. Like the child in the story above, many children are ignored until they do something wrong, so they unconsciously are motivated to strive for even negative attention (such as criticism) just to get some attention. But a healthy family will give a child positive recognition both for behavior that tends toward the desired behavior and for not breaking the rules:

- "I like the way you [hung up your jacket, did your homework, helped your sister, etc.]. That shows [consideration for others, integrity, compassion, etc.]."

- "I notice that you haven't [fought with your sister, used foul words, thrown a tantrum, etc.]. Blessings for [your good manners, being kind, using self-control, etc.]."

Note that this positive recognition, though largely verbal, is best offered with affectionate touching as well (see Chapter 14).

> Some theories of managing difficult children advocate the use of a credit system, or "token economy," in the school classroom and in the family. Such systems, however, tend to reduce human interactions to the level of commodities to be purchased. Token economies may be necessary in some classrooms to keep order, but in families, token economies, though they may seem to be convenient, ultimately subvert the deeper values of life, such as self-discipline and mutual cooperation.

Fair Punishment. Families need a fair and defined way to punish broken rules. But the punishment must be clean; it cannot be given in anger, and it cannot belittle or shame the child. It must be a simple fact—and then family life can resume.

19   GROWTH

The beginning of the solution to all family problems is to realize that just as plants can't grow in chalky soil unless you add to the soil whatever is needed to make it healthy, so children—and husbands and wives—can't grow unless they are given whatever support and encouragement they need to become independent and responsible individuals. No child or spouse can grow in the "chalky soil" of your pre-existing desires and expectations, because what a child or spouse needs for emotional growth might not be what you had expected—or wanted.

It's a tragedy, but parents who do not raise their children with the blessings of real love impede the child's reverence for the holy and thereby contribute to the child's tendency to fall into perversion in seeking acceptance from the world—and then these wounded children have their own children who start the cycle all over again.

So, let's consider what you can do to raise a child with blessings and healthy communication so the child will grow to revere the holy right from birth.

Raising Children to Revere the Holy

Teaching a child to revere the holy should begin in the womb, with blessings, and should continue through infancy and childhood with blessings, prayer, and teaching.

Blessings

At the very beginning, give your child the blessing of a holy conception, rather than the burden of being conceived as an "accident" of lust. Without this blessing, a child can be crippled with pervasive insecurity, doubt, and self-hatred throughout life, unless psychological and spiritual healing is eventually sought out for deliverance from the unconscious burden.

While the child is still in the womb, give it a blessing in the morning and evening and several times a day by making the sign of the Cross over the womb and saying audibly, "May our Lord Jesus Christ bless you and protect you, in the name of the Father and of the Son and of the Holy Spirit."

After your child's birth, whenever you put the child to bed and whenever you fetch the child from bed, make the sign of the Cross on the child's forehead with your thumb and say audibly, "May our Lord Jesus Christ bless you and protect you, in the name of the Father and of the Son and of the Holy Spirit."

As the child gets older, you can teach the child to say his or her own prayers before going to sleep and on waking.

Whenever you feed your child, make the sign of the Cross on the child and say audibly, "Bless us, O Lord, and this food which [name of child] is about to receive, in the name of the Father and of the Son and of the Holy Spirit."

As the child gets older, you can teach the child to make the Sign of the Cross himself or herself, and, ultimately, to say along with you the standard Catholic blessing before eating: "Bless us, O Lord, and these Thy gifts, which we are about to receive from Thy bounty, through Christ our Lord. Amen."

Prayer

While the child is an infant, hold the child in your arms or lap while you audibly pray vocal prayers such as the Angelus, the Rosary and the Liturgy of the Hours. This will teach the child to sit quietly during periods of prayer and worship, and it will prepare the child to sit quietly in church during Mass.

As the child gets older, he or she can join you in the prayers.

Wherever you go and whatever you do, let your child witness you praying and giving thanks. For example, before leaving home, go before the crucifix and ask for protection, and give a blessing to your home; on arriving home, do the same, giving thanks. Let your child see you constantly engaged in prayerful interaction with God. Whenever possible, pray audibly, rather than silently, so that your child can learn from you how to pray.

Teaching

Whenever you bathe or clean your child, when you need to touch the genitals, say, with reverence, "This part of your body is holy." When your child is old enough to understand, every time you bathe the child, teach him or her that the genitals are to be kept private because of their holiness before God, and that they are not to played with like toys.

When your child asks about babies and where they come from, explain that the genitals are used by adults in marriage to make babies. Explain that a girl has a special, holy place inside her for a baby to grow, but that it doesn't work until adulthood. Tell the child that just before adolescence, when the genitals begin to work, you will explain the details of marriage and babies.

Healthy Communication

As an aspect of an environment of love and blessings, it's important for all family members to be aware of what other members are experiencing, and healthy communication within a family becomes an essential element of this awareness.

All too often, communication becomes unhealthy and takes the form of unconscious anger through sarcasm, innuendos and hints, or not saying anything at all—and mutual cooperation[1], the basis of family health, is defiled.

In contrast, healthy communication is direct, immediate, and clear, and it is a good model for learning healthy assertiveness. It depends on facts, opinions, emotions, and needs, as illustrated below.

> *Facts*: "I had a very important appointment this morning, and when I got in the car I found that you had left it with barely enough fuel to get to the fuel station. Stopping for fuel made me late."

> *Opinions*: "I believe that none of us should bring the car home at night with an empty fuel tank."

> *Emotions*: "The whole experience left me feeling irritated and frustrated."

> *Needs*: "I need to be able to leave in the morning without having to deal with unnecessary delays, and I need the car to have a reasonable amount of fuel in it at all times, regardless of who used it last."

The Gender-based Communication Bias

In most Western cultures, women tend to depend on emotions as the basis for communication while men tend to depend on thinking and intellect for communication. This gender-based communication bias can cause considerable problems in families and in all relationships in general.

For example, a woman might seek emotional support and a man will offer an intellectual problem-solving response, thus missing the point of the woman's emotional needs. Or a man might seek concrete information ("just the facts") and a woman will offer an emotional response, thus frustrating the man in his need to solve a problem.

Therefore, remember that healthy communication generally involves both emotions and facts—and a charitable attitude of mutual cooperation, rather than sarcasm and criticism, can help to overcome any communication misunderstandings that might occur.

The Mistake of "Gender Equity"

Quite often men are socialized to ignore healthy communication and to be aggressive and hostile in their communication. Sadly, this is a spiritual failure based in the sins of pride and wrath, and even though it tends to be common in Western societies, it is still opposed to the Christian virtues of charity and mutual cooperation. But when women try to attain "equity" with men through aggressive and hostile social attitudes and behaviors it only makes matters worse, not better, because then all communication degenerates into endless arguments and rebuttals, and the underlying emotions get trampled underfoot on the battleground into a social mire of degenerate rudeness and vulgarity.

20   RESPONSIBILITY

Life's real purpose is measured in terms of purification of heart, and this purification occurs both *because of* injuries and *in spite of* injuries. If you fail to achieve a pure heart, it will be because you have failed to utilize the life opportunities God has given you—even in difficulties and disasters—and no amount of blame or finger pointing will justify your failure. It's all on you.

Now, that may seem contrary to common sense. But it's all based in God's love for us, which is directed to our healing, growth, and purification. Training ourselves to love by accepting God's love for us, even if it contradicts our psychological defenses, is the basis of our spiritual purification.

This, then, leads to the psychological meaning of *responsibility*. To take responsibility for your own life means two things. First, taking responsibility for your own life means to endeavor to stop blaming others for anything that befalls you. It means that no matter what pain or suffering is inflicted on you, you have an obligation to pay the price yourself for its remedy. No matter what your parents—or anyone—ever did to you, still you have an obligation to work in the present to achieve your healing. Only you can do the work because it is you who will stand before God in judgment when you die, and part of that judgment will concern how you treated those who hurt you—your enemies—and how well you trusted in God's justice.

> Even self-loathing and self-punishment—even to the point of suicide, believe it or not—are all veiled forms of blaming others as a way to avoid facing up to the truth of your emotional pain, and, therefore, they are all veiled forms of avoiding your own healing.

Second, taking responsibility for your own life means to endeavor to assume spiritual liability for the injurious consequences of your actions. The true acceptance of this responsibility will lead to feelings of sorrow and to the desire to do anything it takes to alter your behavior. To shirk this responsibility, however, will lead you into the dead-end trap of victimization.

Victimization

To achieve healing it is psychologically necessary to feel the pain of what afflicted you, and to come to terms with that pain through intense psychological scrutiny. But you can't blame anyone for that pain without betraying your baptismal vows to reject hatred and evil. Christ, after all, was not victimized [4]—He freely sacrificed Himself for us. So no one who genuinely lives a Christian lifestyle can be victimized. For the sake of their faith, martyrs freely accept death, and saints patiently endure persecution. But they are not "victims."

In the ancient sense of the word, *victim* means an animal offered in sacrifice. These sacrificial animals, however, did not offer themselves—they were taken from the flocks—and so, through the ages, the term victim became associated with the idea of someone who (a) loses something against his will or (b) is cheated or duped by another. Consequently, in modern secular society at least, the ancient meaning of a victim has been lost to us, and our use of the term carries with it all the unconscious resentment we feel for being cheated, duped, or unfairly treated. In essence, according to today's language, a victim is someone who has been victimized.

So, when we call someone a victim today we imply that the person suffered unwillingly and unfairly; moreover, according to modern sensibilities, we assume that this injustice deserves some social compensation. If the compensation does not come freely, we demand it. We sue. We protest. We kill. We fall into victim anger.

This very attitude—this bitterness and resentment for having been treated unfairly—is a poison that prevents emotional wounds from healing. It stunts the psychological and spiritual qualities of patience, understanding, compassion, forbearance, mercy, and forgiveness that are necessary for emotional healing.

In contrast, those who entrust their pain to God free themselves from resentment and blame; in letting their suffering flow through them in imitation of Christ as the true holy victim, they choose not to feel victimized. No matter what occurs around them, they never lose the mystical peace of healing through divine love.

> Some individuals, however, will avoid the work of their psychological healing because they incorrectly believe that admitting the truth about others' lack of caring amounts to blaming those persons. But healing depends on admitting the truth, whatever it may be. To deny the truth only drives resentments out of sight into the unconscious. Hence it can be that those who hide the truth to protect others from blame lock themselves into an unconscious blame which prevents them from taking responsibility for their own lives. Thus, even as they tell themselves that their lives are failures, they really have succeeded at something: they have become successful at blaming others while hiding that fact from themselves.

Blame and Hiding

Now, the story of Adam and Eve (see Genesis 3 : 1–24) is actually a story that makes a very good point about the original sin of finger pointing and blame. Look at the story. The serpent tempts Eve, and she in turn tempts Adam. God finds Adam hiding and asks what occurred. Adam points his finger at Eve and blames her. Moreover, he blames God in the process : "This woman *you* gave me—she made me do it." God turns to Eve. "Is that true ?" Eve points to the serpent : "*He* made me do it."

So what is the sin here ? It's the failure to trust in God and forgive others after having been hurt or misled—and the failure to trust in God and seek forgiveness after having made a mistake. It's the hiding and the blaming—out of fear—that turns away from God's mercy and points a finger at others to make them responsible. Adam and Eve victimized each other, and all of humanity followed. But in His freely choosing to be a holy victim—the Paschal sacrifice—Christ offers us freedom from the poisoned trap of victimization.

Notice well : Adam and Eve *both* fail. The story's meaning is not about whom to blame, it's about the emptiness of fear and blame itself. When, because of our pain, we fear the world, we end up blaming the world. But, when we fear God in the true theological sense—that is, when we stand in awe of His majesty and mercy—we are then led to the pure and healing fragrance of His divine love and mercy.

A Question

I am puzzled by something you wrote. . . . You claim that in order to change, a person must feel sorrow for the pain he or she has inflicted on others—and to no longer blame others. That makes sense regarding instances where we injure others; but I am reading from the perspective of someone whose parents were verbally abusive and emotionally negligent, who is now trying to recognize the feelings and beliefs buried in childhood. While adults should consider whether their abusive parent(s) might have suffered child abuse (leading to their own feelings of unworthiness), do you expect a victim of child abuse to feel responsible for sorrow felt by the parents/perpetrators and to not blame the abusive parents/perpetrators for the pain they inflicted ?

When I speak about psychological change, I'm addressing the person who wants to change. In your case, that's you. If you were abused as a child, then you probably responded to the emotional pain of the abuse in various ways, including blame, resentment, and anger. Now, as an adult, the sorrow you may feel for all the mistakes you made in the past can motivate you to change your behavior.

In regard to the abuse that was inflicted on you as a child, your healing depends on your understanding that the abuse was not your fault and that you were not responsible for the behavior of those who abused you. Your abusers had their own reasons for acting as they did, but that's their responsibility. Someday they might feel sorrow for what they did, and, even though it may seem unlikely, they might even apologize to you some day. But you are neither responsible for making them feel sorrow nor for mitigating the pain of any sorrow they might feel. Their sorrow, if they have any at all, is all on them. The only thing you can do to help them is refuse to hate them, because your hatred will drive them deeper into their own sin.

Eventually, as your healing progresses, and you understand yourself better than you do now, you may be able to understand your abusers better; this is called *empathy*. It's a good thing, but don't rush it. If you try to force it before you're ready for it, then it won't have any meaning other than that of a distraction from real healing.

Finally, it's important to understand something about *blame*. Being open about the facts of what afflicted you as a child is necessary for your healing. For the sake of psychological honesty, it's important to be able to state the facts of your childhood objectively and without prejudice, such as, "They did this or that," or "They failed me." It's also important to be honest about how those parental failures hurt you and inhibited your psychological growth. But stating facts like this is not a matter of blaming your parents.

In *blame* you don't just state the facts, you gloat over them, clinging to your resentment of others in the unconscious hope that, in your making a big enough stink about it, maybe God Himself will make your abusers suffer for what they did. Blame is a mistake, though, because when you cling to resentment you keep your focus on what "they did," rather than putting your focus on what you can do to reclaim your life *despite* what "they did."

When you let go of blame you let go of the belief that it's your responsibility to bring justice upon others by your making them suffer. Justice is God's responsibility. Your responsibility is only to recover your dignity despite what others did to you, regardless of why they did it.

Practical Examples

To learn how to take responsibility for your own life, it can be helpful to distinguish several aspects to the concept of *responsibility*: recognizing your own imprudence, respecting the time of others, respecting a promise you make, and not trying to protect others from their own feelings.

Imprudence

There can be times when it is necessary to take responsibility for any loss or injury you cause because of your imprudence.

- Let's say you make a reservation for an event that has a 24 hour cancellation policy; that is, if you don't give at least 24 hours advance notice to cancel, you must still pay the fee. On the day of the event, you decide that you could do some errands before the event and still be able to arrive just at the start of the event. While doing the errands, you lose your wallet and your mobile phone. You fall into a panic as you try to deal with the loss, and you miss the event entirely. The next day you try to explain what happened and that your missing the event was not your fault. But you are still charged for the event. So, are you responsible for paying?

Yes, you are responsible. It was imprudence on your part to have expected that everything would go as you planned. You did not consider that anything could have gone wrong, and that your plans could have been thwarted. Had you been prudent, you would have considered the loss you would have incurred if you did not arrive on time for the event, and so you might have left more time between the errands and the event, or you might have scheduled the errands for some other time, such as after the event.

Respecting the Time of Others

There can be times when it is necessary to take responsibility for causing the loss of someone's time (and financial loss).

- Let's say you make an appointment with someone who

charges an hourly rate. He blocks out that time for you on his schedule and promises to wait for you. On the day of the appointment, you have a family emergency, and you forget about the appointment entirely. Several days later you try to explain to the man what happened and that your missing the appointment was not your fault. But he explains that he waited for you for the entire hour you had scheduled and that he is charging you for his time. So, are you responsible for paying?

Yes, you are responsible. Certainly you suffered distress because of the family emergency, but this person suffered the loss of his time as well as a financial loss because you did not notify him that you would not keep the appointment.

Respecting a Promise You Have Made

There can be times when it is necessary to take responsibility for causing inconvenience to someone because you fail to keep a promise.

- Let's say you have promised to drive someone to the airport, but on the day of the flight some unforeseen obligation occurs and you have to change your plans. What do you do?

  You can take responsibility for your promise. You can tell the person what has occurred, and then you can offer to pay for any alternate form of transportation.

The matter of keeping a promise is not just an insignificant thing. In dysfunctional families, though, children will often say anything to appease their parents, and so the act of telling a lie becomes a commonplace reality for the children. Nevertheless, a broken promise is actually a sinful betrayal of the truth.

Therefore, someone endeavoring to live a holy life—and a responsible life—will maintain a constant, prayerful scrutiny of anything he or she says and will resist any temptation to automatically say anything just to appease another person.

Not Taking Responsibility for the Thoughts and Behaviors of Others

There can be times when you cause distress and anxiety to yourself because you are always "walking on eggshells" in fear of how other persons will react to something you do or say.

- Let's say you are at work and someone brings in a plate of homemade baked goods. She holds out the plate proudly and asks you to have some. But you are careful about your health, and so you don't eat between meals, yet you are afraid of hurting her feelings. So what do you do?

You can thank her for her efforts and say politely that you do not eat between meals. You are not wrong or cruel or insensitive for declining to eat anything you do not want. Your coworker's feelings are her responsibility, not yours, and it's her responsibility to learn to cope with them in a psychologically and spiritually healthy manner and not get entangled in negative thoughts and behaviors related to you or to herself.

Summary

If you want to be spiritually healthy and take responsibility for you own life, then keep the focus on *your* life, not on the lives of others. Learn to recognize the ways in which you can be tempted to shirk responsibility for your life by subtly pushing blame onto others or onto external circumstances, and at the same time be careful not to believe that you must take responsibility for the thoughts and behaviors of others.

In families where there is physical abuse, irrational outbursts of anger, or "discipline" that uses shaming to control children with fear, a child will be unconsciously trained to be wary of doing anything that might "cause" an unpleasant reaction in a parent. When these children become adults it can be difficult to overcome the fear of "hurting the feelings" of someone. In such cases, these persons are really more afraid of getting hurt themselves than of hurting someone else. That is, they are afraid that if they speak honestly then they will be shamed for being selfish or stupid, or that the other person will get angry.

In such a situation, the psychological task is to learn how to cope with the dysfunctional behaviors of others rather than take the blame for them.

Therefore, you don't have to fear speaking the truth even if someone might go into a silent sulk for several days or fly into a rage. Remember that the inappropriate behaviors of others are not caused by you, they are acts of free will on the part of the other; that is, they may be unconsciously motivated, but, if they become outward acts, a conscious choice has been made to not restrain them. Hence such acts are offenses against charity and so are spiritually directed against Christ, not against you. So pray for the courage to remain firm in protecting your boundaries and not be manipulated with fear, guilt, and shame.

21 BOUNDARIES

By definition, a boundary is anything that marks a limit. A psychological boundary defines personal dignity. When we say to someone, "You just crossed a line," we are speaking about a psychological limit that marks the distinction between behavior that does not cause emotional harm and behavior that causes emotional harm.

We all need to protect ourselves from emotional harm. Psychological defenses are created in childhood to serve that purpose unconsciously, but they can also lead us into unhealthy and unproductive behavior. Boundaries, unlike psychological defense mechanisms, are conscious and healthy ways to protect ourselves from emotional harm.

The ideal of life is mutual cooperation, but if you must interact with others who are not cooperative and rather are hostile or manipulative then it is necessary to have strong boundaries to protect yourself.

Some persons, however, have great difficulty setting boundaries—they may even believe that setting boundaries is rude—and this difficulty usually derives from child abuse. But let's be clear that abuse can range from subtle emotional manipulation to severe sexual and physical abuse. To the unconscious, though, any abuse, no matter how mild or severe, is an insult to personal dignity. It's precisely this insult to personal dignity that explains why adults who were abused as children lack the ability to set appropriate boundaries. As odd as it sounds, their *not having boundaries* served them as a defense mechanism in childhood. Most abused children know intuitively that if you try to do anything to resist the abuse, you just get hurt all the more. So setting aside any resistance means less hurt.

Sadly, defenses that served you very well as a child to ensure your survival can actually cripple you with fear, dishonesty, and self-sabotage when carried into adulthood. With persistence and courage, however, any psychological defense can be overcome. So if a lack of boundaries has gotten you into trouble in the past, take heart, for the problem can be remedied.

A False Belief

First it will be important to overcome the pernicious belief that you are worthless. Like any frightened child you created this belief unconsciously to tolerate your lack of resistance to childhood mistreatment. The psychological logic is this: if you can convince yourself that you're worthless and therefore don't deserve any protection from degradation, then you can more easily justify not resisting anything that degrades your value.

Note carefully, though, that the belief that you are worthless is a negative belief that you created yourself; therefore you can just as well create another, positive belief to replace the negative belief. As a first step, you might begin this process by repeating to yourself, over and over, "I am not worthless." So let's continue from there.

Boundaries Derive from Love

Healthy boundaries derive from love, not from fear. For example, you will often see so-called "nice" persons who always appear to sacrifice themselves for others. They give the impression that capitulating to others promotes peace and that boundaries are selfish—but many of these persons are motivated by an unconscious need to keep the "peace" because of their fear of conflict. Such persons usually come from dysfunctional families, where they may have played the unconscious family role of "peace keeper." They're angry at their parents, they feel guilty for being angry, and they fear any conflict that might reveal the truth about their anger. The real motive for their "nice" behavior, then, is fear, not love.

On the other hand, you can find persons who, knowing full well that they are being hurt, will sometimes set aside their boundaries as an act of charity for others. For example, if people push past you to get on a bus, you might decide to say nothing, knowing that people who would push past you to get on a bus will also react with hostility if you say anything to them about their rude behavior. In this case you can set aside your boundaries and tolerate their rude behavior with forbearance, praying that they might someday learn to act with charity to others. Yet the same persons who can willingly set aside their boundaries can just as well defend them. For example, if someone at work uses foul language, you can state that you do not like to hear such talk; if the talk persists, you can get up and walk away.

Thus there is a big difference between someone who has clear boundaries and is willing to protect them—and who can willingly set the boundaries aside for the good of others when necessary—and someone who, because of fear, tolerates anything. Therefore, acting out of fear only leads to a wasted life because it unconsciously supports rudeness and disorder. Acting from love, however, can bring genuine good into the world through your personal example. But only with healthy boundaries can you act from love. Let's see why this is so.

The Lack of Boundaries:
A Refusal Based on Hatred

Consider that boundaries have a fundamental place in life

itself. Look around you, and you will see that every living creature has its own territory which it defends against intrusion. Boundaries are so fundamental that even criminals who thrive on violating the integrity of others have their own internal code of ethics, their own "boundaries."

Considering, then, that boundaries have a core purpose in civilization, an individual's lack of personal, psychological boundaries isn't really a true lack—at least, it's not a lack in the philosophical sense of something "missing." Instead, this apparent lack is really a *refusal* to defend one's own dignity, and it's a refusal based on hatred. This hatred, though, is double-edged: it's a hatred for the self as well as a hatred for others.

It's a hatred for the self that results from living always in fear because of having been mistreated or abused as a child. Unable to make sense of senseless hurt, a child, using its best, but still imperfect, childhood logic, arrives at the only "logical" conclusion: "It's all my fault. I'm just a worthless person. I deserve condemnation for being worthless, and I deserve condemnation for always being so afraid." And there you have it: self-hatred caused by fear that is caused by abuse.

All of this self-hatred, however, derives from a hatred for others. For example, when a child is mistreated by a parent, the child will be angry with the parent, but, because it will feel dangerous to be angry with someone the child depends on for food and shelter, the child will hide the anger—and hate—by turning it against itself. Nevertheless, as hidden as it may be, the original focus of the anger is on the parent, not the on self.

That hidden hatred, therefore, hurts others as well as yourself. When others mistreat you now, as an adult, your dignity is insulted, yes, but by keeping quiet and allowing the mistreatment, you deprive them of what would essentially be a spiritual warning[1] about their sin; that is, if you were to defend your boundaries and speak up about the mistreatment, you would at least give the offender the opportunity to recognize and repent the hurtful behavior.

To re-establish healthy boundaries, then, endeavor to stop *refusing* to defend boundaries. You can do this by starting to refuse to hate—and that includes refusing to hate or defile yourself.

Examples of Healthy Boundaries

Refusing to break the law.

The law is absolute to a particular city, state, or country.[2] Breaking the law is not just an act of hatred to authority, it is a criminal act with unpleasant penalties. If you break the law, even if others manipulate you into doing it, you are the one who has to pay the price. Getting yourself into trouble like this defiles everyone.

Refusing to bend the rules.

Unlike the law, which is absolute, rules of conduct are relative to a particular social context. Rules allow things to function smoothly because everyone within a particular context agrees to them. Rules can refer to a game, to office procedures, to family conduct, or even to the celebration of liturgy. But if you allow rules to be bent, then the whole social context becomes defiled.

Refusing to betray your moral values.

Your moral values provide your own internal guidance about something that is wrong to do, even if it might be legal or even if society encourages it. Moral values derive from an abstract sense of the "good," which has its origin in God. If you betray your moral values, such as by allowing yourself to be pressured into doing something immoral, you betray God and defile the good.

Refusing to allow someone to pressure you to get too close to you emotionally.

We do not live in a world of true love; we live in a world of selfishness, where others try to get their needs met even at the expense of your needs. People will try to get you to "open up" when you don't want to, and they will try to get you to "spill your guts" when it can be used against you.

Allowing yourself to be pressured like this defiles love.

Refusing to subject your body to indignity.

We are physical creatures. Our bodies are made of bones and flesh. Each of us has a physical presence that makes us unique and contributes to our sense of individuality. Moreover, the body of every Christian is a temple of the Holy Spirit. Your body, therefore, needs to be protected with modest behavior and clothing.

> Keep in mind that Christians wear clothing not to hide their nakedness but to give dignity to their bodies. In contrast, Satanic rituals are conducted in the nude because a body stripped of clothing has lost its holiness and is just a spiritually anonymous object.

Therefore, dressing immodestly, tainting your body with tattoos,[3] allowing your body to be touched with lust, or allowing your health to be threatened (for example, smoking cigarettes or breathing second-hand cigarette smoke, eating junk foods, using drugs, or abusing alcohol) defiles your body and your soul.

Putting It Into Practice

PROTECTING YOURSELF FROM WHAT OTHERS WANT
FROM YOU: *SAYING "NO."*

Here are some examples.

- I cannot do that right now; I will get to it in due time.
- I prefer not to discuss this right now.
- I understand what you want, and yet it's against my values, and so I will not do it.
- That's a private matter that I don't want to discuss.
- It's none of your business.
  (*This is a legitimate response if it is said gently and calmly.*)
- I've already explained my opinion about the matter; I don't want to discuss it further.
- I have already said "No," and I'm not going to argue with you about it.
  (*If the other person keeps making objections, then just keep repeating, after every objection, "I said I'm not going to argue with you."*)

PROTECTING YOURSELF FROM WHAT OTHERS DO TO
YOU: *STATING CONSEQUENCES.*

Note that if you tell others what to do, it will lead to opposition and conflicts. Therefore, the most effective strategy is to make statements in which you state what *you* will do if the other person does something contrary to your preferences.

Here are some examples.

- If you keep using foul language, then I will get up and leave.
- If you're going to complain about how I drive, then I will stop the car and won't drive any farther until you get out or be quiet.
- If you keep yelling at me, then I will hang up the phone.
- If you send any more offensive text messages, I will block your number.
- If you intend to dress like that, then I won't go with you.
- Listen, there's a complicating factor here that you're not aware of. [*Specify.*] I'm just trying to clarify things. If you're going to be sarcastic and call me stupid, then I'm not going to help you with this task.

Summary

Life often involves counter-intuitive principles. For example, to drive from one place to another you may have to drive for a while in a direction away from your destination. Psychology, too, is like this. Boundaries can have a counter-intuitive element to them. When others make demands of you, you demonstrate that you care about others by resisting the temptation to cross certain boundaries in an attempt to fulfill the others' demands. To the other, your protection of your boundaries can feel restrictive—even confusing or rude—but to you it's a job well done.

The explanation for this can be found in the psychology of infant development.

The time of infancy brings with it the expectation that the child's expression of his or her needs will lead to the fulfillment of those needs. A child cries, and a mother—a good mother—will come running to feed the child, change the diaper, relieve pain, or do whatever else must be done to attend to the child. After all, a good mother can interpret the meaning of any cry.

As infancy progresses into childhood, a new task begins. Rather than be dependent on having their needs fulfilled in all things, children learn how to fulfill their own needs. They want to hold their own cup and tie their own shoes. This prepares children to grow into mature and responsible adults.

In a dysfunctional family, however, little of this healthy learning takes place. If infants are denied the comfort of feeling understood, they will not be able to take up the task of wanting to fulfill their own needs. Never having felt understood, they will feel burdened by always having to take care of themselves. The mature obligation of fulfilling their own needs as adults will seem like a curse.

Consequently, if you acquiesce to the temptation to give to others everything they want, you will infantilize them. Instead of being an example of mature confidence and independence, you will psychologically cripple others. If you make this mistake, you will show that you do not really care about others.

Thus the full irony becomes revealed: only by maintaining your boundaries can you give real love to others. Furthermore, when parents have good boundaries, they can teach their children to develop healthy boundaries and to encounter life with full confidence.

22   HOW TO SAY "NO" TO A CHILD

It's always a sad thing when someone attempts to discourage a child's behavior by saying, "You don't want to do that." But of course the child wants to do that! It's perfectly obvious he wants to do it, or he wouldn't be trying. So why confuse the child by denying what you both know is perfectly true?

Here, then, is a special hint on how to say "No" to a child without causing psychological hurt. You do this by *acknowledging* what the child wants and then, without making the child feel guilty or bad simply for having his or her desires, *explain* why the child cannot have what he or she wants.

To a young child say the following:

> "I know you want to [have some candy, play in the water, chase the birds, whatever . . .] *and* there are times when you can't always have what you want because other good things have to come first."

To an older child (or another adult, for that matter) try saying something like this:

> "I know that you really would like to [stay out past dark, bungee jump off the Golden Gate Bridge, or whatever ...] *and* [the danger of getting mugged, the law, insurance regulations, etc.] just won't allow it."

The point of such statements is to show the child that you recognize and respect the child's desire *and* that since the world is filled with conflicting desires, one's own desires can't always be fulfilled. This is an important lesson for children to learn. (It's too bad most adults haven't learned it.)

Said in another way, it's not that the child's desire is wrong, it's simply that, because the world is unfair, all desires cannot always be fulfilled. It's important to learn that "unfairness" is, in many cases, a conflict between two "goods." This is why you use the word *and*, rather than *but*, between the two parts of your statement.

What if ... ?

What if, after taking the precaution of saying "No" properly, a child were to respond, "If you don't give me what I want, I will kill myself!" Or what if you were afraid that a child might commit suicide if his or her desires weren't fulfilled? What then? Should the fear of violence hold you hostage?

Well, it's important to remember that no one can make another person get angry. Even though a person might feel hurt by something, anger is a response to that hurt, a response freely chosen for the purpose of causing harm in retaliation for that hurt. It's not a response that someone can be forced into; it's a response that a person chooses.

So even though a parent might have to do something for perfectly good disciplinary reasons that a child experiences as hurtful, the parent is not responsible for causing any anger the child might express, even if the anger takes the form of a suicidal threat—or even if the anger takes the form of actual suicide.

When a child considers suicide to be a justifiable response to feeling hurt, it points to a grave disorder that derives from a combination of two things. First, it demonstrates that the child has been brainwashed by the contemporary culture of hedonism and entitlement, such that the child has come to accept the false belief that "anything is acceptable, and if I want it, I'm entitled to it, and, if I don't get it, I'll make a big enough stink about it until I do get it." Second, it demonstrates that moral values and discipline have been so lacking in the family life as to let false beliefs take root and grow in the child.

Here, then, is where parents do have responsibility. If a

child gets angry when parents have to say "No," then the parents have failed in either, or both, of two ways. On the one hand, parents can fail to provide necessary oversight to restrict the child's access to video games, TV, movies, popular music, magazines, social media, etc. and to correct and reverse any brainwashing the child receives from school; on the other hand, parents can fail to assert the discipline of making Christian moral values—such as love, humility, patience, and mutual cooperation—the core of the family life.

23 THE LOSS OF INNOCENCE

Once a child is born, its continued survival depends entirely on someone to feed it and care for it. Consequently, the child comes to expect the world to be caring. As the child grows and develops, its mental health and sanity depend on the innocent belief that the world is not completely irrational and hostile.

So what is a parent to do when social violence and natural disasters around the world shatter the child's sense of innocence? Well, here are several guidelines.

1. *Be careful not to hide anything from the child.* Parents sometimes believe that if they don't talk about tragedies then it will protect a child from fear. But children, in one way or another, know as much, if not more, about what is occurring in the world than their parents. So when a parent tries to hide reality by not talking about something, the parent's silence only increases a child's inner, unspoken anxiety. Moreover, parental silence "tells" the child that because of the parent's evasiveness the parent can't be a trusted source of support.

2. *Talk about the event from the child's perspective.* Parents often believe that "talking about" something means telling the child what they themselves believe. But usually the parents are more anxious than the child, and so they end up making the child anxious. The fact is, children think about things that might not even occur to an adult. For example, hearing that an entire family was killed in a terrorist attack, a young child might not be concerned at all about his or her own death in a similar situation but might be worried about who will take care of the family cat that will be left alone in the house without food if anything occurred to the family. Therefore, to "talk about" something with a child, it is necessary for the parent to listen carefully to the child's unique concerns and help the child understand the meaning of those concerns.

3. *Help the child express emotions.* Children need help putting complex emotions into words. By listening carefully to the child's concerns, parents can help the child distinguish anger from fear from anxiety from vulnerability from frustration from sadness and so on. Of course, you, the adult, are perfectly capable of sorting out your own emotions, aren't you? Aren't you?

4. *Be careful not to overwhelm—or brainwash—the child with your own anxiety.* Parents who become overly protective of a child after a tragedy are looking after their own needs, not the needs of their children, and so they instill a sense of paranoia in the child. If a child is

kidnapped in your city, your bolting the doors, keeping the drapes closed, and refusing to let your child out of the house will only cause additional trauma in your child.

5. *Speak of positive and good things.* Bad things occur, yes, but far more good things occur each day. Thousands of airplanes take off and land every day without incident. Hundreds of millions of children go about their lives every day without being attacked, molested, or abducted. Teach your child to trust in the good, not to fear the bad.

6. *"Why do bad things occur?"* Parents often freeze when a child asks this question—or they offer a cynical answer that reflects their own bitterness. Here's the best and simplest answer of all:

> God is love, and God created the world to share that love with us. But love can't be commanded; if we are to love, we must love by our own free will, and that means we must have the capacity to not love. Therefore, God gave all of us free will; with it came the freedom to love, but the freedom for bad things to contradict love also came with it. So the more you see bad things occur around you, the more you should be reminded to love from your own heart.

24 HELPING CHILDREN HEAL

Consider the way a dysfunctional father treats his family. Instead of being a good father—that is, sympathetic, loving toward others, compassionate, humble, and always returning a blessing for an insult (see 1 Peter 3:8)—he will, overtly or subtly, wear down his wife and children with lies, criticism, and faultfinding. He will manipulate them and play "mind games" with them, denying their reality and their feelings even as he smiles at them.

In his selfishness, he denies his children's reality. That denial will wound the children deeply. But, because the children can't just go find another father, and because they lack the psychological capacity to understand the games that are being played with their minds, their emotional pain will be driven down into their unconscious, forcing them to defend themselves internally and intellectually. They will teach themselves to suppress their true feelings. They will view the world with cynicism. And the residue of that defensiveness will continue on in their unconscious even into adulthood to affect all of their interpersonal relationships.

This continuing dynamic will be seen especially in the way these adults now treat their own children.

Maybe you are one of these adults.

Instead of validating the reality of your children's pain, you will tend to deny it. When your child is hurting, you will tend to say, "Oh, it's not that bad. Stop whining."

What does this do to your children? Well, they know very well the reality of their pain. And they know very well that you're denying it. So they lose trust in you. Then they will unconsciously develop ways to keep testing you with their behavior, trying to "get you" to finally acknowledge their reality. Yet the more you see them as a nuisance, the more they see you as a failure.

So what's the proper way to help children heal from pain?

First, validate the children's reality.

- For physical wounds, say something like this: "Yes, it hurts, doesn't it? And, oh, look at that good blood! What good, strong red blood! You're doing a very good job of bleeding!

- For emotional wounds, be upfront and never try to protect children by hiding the truth—be assured, they already have a good idea of what's going on anyway. All they need from you is the truth so that they don't have to concoct their own imaginary explanations to fit the situation. You might say, for example, "Yes, it's scary, isn't it? Grandma is in hospital because the doctors think she has cancer. Right now, we don't know any more than that. There will be medical tests in the next couple of days. Then we will know more."

Second, teach the children to trust in God and teach them that all things—even pain—will pass.

- For physical wounds, say something like this: "It won't hurt forever. The bleeding will stop when it's ready to stop. So let's say a prayer to God for your healing, and then we will go and do what needs to be done to clean up the wound."

- For emotional wounds, don't lie and say that everything will be OK. Instead, admit that you really don't know what might occur next and teach the children to pray and trust in God. "Yes, Grandma could die. So let's pray that she will be OK. But whatever occurs, we must trust in God that He will have mercy on her soul and that He will help us cope with our feelings."

What a gift to a child! Reality and faith!

How many of us never received these gifts? What a wounded mess our world is because of it.

When seeking out my help in the face of some sort of

family crisis, parents often admit to me that they have
hidden the truth from their children. Then they quickly
add, "I was trying to protect them."

Well, you cannot protect children by hiding anything
from them. You can protect them only by teaching them
to trust in God's providence.

Part Two

QUESTIONS & ANSWERS

Gird up your loins now, like a man; I will question you, and you tell me the answers!

Job 38:3

25 WHEN CHILDREN FALL

I'm a devout Catholic, but my adult children have fallen away from the Church. I pray for them, but is there anything else I should be doing?

Someone once sent a question like this to a columnist in one of those diocesan newspapers, and his response was something like this: "Children have free will, and this sort of thing happens. It's not your fault. Just pray for them."

Well, an answer like that misses the point entirely. Things don't just "happen." Everything we do with our free will has an unconscious motivation, and if we are to live genuine Christian lives we have to discipline ourselves through sacrifice, obedience, and prayer so that unconscious motivation does not draw our wills away from God's will.

Drawn Away from God's Will

Christian parents have a prime duty to raise children to love and to fear God. And one of the parents' prime obligations is to teach their children to do God's will and to protect their children from being drawn away from God's will.

In the times of the early Church, Christian families tended to live in Christian communities, and, because of the general lack of mass communication, these communities tended to be relatively insulated from the pagan influence surrounding them. Therefore, children lived well-protected within the communities. Still, Christians had to be vigilant; their faith became their real protection from the evil of the hostile world around them, and children learned by their parents' example to put their trust in a living faith.

But once the emperor Constantine made Christianity the formal religion of the Roman Empire, everything began to change. Over the years, as societies became more and more Christian, and as Christianity became more and more incorporated into secular politics, individual Christians tended to let their guard down. No longer threatened by a hostile non-Christian environment, their faith tended to become less emotionally intense and more intellectual. In essence, faith was gradually taken for granted. Faith began losing its identity as a personal battle against evil, and it started to become a mere social identity—a requirement, as it were—for social status and acceptance.

Now, in recent years, because previous generations have allowed their Christian faith to become lukewarm and hypocritical, anti-Christian ideology has had ample space to grow. The secular world, with all its weapons of entertainment, has been attacking the Church as an angry reaction to the social effects of Christian values having taken on secular political power. The secular world is actively trying to shake off the "burdensome yoke" of Christian morality. Children are being assaulted and brainwashed by anti-Christian—and especially anti-Catholic—television, movies, magazines, advertising, social media, music, video games, and sports, along with education itself.

When so much of the world today is based in such evil— that is, opposition to God's will—Catholic children need to be protected from this evil. They need to be given a living faith that teaches them clearly, yet compassionately, what evil is. They need to be given a living faith that protects them from being drawn away to their destruction in an evil world. Children need to learn true, heartfelt trust in God.

Trust in God

Full trust in God is composed of two separate but interrelated components: trust in God's justice, and trust in God's providence.

1. **Trust in God's Justice.** We have all encountered individuals who commit offenses and seem to "get away with it." Although the irritation that we feel is

justified, we can also be drawn into the desire to take matters into our own hands and get revenge. If we remember, however, that every crime—every sin— every offense against love—that a person commits is an offense against God that will be accounted for during his or her judgment at death. All sins will be paid for. If the sins are not repented, they will be paid for in hell, but if the sins are repented they will be paid for in Purgatory, thus demonstrating that *mercy* is a fundamental part of God's justice. To trust in God's justice, then, is to set aside our anger for the injuries inflicted on us and to let God administer His own justice according to His will.

2. **Trust in God's Providence.** Some individuals have the mistaken belief that "trust in God" means to sit around doing nothing in the expectation that God will do everything for us. But this false belief is based in an avoidance of our taking full responsibility for living holy lives that bear spiritual fruits.[1] To trust in God's providence, therefore, does not mean that we do nothing; it means that we believe that, in answer to our prayers, God will guide, protect, and encourage us as we take responsibility for developing and using our talents to serve God.

With a fully-developed trust in God, children will be protected from everything that can assault their faith. To develop this trust in God, however, children need the example of parents who themselves trust in God. But if their parents' lives do not reflect trust in God, the children will see the fraud and will end up trusting in nothing but their own power of manipulation.

What Your Children See

So, let's be honest here now. What unconscious motivation has led your children to "fall away" from the Church? Well, maybe you see yourself as a "devout" Catholic because you attend Mass daily. Maybe you even go out of your way to attend a traditional Latin Mass. Maybe you pray the Rosary daily.

But what do your children see?

Do they see both parents with a living faith engaged in an all-out battle with the evil of the world? Do they see both parents living in contemplative love for God and constant awareness of His presence? If they did, they would look to their parents' faith and, like Peter looking to Christ (see John 6:68), they would say, "Where else can we go? This is the real thing."

No, your children don't see living faith. Your children don't see protection from evil. Your children don't see genuine, fruitful devotion. Your children don't see genuine love for God. Instead, they see your external acts of devotion as meaningless because they see all the other things you do, or your husband or wife does, that contradict the true faith. Thus you lose credibility—and when the parents lose credibility, the children will become cynical, angry teenagers who turn to the secular social world around them for identity and acceptance. They will have more concern for gaining their friends' approval than for loving God.

How You Lose Credibility

Do you or your spouse raise your voice or argue with your children? Do you or your spouse manipulate your children with guilt or tell them that they will go to hell if they don't do what you want them to do? Ding! You lose credibility.

> In Ephesians 6:4 we are told not to provoke our children to anger, but to bring them up with the training and instruction of the Lord.

Do you or your spouse instruct your children with a focus on duty and rationality, using intellectual defensiveness to maintain your authority, all the while lacking emotional awareness and patient sensitivity to the personal experiences of your children? Ding! You lose credibility.

> In Colossians 3:12 we are told to put on heartfelt compassion, kindness, humility, gentleness, and patience when interacting with others.

Do you or your spouse sulk in silence or in sarcastic

criticism when others mistreat you? Ding! You lose credibility.

> In James 1:3 we are told to consider it all joy when we encounter various trials, and to know that the testing of our faith produces perseverance.

When you or your spouse are driving, do you curse or honk at other drivers? Ding! You lose credibility.

> In 1 Peter 3:8–9a we are told to be of one mind, sympathetic, loving toward one another, compassionate, and humble, and to not return evil for evil, or insult for insult, but, on the contrary, a blessing.

To be fashionable, do you or your spouse wear immodest clothing that invites others to lust for your body? Do you have tattoos? Ding! You lose credibility.

> In 1 Corinthians 6:19–20 we are told that our bodies are temples of the Holy Spirit within us, Whom we have from God, and that no one is his own.

Do you or your spouse gossip about friends or co-workers? Ding! You lose credibility.

> In Philippians 2:3–4 we are told to do nothing out of selfishness or out of vainglory, but instead to humbly regard others as more important than ourselves, each looking out not for his own interests, but everyone

looking out for the interests of others.

Are you or your spouse overweight? Do you or your spouse eat junk food throughout the day? Ding! You lose credibility.

> In Philippians 3:18–19, Saint Paul, speaking in tears, said that many so-called Christians conduct themselves as enemies of the Cross of Christ. Their end is destruction, he said; their "god" is their stomach and, in the pride of self-deception, their "glory" is really their "shame," all because their minds are occupied only with earthly things.

Are you or your spouse a tobacco smoker, enslaved to nicotine? Do you use marijuana, which is for atheists (those who reject the idea of God) and Satanists (those who reject God)? Are you a heavy drinker or an alcoholic? Ding! You lose credibility.

> In Galatians 5:1 we are told that for the sake of freedom Christ set us free; so stand firm, he said, and do not submit again to the yoke of slavery.

Do you or your spouse crave eroticism? Do you or your spouse look at pornography on your computer or mobile device? Ding! You lose credibility.

> In Romans 1:25 we are told that through the ages the wicked have exchanged the truth of God for a lie and

have revered and worshiped the creature rather than
the Creator, Who is blessed forever.

Do you or your spouse overlook sins, in the belief that
the ends justify the means, as in saying, "Sure, there's foul
language and sexual scenes in this movie, but it has a good
message." Ding! You lose credibility.

> In Ephesians 4:17–19 we are told that we must not live
> as the Gentiles do, in the futility of their minds, dark-
> ened in understanding and alienated from the life of
> God. Because of their ignorance, and because of their
> hardness of heart, they became callous and handed
> themselves over to licentiousness for the practice of
> every kind of impurity to excess.

Do you or your spouse ever skip the blessing before eating
because you're in a hurry or because people might look at
you with scorn? Ding! You lose credibility.

> In Romans 1:21 we are told that although the wicked
> knew God they did not accord Him glory as God or
> give Him thanks. Instead, they became vain in their
> reasoning, and their senseless minds were darkened.

Do you or your spouse ever say, "Let's skip Mass today.
I don't feel like going." Or do you or your spouse arrive
at Mass late (after the priest begins with the sign of the
cross) or leave early (before the dismissal)? Ding! You lose
credibility.

> In Galatians 6:7–8 we are told sternly that God is not
> mocked, and that a person will reap only what he sows;
> the one who sows for his flesh will reap corruption
> from the flesh, but the one who sows for the spirit will
> reap eternal life from the spirit.

When you or your spouse hear of some person in the news who has done something despicable, do you say, "Scum like that should be wiped off the face of the earth!" Ding! You lose credibility.

> In James 2:13 we are told that judgment is merciless to
> one who has not shown mercy.

Do you or your spouse ever shout and cheer for a sports team? Ding! You lose credibility.

> In Galatians 6:14 Saint Paul asserted that he would
> never boast except in the cross of our Lord Jesus Christ,
> through which the world has been crucified to him,
> and he to the world.

Do you or your spouse worry about things to the point of anxiety or insomnia? Ding! You lose credibility.

> In Matthew 6:34 we are told not to worry about tomor-
> row because tomorrow will take care of itself.

Do you or your spouse participate in protests, or start tort lawsuits? Ding! You lose credibility.

> In 1 Peter 2:23 we are told plainly that when Christ was insulted, He returned no insult, and that when He suffered, He did not threaten; instead, He handed Himself over to the one who judges justly.

Do you or your spouse come home from work in a dark funk, warning everyone to "Get out of my way! Leave me alone!" saying, "What a horrible day!" Ding! You lose credibility.

> In 2 Corinthians 1:5 we are told that as Christ's sufferings overflow to us, so through Christ does our encouragement also overflow.

Do you or your spouse turn your back when beggars ask for money? Ding! You lose credibility.

> In Luke 6:30 and Matthew 5:42 we are told to give to everyone who asks of us.

Have you or your spouse allowed atheistic, anti-Catholic public "education," social media, television, movies, magazines, rock music, and video games to hijack the moral development of your children? Ding! YOU HAVE LOST CREDIBILITY!

> In Matthew 18:6 Christ told us that it is such a great spiritual crime to cause a child who believes in Him to sin that it would be better for that person to have a great millstone hung around his neck and to be

drowned in the depths of the sea.

Now, this list could go on and on—and it does, and it's not pretty. Many persons who call themselves "devout" Catholics have lost credibility with their children over many things. Even if they have changed their behavior now, they still failed in the past, when their children were younger.

Exposing the Fraud

Many children don't see devotion in their parents. They see hypocrisy and, to their eyes, empty, superstitious rituals. Though they might claim to be angry with the Church, they are unconsciously angry with their parents for living a fraud instead of a true Christian lifestyle that bears tangible spiritual fruits—and their anger is directed to one purpose: to expose the fraud.

> So what are these tangible spiritual fruits of the Holy Spirit? In Galatians 5:22–23 Saint Paul names them: love, joy, peace, patience, kindness, generosity, faithfulness, gentleness, and self-control. Church Tradition lists twelve fruits of the Holy Spirit: charity, joy, peace, patience, kindness, goodness, generosity, gentleness, faithfulness, modesty, self-control, and chastity (see the *Catechism of the Catholic Church*, 1832).

Therefore, the children's unconscious motivation is to

show the world, through their own wretched behavior, that their parents are lacking in compassion and real love and that their "devout" parents have failed to produce any tangible spiritual fruits.

What You Can Do Now

So what can you do now if you have lost your children's credibility and they have lost their faith? Is there no hope? Well, there is always hope, as long as you are not afraid.

So, first, admit your mistakes, and the mistakes of your husband or wife, honestly and openly. Tell your children that you were wrong. Tell Christ that you were wrong. With a sorrowful heart, repent and confess your errors.

Only one thing, though, has any chance of reaching past your children's apathy and resistance: your tears of contrition. Weep. Weep for the damage you have done to your children. Weep for their souls. Weep for your mistakes. Let your tears speak from your heart.

Then begin to live the faith as it is supposed to be lived. Live the suffering, self-sacrificial love that Christ taught and that the Catholic mystics have experienced through the ages. Let that love fill you from the inside and envelop you from the outside, becoming the entire reason for your life. Let this love manifest for both you and your spouse as a chaste life of sacrifice, obedience, and prayer—from your heart, not intellectually—every moment of every day. Live it with patience and humility, seeking God's blessing for everything you do, being grateful for all you receive, and bearing all trials with absolute trust in God. Then, with emotional honesty and tears of contrition, demonstrate that love to your children.

Living a life of real Christian faith is relentless hard work for both parents—it's a true spiritual battle against evil. But when your faith becomes your life then maybe—even though it may take 10 years or 20 years, or more—your children will take you seriously.

Then, maybe, once your children take you seriously, they will see that their anger can be healed. Then, maybe, they will want the Good Shepherd to find them. What greater hope is there than that?

I am desiring to seek assistance for my 10 year old son. It is a long story but to come to the present my son is not acting normally. I believe he can be but is showing abnormal behavior I believe because of emotional problems, mainly because of our home environment. I am a devout Catholic and am seeking guidance that will help me come aligned with the will of God. I want to help my son and the rest of my family, including myself, and I know I can only do it with God as part of it.

A branch of psychotherapy called "Family Therapy" holds a fundamental premise that all children's symptoms are the result of larger family problems. So, if a child's behavior needs to be changed, the whole family must change.

Now, in your message you acknowledge the role of the family in your son's abnormal behavior. That's a good start. Furthermore, you recognize the need to seek a solution with God as part of it. That's even better.

So what can you do? Well, you say you're a devout Catholic.

Yet, from what you have written, it would seem that your husband is not a devout Catholic; if he were, he would be a proper father and you wouldn't be having these problems. So that puts you in the role of a Saint Monica or a Saint Rita, doesn't it?

Therefore, let's ask some questions to see whether your current family life fits the description of a genuinely devout Catholic family life. If not, then you will know what changes to make, so that, while praying for the conversion of your husband and children, you can be the defender of faith within your family.

- Have you read the *Catechism of the Catholic Church* so that you have a solid intellectual understanding of the Catholic faith? Do you understand the faith well enough yourself that you can explain it to your son in language that he can understand?

- Have you taught your son how to sit quietly in reverent respect while praying at home so that he can sit quietly and reverently in church during Mass, rather than cause a disturbance like all the other children making noise in church because their parents haven't taught them at home to sit quietly in prayer?

- Do you spend time every night with your son reading Scripture and explaining it to him? Before every Mass do you read with your son the Scriptural readings and explain their meaning to your son, so that he knows the theme of that day's Mass?

- Do you allocate special time each day with your son to pray some form of morning prayer, evening prayer (before or after dinner), and night prayer (before bed)?

- Through your personal example, do you teach your son to trust always in God's justice and providence? (See pp. 133–134.)

- Do you teach your son, through your own personal example, that whenever anyone says or does anything unkind to you, you respond with a blessing and a prayer for that person's repentance?

- Are you careful never to curse or speak harshly, critically, or sarcastically to anyone?

- Do you discuss openly and objectively with your son all of his experiences, so that he can learn to see both the positive and negative qualities in everything human?

- Do you teach your son that if he chooses to live a genuine Catholic life, he will most likely have few friends and will suffer much social persecution?

- Are you careful never to lie to your son?

- If you make a mistake, do you admit it honestly and then teach your son how you can learn from it?

- If you ever hurt your son emotionally, do you explain what occurred and why it occurred, and then promise to do everything you can to not do it again?

- Do you show your son through your own personal example that you do not have any desire for materialism or social approval, and that instead of seeking out your own pleasure you always look to the good of others?

- Do you explain to your son that most everything he will see on TV or in movies or read in comic books and newspapers, or, for that matter, be taught in school, is hostile to the Catholic faith? And do you then correct the errors he has learned from others?

- Do you explain to your son that you do not watch TV or movies because the entertainment industry wants to destroy the Church by brainwashing everyone, especially children, and that you prefer to live a holy life of prayer and study so as to develop your personal talents for God's service?

- Do you teach your son that competitive sports and video games are based in pride and strife, and that instead of competing with his neighbors he should be praying for their enlightenment and conversion?

- As a personal example to your son, do you dress modestly? Do you tell your son that it is necessary to avoid tattoos and piercings? Do you explain to him how modesty is central to the Christian faith, and how many persons in this world are deceived by the social worship of lust?

- As a personal example to your son, are you a non-smoker?

- As a personal example to your son, do you avoid marijuana and other drugs and use alcohol only with careful responsibility?

- As a personal example to your son, do you eat simple, healthy food and maintain an ideal weight?

- As a personal example to your son, whenever you can, do you walk short distances rather than drive, and take stairs rather than elevators, for exercise?

- Do you discipline your son properly? (See Chapter 16.)

- Do you teach your son, through your own personal example, to treat other family members with kindness and dignity, as a aspect of Christian mutual cooperation?

- If your husband does anything immoral or unfaithful, do you explain to your son honestly and compassionately exactly what your husband is doing, and why it is wrong, telling your son not to blame his father but to pray constantly for his father's conversion?

Therefore, if, as you have said, you really want to help your son and the rest of your family, including yourself, doing it with God as part of it, then set about now to change your lifestyle according to the above principles. With prayer and sacrifice, you can do it.

27 CULTURAL SUBVERSION

Wait a minute. Christ never told us not to smoke or not to drink our diet colas. What does giving up these things have to do with a spiritual life?

Very much, actually.

Lack of Trust in God

Many of these things are symbolic of our turning to material satisfactions in difficult times rather than turning to God. How can someone even claim to trust in God's providence and justice if, at the first hint of vulnerability, he or she immediately reaches for a cigarette or for food that isn't really needed for nutrition?

So, despite what is written on our money, hardly anyone in this country really trusts in God. In fact, it may only be a matter of time before the courts declare that printing "In God We Trust" on money violates the constitutional rights of atheists.

151

Realize, therefore, that we live in a culture as morally depraved as ancient Rome. In the context of a government that is fundamentally anti-Catholic,[1] the news media and the arts and entertainment industries are all fundamentally anti-Christian, and their underlying "progressive" liberal agenda (see Appendix I) is to reduce the moral sensibilities of this country to the lowest common denominator of secular hedonism. In the language of atheistic politicobabble, this is called "diversity."

We live in a world that has so forsaken the divine that most individuals now extol trivialities so as to provide at least some illusion that their lives have some meaning.

Jesus criticized the Pharisees and Herodians for following the illusions of their own time. But when He warned His disciples to beware the "leaven" of the Pharisees and the "leaven" of Herod (Mark 8:15), even they didn't understand. And so it is today. Most Christians today just don't get it when they are warned to guard against the "leaven" of popular culture; moreover, they go so far as to make heroes of individuals whose lives are given over to flagrant mortal sin.

Unconscious Infection with Subversive Desires

We are always in danger of being unconsciously "infected" by the subversive social desires around us that eat away at religious values like a malignant cancer. First it was endorsement of divorce, "free sex," surrogacy, and abortion; now the agenda centers on lifestyles defiant of chastity, and soon—if not already, in some places—there will be the legalization of marijuana, prostitution, public sex, infanticide, assisted suicide, and euthanasia.

If you were to look at sin epidemiologically—that is, in the same way as investigators seek the origins of a medical epidemic—you would have to consider the vectors of its transmission. And it should be perfectly obvious that the cultural desires which lead to sin—desires such as pride, hate, lust, greed, blame, competition, and self-gratification—are spread rampantly by popular entertainment and sports. Those who are not on guard against the leaven of popular culture are easily infected. As Saint James said, each person is tempted when he is lured and enticed by his own desire (see James 1:14).

> . . . I see that God is ever ready to give us all the interior and exterior aids necessary for our salvation, and that He observes our deeds solely for our own good . . . on the other hand, I see man continually occupied in useless things, contrary to himself and of no value; and that at the hour of death God will say to him: What is there, O man, that I could have done for thee which I have not done? . . . and I am amazed and cannot understand how man can be so mad as to neglect a thing of such vast and extreme importance.
>
> — Saint Catherine of Genoa[2]

Moreover, when parents surrender their moral authority to the popular culture around them, they allow their children to be brainwashed with popular ideology; families then disintegrate into moral indifference and corruption—and the children are left with gaping emotional wounds of unconscious confusion and anger, social disobedience, and a crippling lack of faith.

Even though many families may have the tacit acceptance of Christ on their lips, in their hearts they are scooping up all the subversive anti-Christian satisfactions and amusements that our culture offers us in its veiled hope of seducing us to our own doom.

> Have no love for the world, nor the things that the world affords, wrote Saint John. If anyone loves the world, the Father's love has no place in him, because nothing that the world affords comes from the Father. Carnal allurements, enticements for the eye, the life of empty show—all these are from the world, and the world with its seductions is passing away but the man who does God's will endures forever (see the First Letter of the Apostle John, 2:15–17).

Note, however, that when Saint John speaks of "the world" he refers to the social world of human construction, not the beautiful physical world of God's creation. The social world defiles God's beauty by infecting us with unconscious desires that lure and entice us into sin. As Saint James said, desire conceives and brings forth sin, and when sin reaches maturity it gives birth to death (see James 1:15).

Sweetness to Fill Emotional Emptiness

Christ redeemed us from our slavery to sin through His Passion and death, and each of us enters into that redemption at baptism. Most often this is infant baptism, though, and most parents do almost nothing thereafter except indoctrinate their children into popular atheistic culture and a life of continuing sin. So in most modern families children imitate their parents' hypocrisy and commit a multitude of sins after their baptism.

Cultural frivolities, whether soda pop or lust, are nothing but "sweetness" to fill the emotional emptiness of a soul that has forsaken Christ. In fact, much that calls itself "Christianity" today is just an imitation of the world and, like soda pop, is just sugar water of no substance.

Therefore, rather than follow the "sweet and satisfying paths" of spiritual mediocrity that Saint John of the Cross warned us about,[3] learn to quench your thirst for truth and holiness with the living water from Christ's merciful heart.

> How were some of the saints so perfect and contemplative? They strove to subordinate all their earthly desires to heavenly ones, and by doing so they could cling

to God from the very depths of their hearts and freely attend to him.... If we were not so absorbed in ourselves and if we were less confused in our own hearts, then we might savor divine things and experience something of heavenly contemplation. The greatest hindrance to our spiritual development—indeed, the whole hindrance—is that we allow our passions and desires to control us ... When we meet the least adversity, we are too quickly dejected and we turn to other people for comfort, instead of to God.

— Thomas à Kempis[4]

The Influence of Demons

When cultural subversion entices us onto those "sweet and satisfying paths," we also become vulnerable to the influence of demons. As used here, the term *influence of demons* can refer to a range of experiences commonly used in the literature of exorcism.[5]

- *Temptations* are inclinations to do something harmful to oneself or to another.

- *Obsession* refers to an intense fixation on particular thoughts or ideas that are troubling to the person being affected by them.

- *Oppression* refers to physical blows or infirmities

caused by demons.

- *Parasitism* refers to demonic presence in a person that can exert harmful influence over that person but that, like a physiological parasite, does not control a person's mind or behavior.

- *Infestation* refers to demonic activity in a particular place or location.

- *Possession* refers to demonic control of a person's body and actions.

Note that temptations are a general part of ordinary human psychology; temptations push us into worldly activities that entice us to engage in the sins associated with those activities, and, consequently, send us right into the grasp of evil. Furthermore, the term *obsessions* is also used in psychiatric terminology. Thus it can be problematic to judge where psychology ends and demonic influence begins. For example, a psychologist must wonder whether a person is tempted by and obsessed with particular thoughts because of psychological defenses created in response to childhood traumas or whether the obsessions have a demonic origin—or whether they may be both.

What You Can Do

Endeavor, therefore, to realize that when you carry in your

heart all sorts of unconscious infection with subversive desires, you are in danger of falling right into all the snares of self-sabotage, disobedience, and sin that demonic influence has laid out for you. Seek, then, to purge from your life all resentment, hatred, and lust, and cling to the following counsels.

- Believe that God desires your healing and will forgive any sin if only you stop hating yourself and turn back to Him in sorrow.

  > It is the trick of demons to tell you otherwise. They will say that you are a bad person, that God hates you, and that there is no point in asking God for help. **If you believe these lies, your *belief* in them will work like a deadly curse that keeps you bound to self-punishment.**

- Nurture a desire to detach yourself from the worldly need to defend your pride, and nurture a desire to trust completely in God to protect you.

- Face everything with patience and humility as you dedicate your life to growing in holiness.

  > To live in humility, desire to live always in confidence of God's love, protection, and guidance and therefore to not be concerned when others insult you—or praise you. Secure in God's love, you don't have to base your identity on whether or not others acknowledge you,

and so you don't have to compete with them and beat them down to make yourself feel bigger.

Humility does not have anything to do with humiliation or self-defilement. Seeking humiliation is a psychological defense against the pain of deep emotional wounds, such that you take unconscious pleasure in being demeaned in the secret hope that you will somehow, someday, earn someone's admiration for your willingness to stifle your dignity by enduring painful abuse.

Therefore, it is important that we never relinquish the noble responsibility of developing our talents to the fullest. Our growth and self-development is a spiritual necessity, and it won't become an act of selfishness if we seek it with proper humility.

- Forgive others as God forgives you; that is, when you feel hurt by others, relinquish your desire for revenge, and put justice in God's hands.

- Respect yourself and your body, especially through a lifestyle purged of competition, immodesty, and lust.

- Pray for deliverance from evil. (See Appendix IV).

Lead Us Not Into Temptation

So, will bodily pleasures, social entertainments, competitive sports, politics, and militarism send you right to hell?

Well, who can say but God, the only one who knows all the secrets hidden deep in your heart? But it can be said with certainty not only that none of these things will lead you to the Kingdom of Heaven, but also that all of them will lead you into temptation.

So, to paraphrase Matthew 26:41, watch and pray that neither you nor your children enter into temptation.

28   TOO BUSY?

I am a lawyer and father of six. I am thus very occupied most of the time. I know being holy is for all the faithful and I strive to incorporate prayer and penance throughout my day, revolving around the Eucharist. My question is: Are the ascetic practices of St. John of the Cross, for example, meant for all or only for the few religious who can devote their entire life to them? Or for occasional periods in our life (e.g. lent, to overcome addictions, etc.)? Is it dangerous for an ordinary mortal like myself to try to scale this Mount? Is it even possible in a normal lay life?

Christ Himself told us what He requires of us:

> When the Pharisees heard that Christ had silenced the Sadducees, they gathered together, and a scholar of the law tested Him by asking which commandment in the law is the greatest. Christ said to him, "You shall love the Lord, your God, with all your heart, with all your soul, and with all your mind." Christ said that this is the greatest and the first commandment, and that the second commandment is like it: "You shall love your

neighbor as yourself." Christ summed it up by saying
that the whole law and the prophets depend on these
two commandments (see Matthew 22:34–40).

So what does it really mean, "You shall love the Lord, your
God, with all your heart, with all your soul, and with all
your mind"? Can an "ordinary mortal" afford to do this?
Well, I can tell you what the Catholic mystics through the
ages have said it takes: everything you have. Furthermore,
that's actually something anyone can afford.

Vocation in the Context of Devotion

Now, as Saint Francis de Sales wrote, it would be "ridiculous, unorganized and intolerable" for married people
to be no more concerned than a religious about increasing
their income or for a working man to spend his whole day in
church like a religious. Nevertheless, each person becomes
more acceptable and fitting in his own vocation when he
sets his vocation in the context of devotion. Through
devotion, family responsibilities become more peaceful,
and mutual love between husband and wife becomes more
sincere. Therefore, in whatever situations we may be, it is
important to aspire to the life of perfection.[1]

In fact, the need for every Christian to aspire to a life of
perfection is the whole point of Christianity. Catholic
mysticism, such as that taught by Saint John of the Cross,
is simply a matter of living a humble and devout lifestyle

so as to seek holiness in everything you do, letting nothing interfere with a life of constant prayer. For example, rather than thinking of family responsibilities as a hindrance to prayer, parents can aspire to a dedicated prayer life in two ways: by performing all daily tasks while *maintaining* a constant awareness of the presence of God (such as by praying the Jesus Prayer[2]) and by *sharing* some of their vocal prayer time (such as the Liturgy of the Hours and the Rosary) and some of their holy reading with their children, as a family activity.

A Final Image

Beyond that encouragement, I can offer you one final image in your own language that you might find particularly understandable. When you say, "Is it dangerous for an ordinary mortal like myself to try to scale this Mount? Is it even possible in a normal lay life?" you express a subtle doubt in a way that sounds as if you were a lawyer arguing a case in court before a judge, with a preconceived negative answer already in your mind.

So imagine standing before Christ the Judge on the last day. You will have to stand in your own defense. If you walk into the court with humility and say, "My Lord, I can offer no defense. I have already given you everything I have—my occupation, my family, all my heart and soul and mind—and I have nothing left with which to defend myself," Christ might just say, "That's true. Case dismissed."

But if you have doubted God's mercy, if you have secretly feared to trust completely in God, if your heart is stained with anger or lust, He might just say, "Well, let's hear what your Accuser has to say." There you will be, empty and broken, with a fool for an attorney, standing next to the opposing counsel: Satan himself. And Satan, a master psychologist, will trample all of your psychological defenses into the dirt. It won't be pretty.

So, if you accept the fact that you—indeed, anyone—can and should ascend Mount Carmel, and if you give "everything you have" to make the climb, then you will discover the ineffable glory awaiting you at the summit.

With Trials as a Teacher

Now, even though anyone can afford to make the climb, you might wonder why some persons are able to grow to such great spiritual heights and why others make so little progress. Well, Saint John of the Cross explains it.

> And here it ought to be pointed out why so few reach this high state of perfect union with God. It should be known that the reason is not that God wishes only a few of these spirits to be so elevated; He would rather want all to be perfect, but He finds few vessels that will endure so lofty and sublime a work.... There are many who desire to advance and persistently beseech God to bring them to this state of perfection. Yet when

God wills to conduct them through the initial trials and mortifications, as is necessary, they are unwilling to suffer them and they shun them, flee from the narrow road of life [Mt. 7:14] and seek the broad road of their own consolation, which is that of their own perdition [Mt. 7:13]; thus they do not allow God to begin to grant their petition. They are like useless containers, for although they desire to reach the state of the perfect they do not want to be guided by the path of trials that leads to it.[3]

29   PARENTAL LOVE FOR A CHILD

There seems to be a theme running through a lot of your discussions which throws a lot of weight on what the parents did wrong during a person's formative and developmental years to cause his/her grown up illnesses, psychological states, issues, behaviors, shticks, personalities, what have you. . . . You know this better than I, but to cite but one example: "Your own inner pain must be understood through the psychotherapy, not hidden away with flashy slight-of-hand. In essence, it will be necessary to learn to treat yourself with the honest, gentle, and compassionate true love that your parents never gave to you."

Is it always what a parent did wrong that informs a person's make-up?

Indeed, I have a wonderful son who is very close to me but still finding himself and dealing with issues of life choices; after growing up in a terribly dysfunctional home in which his mother/my wife (ex) had so many problems that I was unable to cope with and which in turn led to instability, chaos, and a 10 year "war of the roses" divorce; so I know of from "parents doing wrong."

But why the seeming assumption throughout your discussions that this is a given to every person's problems?

Yes, what I say about a person's psychological problems deriving from parental failures in childhood is true for everyone. A fundamental axiom of psychology is that whenever children have psychological or behavioral problems, look to the parents for the cause of the problems. Children intuitively understand the truth of this; parents, understandably so, shudder at it.

Trauma Kept Secret

The sad truth is that many parents have experienced child abuse as children, or have experienced other traumas in the past, or have experienced emotional wounds in the past, but have not sought healing; instead, they have tried to keep their emotional pain secret.

> "It's all in the past," they say. "What's the point of talking about it? Nothing can change it." Well, it's not all in the past. It's still alive, even now. It still lives in the unconscious where it exerts its pernicious, hidden effects on everyone who gets close to it.

Consequently, because of their hidden unconscious anger, these parents will not be able to give healthy attention to their children's emotional experiences, and so they will inflict trauma on their children; that is, the children's lives will be disturbed by the hidden pain of the parents, but because it's all unconscious the children will not be able to articulate it. The children may be plagued by terrifying dreams; they may become depressed or anxious; they may become argumentative or disobedient; they may abuse alcohol, use marijuana or other drugs; or they may engage in criminal activity. It's inevitable—until someone says, "Enough. This has to stop."

And how will it stop? Well, either the parents will go into psychotherapy or the children will go into psychotherapy, but either way, if the truth of the parents' emotional pain is brought out into the open, the children will finally realize that the torment was real and that they weren't crazy for feeling so disturbed all their lives.

Getting to the Problem

Nevertheless, I sympathize with you. In trying to understand what has occurred and what its consequences will be, we need to consider any positive influences in your son's environment. What about anything you have done that has been helpful to your son? What influence did that have on him, and what influence will that have on his future? To begin to answer these questions, let's ask another question: *What exactly does it mean for a parent to love a child?*

Parental Love

What exactly does it mean for a parent to love a child?

From my clinical experience, I have learned that most parents do not know the true answer to this question. Some parents think that because they have feelings of affection for their children they must love their children; but love is more than a sentimental feeling. Some parents will say something like, "Well, I tried my best; I gave them food and shelter, so that means I loved my children." All of this really amounts to a defense rather than an answer. The defense hides a truth, and the truth is not pretty, for the truth is that the parents failed to love their children—that is, to will the good of their children—by giving the children everything the children really needed.

Nevertheless, "giving the children everything they need" requires some definition. To give children every "thing" they need is impossible. No parent can do this, and it's foolish to even think that it's possible.

The Possibility of Real Love

Real love, though, is possible because real love is not about giving "things." Real love for a child means that a parent is willing to go to any lengths—to do anything it takes—to be emotionally genuine with the child. That is not easy because it means that the parent must give everything of his or her own being.

For example, if, during a family crisis, a father were to take his son to a sporting event, the father would be implicitly saying, "This is how I hide my emotional pain behind illusions of grandeur and triumph." In contrast, if the father were to take his son for a hike and were to talk about his current helplessness, acknowledging what the son needs from life and admitting that he cannot provide those things for the son right at the moment, and explaining how a dedication to acts of patience, kindness, and forgiveness will get them both through a difficult situation, the father would be offering a profound model of healthy coping skills.

The Rarity of Real Love

Therefore, notice that I said that real love is possible. Yes, it's possible, but it's also rare. It's rare because most adults are too terrified to be emotionally genuine, and they are too terrified to look psychologically deep enough inside themselves to learn how to become emotionally genuine and to give of themselves honestly in real love.

Why? Well, most adults have suffered the emotional pain of having parents who were not emotionally genuine. Most adults were not loved by their parents, and so they are terrified of loving their children. Thus we come full circle: emotionally crippled children come from emotionally crippled parents.

Note that this does not mean that parents have to be perfect. We all make mistakes, but if parents are willing to admit their mistakes and learn from them and keep trying to do what is good for their children, then real love will be possible.

Giving of Yourself Genuinely

If you—the parent—want to know what good you have done for your children, look not to the "things" you did for them but to the way you gave of yourself genuinely to your children. If anything falls short, then resolve now to do anything it takes to remedy your failures of emotional genuineness: learn about the psychology of the unconscious, scrutinize your inner motivations, overcome your fear of emotional honesty and humility, and seek out healing for your own childhood emotional wounds, even if you must enter psychotherapy.

In short, to be a good parent—a successful parent—be willing to do *anything it takes* to help your children, now, while you have the chance. That's real love for your children.

30 BREAKING A CYCLE OF HATE

Recently my husband started to yell at our son and I tried to stop it. It ended up with his becoming angry, yelling and accusing me. He called up his mother and canceled her coming over to have dinner with us and the kids because he said there was a commotion going on at our home (I couldn't believe it) and proceeded to talk to her about me. I heard all this and what he was saying. To top it, I know my mother-in-law doesn't keep things to herself. I know that she will talk about this with others in the family. What I was trying to settle turned out worse.

I am so beyond this. I feel it inside. For years now I have been trying to live this marriage vow that I took so long ago so blindly. My instinct is not to be a part of all this. It's wrong and so immature and I certainly don't want to act immaturely either. I feel caught in this.

What would Jesus do? I have been accepting this as a suffering, offering it up to God to use to redeem since I know about this. But I feel such a humiliation. My instinct is to become aloof to this immature man and now if they invite us to any of his family things I wouldn't want go anymore. I have been aloof to my husband since this and pondering it and praying for my direction here. My husband makes *it like nothing ever happened and life goes on. I don't want this occurring anymore. How can I be an instrument here of God's unconditional love and break this cycle?*

Your role as the wife and mother in a Christian family has two aspects to it.

Breaking the Cycle of Hate

In regard to your own behavior in breaking the cycle of hate, endeavor to imitate Christ in all things. Therefore, when you are insulted, learn to accept all insult gracefully (that is, with God's grace), remain calm, give a blessing in return to a curse, and pray for the repentance of the offender. This is how Christ acted, and this is how He commanded His disciples to act.

> In 1 Peter 2:21–23 we are told that Christ suffered for us, leaving us an example that we should follow in His footsteps. He committed no sin, and no deceit was found in His mouth. When He was insulted He returned no insult, and when He was made to suffer He did not counter with threats; instead He handed Himself over to the One who judges justly.

That's a hard example to follow because you will experience recurring temptation to seek revenge on others when your pride or honor is threatened; it takes constant patience and perseverance to trust in God's justice (see pp. 133–134) and to respond to all injuries with love instead of hate.

Protect Your Children

In regard to your children, be careful to attend to their physical, mental, and spiritual protection. Here are four things to guide you.

1. **Explain.** Whenever your husband does anything inappropriate, explain to your children (at an appropriate time) that he has acted in a way contrary to Christian behavior. You do not have to be critical of him as a person; just explain to the children why the behavior is wrong, citing Biblical examples as illustration. You cannot do this, however, unless you have read and understand the Bible sufficiently yourself to explain it to your children.

> It is important, however, to ensure that nothing in the family ever degenerates into domestic violence (see Chapter 7) or child abuse (see Chapter 8); if it does, then seek safety immediately, calling the police for help if necessary.

2. **Reassure.** Once things have calmed down, reassure the children that you are OK and that you are not afraid of your husband. Convey to them your faith in

Christ as your protector—and as the protector of the family.

3. **Apologize.** Admit to the children your role in what occurred and how your attempts to help may have gone wrong. Tell the children that you will do all you can to prevent such a problem from reoccurring, and ask for their help and understanding.

4. **Promise.** Let the children know clearly that you have no intention of leaving the family. Ask the children to pray with you for the conversion of their father so that the family can become a real Christian family.

The Cross is the supreme reminder of the Christian refusal to hate.

31   BOTCHED

So what happens if parents messed up their children? Is it a life sentence to hell?

No one goes to hell who truly loves God with a pure heart. Nevertheless, many individuals fool themselves into believing they love God—just as they deceive the world around them into believing they love God—when they are really doing many things contrary to love that only push God away. Still, there is always hope for eventual enlightenment and repentance, no matter what the original mistakes may be.

Worldly Vanity

Saint Teresa of Avila, for example, lived for 20 years as a nun before she discovered real love. She spent the early years of her vocation engaged in vain gossip, attractions to worldly status, and superficial prayer—until an experience of mystical love set her heart on fire. Finally understanding what it means to stand in the real presence of Our Lord, she set about reforming her own life, along with her own religious order.

Perversion

Saint Catherine of Genoa grew up with a yearning for holiness, but once she got married she turned from God into a life of perversion. After about ten years of self-gratifying "love" for the world, she had visions of God's pure and patient love for her. This is how she responded:

> Lord! I give myself to Thee. I know not what I am fitted for but to make a hell by myself alone. O Lord! I desire to make this compact with Thee: I will give this sinful being of mine into Thy hands, for Thou alone canst hide it in Thy mercy, and so dispose of me that nothing of myself can anymore be seen. Occupy me wholly with Thy love, which will extinguish in me every other love and keep me wholly lost in Thee, holding me so engrossed by Thee that I shall find neither time nor place for self.
>
> — Saint Catherine of Genoa[1]

The Conditions of Discipleship

The example of the saints might sound like a radical proposal to many persons today—especially to those under the pernicious influence of liberal, watered-down "Christianity"—yet remember what Christ told us Himself about the conditions of discipleship.

> He told us that whoever loves father or mother more than Him is not worthy of him, and that whoever loves son or daughter more than Him is not worthy of Him. Moreover, whoever does not take up his cross and follow after Him is not worthy of Him. In short, whoever finds his own life will lose it, and whoever loses his life for His sake will find real life (see Matthew 10:37-39).

Raising Children Properly

In regard to your question, then, this all means that if parents want to raise children properly it is necessary to love God more than they love their life and more than they love their work in the world. By loving God as Saint Catherine describes, parents make it possible to show their children how to love and to serve God. Otherwise, the parents botch the whole job.

Therefore, if, after living a life of self-gratifying "love" for the world, you finally discover that you have botched the job of raising your children, then you have one choice: return to God as Saint Catherine describes. In other words, take that cross you wear around your neck like a piece of jewelry and start carrying it. This necessitates three steps.

1. Make reparation to God for your past mistakes, and for the sins your children have committed as a result of your failure to direct them properly. By making this reparation to God you make it possible for your children to recognize real love and to return to God as well.

2. Admit openly to your children that your previous behavior was wrong, and that you're sorry for the mistakes you made. Much of the psychopathology of children who feel victimized derives from their unconscious desire to show their parents how much they have been abused and to hear their parents acknowledge their pain. Anyone who has ever been injured, therefore, really wants nothing more than to hear the one who hurt him admit he was wrong and to apologize. So give your children the honesty they deserve.

3. Set about living a truly holy life, free of every shred of hypocrisy that your children can point to in scorn. In all of this, pray for your children with the intensity of Saint Monica and Saint Rita. After heartfelt contrition, much sacrifice and prayer, deep sorrow, and many tears, you might find your children coming around back to the Church.

Paying the Price

This is all a heavy price to pay for your past mistakes. But if you don't pay the price, you will spend the rest of your life getting angry at anyone—including God Himself—who points out your self-deceit. And being angry at God is, well, not the path to heaven.

32   HONORING YOUR PARENTS

*I have been dealing with a mother with Borderline Person-
ality Disorder for a long time. She has not been diagnosed
by a professional, but I have talked with professionals who
have said she probably has that. I have also been diagnosed
with tendencies towards Dependent Personality Disorder.*

*I have been working hard to maintain a relationship with
my mother; however I sometimes feel emotionally abused by
her. I have attempted to set boundaries and be less attached
and to not take things personally from her.*

*It is very frustrating to me that she can say whatever she
wants to me without any regard for my feelings, but when I
try to tell her she's hurting my feelings she basically tells me
I deserve it and that she has a right to talk to me however
she wants. I have been a very good daughter to her. I want
to love her without enabling her and have been trying to
set boundaries for many years, but struggle with enforcing
boundaries because I don't want her to view me badly. I
struggle with the knowledge that everyone is entitled to his
or her own opinions and freedom of speech, but her speech
hurts me. I understand I can't change her and that I have to
tell her what I will accept, but when I try that, she tells me
that if I wouldn't have done this, that, or the other thing, she*

wouldn't be acting the way she is, and she never acknowl-
edges that she is hurting my feelings and always makes an
excuse for it.

How do I maintain a relationship with her without al-
lowing myself to be emotionally abused? How do I allow her
to have her opinion but still express mine? Also, I am getting
married soon and a lot of her anger is directed toward my
husband. How do I protect my marriage?

Throughout the Bible, we are told to "honor your father
and your mother" as a reminder of one of the Ten Commandments (see Exodus 20:1–17). Many domineering
parents, however, try to use this commandment to demand
a child's obedience to their every whim, and many children
blindly and obediently try to follow this commandment
without understanding the implicit meaning behind it.

Therefore, let's look at the psychology of it all.

Honoring Love

What is the purpose of honoring our fathers and mothers? Well, by honoring them we make it possible to learn
from them, so as to acquire their wisdom and their love
for God. This shows that the assumption made in the
commandment about honoring parents is that fathers and
mothers love God, are living holy lives, and care for their
children and want their good—and are therefore engaged

in patiently and gently teaching their children to love God rather than criticizing them and controlling them so as to make them serve their parents. Hence, to honor your father and your mother is to honor their love for God.

When Parents are Enemies of Love

So what occurs when parents don't really want the good of their children? What occurs when parents constantly criticize their children, abuse them, and essentially stifle any good that the children could achieve? In short, what occurs in dysfunctional families when parents don't really love their children but manipulate and control them? Well, parents such as this don't love their children because they don't love God either. These parents have broken the first commandment, and, to their children, that makes them enemies, not parents worthy of being honored. Trying to honor parents such as this amounts to trying to carry out a fraud. After all, how can you honor your enemies?

Praying for Your Enemies

Nevertheless, even though it is foolishness to honor our enemies, we still have to pray for them. Christ told us to pray for our enemies; moreover, through His own behavior, He showed us how *not* to do it.

- Praying for your enemies does not mean *accepting*

everything they do.

- Praying for your enemies does not mean *ignoring* the danger they cause to you and to others.

- Praying for your enemies does not mean *forgetting* the harm they have caused.

- Praying for your enemies does not mean *resigning* yourself to injustice, because praying for your enemies does not mean that they will escape divine justice.

Praying for your enemies, as Christ made perfectly clear right from the Cross, means that, because you are aware of the divine justice they will eventually have to face, you care about their salvation and wish for their repentance. Even as He was being crucified, Christ was not plotting revenge on His enemies; instead, with a broken heart flowing with mercy, He yearned for their repentance.

A Relationship of Truth

Consequently, considering what you have said about your mother's treatment of you, the only "relationship" you can have with your mother is a relationship of truth. See the truth, then: understand that she does not love you.

If you don't see the truth, you will be endlessly trying to appease your mother, to do something to make her love you. You will be dependent on your hope for her love. You will be like a dog begging for table scraps and dying of hunger because the scraps are not real food.

If you do see the truth, you will realize that making your mother love you is impossible. She will never love you unless she changes psychologically; she will never love you unless she sees the truth of her own brokenness and wants to be healed.

You can't make her change, and you can't heal her yourself, but you can stop encouraging her to remain stuck in her dysfunction. So how do you stop encouraging her? Well, you stop being nice.

Stop Being Nice

Christ wasn't "nice." He loved us—He spoke the truth—He was the truth—but He wasn't nice. To be nice is to accept anything, even sin itself. Why? Well the deep unconscious motive for being nice is *fear*, the fear that if you speak the truth you will be rejected and abandoned because you offend someone. If you're afraid, then, you won't be able to love, because to love is to speak the truth and, with non-judgmental bluntness, to call a sin a sin.

Imagine your mother talking to a friend, complaining about how difficult it is for her to have a problem daughter like you. If the friend were merely nice, the friend would say, "There, there, you're doing your best to be a good mother." But if the friend were to speak the truth, the friend would say, "Well, no wonder your daughter has so many problems! Look at how miserably cruel you are to her!" So there's the difference between being nice and speaking the truth from a heart filled with love. Therefore, stop being nice and start being genuine.

To be genuine with others, though, you have to do your own psychological work first, so that you can be genuine with yourself. You can do this through psychological and spiritual scrutiny, though you might also need psychotherapy. In any case, once you can see how you deceive yourself, you can help others see how they deceive themselves.

Mind you, being around your mother while you are still in the process of your own healing can be psychologically precarious and dangerous. Your best protection, at least temporarily, may be to distance yourself—emotionally, and even physically if necessary—from your mother. In addition, if you enter psychotherapy, you can rely on frequent guidance and coaching from your psychotherapist about what to say and do in regard to your mother.

You Go Where You Are Praying

Keep in mind that as you change and become more and more genuine, your mother's behavior might eventually change as well. Initially, though, she will accuse you of being mean and ungrateful, and she will try to make you feel so guilty that you will come crawling back on your knees to her domination. So pray constantly that you can remain confident in the truth and can speak always from a place of love; also pray constantly for your mother's enlightenment and repentance. In the physical world we go where we are looking; in the spiritual realm, we go where we are praying. So if you're not praying for what you want, you don't really want it.

As for the success of your marriage, much depends on your husband. If he is psychologically strong, confide in him and ask for his help in maintaining a distance from your mother and in your becoming more emotionally genuine. Pray together for the strength to resist your mother's subversion. If your husband is not psychologically strong, well, beware, because your mother will prey upon his weakness to undermine your marriage.

33   ANGER AT PARENTS

I was taught that anger is a bad thing. I've had an abusive childhood but it is hard to feel any anger about it because I feel guilty and afraid about offending God or blaming my parents.

Anger is always a reaction to some sort of hurt or insult. But when you look at this reaction more closely, you will see that anger does not have to be the only reaction to hurt.

Physiological Arousal

The most immediate and primary response to hurt or insult is a physiological arousal of the sympathetic nervous system. Your heart rate jumps. Your blood pressure surges. These things, however, are just immediate self-defensive reactions—often called a "fight or flight" response—that prepare you to take some action to respond to the threat, such as by holding your ground and fighting off the intruder, or by running away from the intruder to get to a place of safety.

Definition of Anger

Now, to be technically precise here, *anger* does not refer to the feeling of physiological arousal itself; anger is a particular response to that arousal that is grounded in hostility and hatred. In essence, anger is a wish to hurt someone because someone has hurt you. Anger does not even have to be experienced as the strong emotion of rage; it can just as well be a thought or a wish to hurt someone. In this sense, then, anger is a "bad" thing because it is an offense against love, for love is a matter of willing the good of others, not a matter of wishing them harm.

Experiencing Anger in the Healing Process

When you are told to acknowledge your anger within the context of psychotherapy or spiritual healing, however, you are not being told to do something that is morally wrong. Nor are you being encouraged to "get angry," such as by yelling, cursing, throwing things, breaking things, or hitting someone. Instead, you are being told to recognize *something that is already within you,* so that you can stop deceiving yourself about your own reality. So let's see what that "something" might be.

Unconscious Anger

The trials of childhood, whether as severe as outright

child abuse or less severe as manipulative mistreatment in dysfunctional families (see Chapter 12), provoke feelings of hurt and insult in the child, and almost inevitably that hurt leads to hate and a desire for revenge. In fact, even many ordinary, non-abusive frustrations of childhood will provoke feelings of hurt and secret fantasies of revenge.

But because children are not usually taught to express hostile thoughts and feelings by speaking about them—and because they aren't taught the psychological meaning of anger, and because they aren't taught the real meaning of mercy and forgiveness and reparation—children quickly learn, through fear, shame, and guilt, to hide their true feelings from their parents.

The ultimate psychological problem, however, is that these unexpressed thoughts and feelings get pushed into the unconscious where they grow in darkness, like mold on the walls. Moreover, even though it all starts in childhood, unless there is some specific psychotherapeutic intervention the unconscious anger will continue right into adulthood. It may be hidden from conscious sight, and it may be hidden from public view. But it can't be hidden from God.

That is, unconscious anger, no matter how much you try to deny it, will stain all your interpersonal relationships. With this anger festering inside of you, it becomes almost impossible to give real love to anyone, including God, even in confession. So when you experience difficult things, you fall kersplash! right into the swamp of childhood anger.

The Healing Process

The whole point of the healing process is to learn that there are very specific environmental triggers for your thoughts and feelings. In the healing process, you first learn to recognize the triggers of anger; then you learn to recognize the emotional "bridge" that goes back to childhood wounds; then you learn to do something constructive about the triggers, rather than succumb to hostility.

The Triggers of Anger

To start the healing process, learn to look for the actual events (notice the plural) that have been bothering you recently. Take each one separately. What are all the feelings about that event? Frustration? Helplessness? Abandonment? Betrayal? Fear? (It won't be anger, because anger is the final, hostile reaction to all the other feelings.)

The Emotional Bridge

Next, follow each example of hurt back into its roots in the past to all those times and circumstances when you felt the same way. Carefully scrutinize your childhood and examine your memories of painful events to discover what you were really feeling then.

> Remember, your impulsive reactions to present injuries
> are the unconscious expression of the original emo-
> tions and fantasies you experienced, but suppressed,
> in childhood.

After scrutinizing their childhood, some persons will say
that they feel sad or lonely but do not feel any anger at
their parents. In these cases, the anger will be recognized
not through the emotion of rage but through specific behaviors of hate.

But before describing these behaviors of hate, let's note
here that *hate* does not necessarily mean a passionate
loathing; it can just as well be a quiet, secret desire for
harm to come upon someone or something. Hate can be
a subtle thing, therefore, and it often is experienced more
unconsciously than consciously. Consequently, it will
often be very easy to deny that you have any hatred for
anyone simply because you do not feel anything.

Note also that hatred and anger are theologically syn-
onymous. Christ Himself taught the crowds, "But I say
to you, whoever is angry with his brother will be liable
to judgment" (Matthew 5:22). Moreover, Saint John the
Evangelist reflected this sentiment when he said, in one of
his letters, "Everyone who hates his brother is a murderer"
(1 John 3:15). The theological implication of these texts,
therefore, is that any desire for harm to come to another

person—whether through active loathing or through passive resentment—is, in its spiritual essence, an evil desire to remove the fullness of life (with its possibility of love and forgiveness) from that person.

Here, then, are some specific behaviors of hate.

- Hatred for authority can be expressed through criminal activity; terrorism; political protest; pornography;[1] abortion; shoplifting; speeding; being late for appointments; living in clutter or filth; and so on.

- Hatred for the self can be expressed through the self-sabotage of one's potential such as by chronic procrastination; the inability to support oneself by working; overdependence on others; substance abuse; obesity; codependence (such as marrying an alcoholic); emotional disability; and so on.

Nevertheless, whether the end result be hatred for authority or hatred for yourself, the underlying cause of the hatred is anger at your parents because of their failures in love; that is, in their failures to understand your emotional experiences and to guide you rather than control and manipulate you to serve their desires.

The Constructive Choice

Having understood the triggers of your anger and the

emotional bridge to your past, now deal with each troubling event separately, according to the thoughts and emotions specific to that event. Do something constructive and creative about each problem individually. Choose something different from the prevailing culture's Satanic Rule: "Do to others what they do to you." Choose something based in true Christian values.

> In 1 Peter 3:8–9a we are told that all of us should be of one mind, sympathetic, loving toward one another, compassionate, and humble, and that we should not return evil for evil, or insult for insult, but, on the contrary, a blessing.

Remember, it's your choice. You can do something healthy and constructive, or you can get angry about everything and stew in it. Up till now you have been stewing in it, because everything in your life is caught up in a big snarl of childhood hurt, and that's why everything seems so oppressive and foul underneath the surface of a nice, devout demeanor.

Summary

If you go through this healing process, you will learn to free your hidden anger from its dark, silent prison. Having thus set it free, and having thus cleansed yourself of its stains, you will also be free of something else. You will be free of feeling victimized and free of secretly blaming your parents, because as long as you keep your anger hidden, you remain emotionally disabled, and as long as you remain emotionally disabled, you are throwing your disability in your parents' faces to accuse them of their faults.

Once you acknowledge the core of your anger, and understand it, and stop unconsciously wishing harm on your parents, then you can forgive—that is, stop hating—your parents. Then you will be healed, and then you can turn to God with real love in your heart. You may not be reconciled with your parents—that is, you may not be able to trust them unless they apologize and change their behavior—but you will be reconciled with God.

34 UNCONSCIOUS ANGER

You need to be clearer about your material—not all people who suffer with anxiety or depression are going to hell. If a person unconsciously desires to harm, then this is unconscious (not in one's consciousness, therefore, not a volitional act). How can something unconscious be a sin?

You need to revise your theology. You are more or less saying that unless people know their need to heal from childhood hurts, they are doomed to hell. This is a grave misunderstanding. What about the many people who lived in the times before psychodynamic theory was even thought of?

You cannot tell people, "Well, turn away from the satisfaction of thinking that you are in a state of grace when you unconsciously desire to harm yourself and others." Unconscious "desire" cannot be sinful—it is not volitional.

I just don't want to be carrying a false sense of guilt.

If what you are saying were true, then by all means, I would accept it. But it undermines Catholic doctrine. You have not given me anything Catholic to support what you are saying except an opinion based on psychotherapeutic studies.

Where there is confusion between opinion and Church

teaching, I rest with the Magisterium.

There's nothing more Catholic than putting your trust in God's mercy and love. How beautiful to accept your wretchedness gracefully and trust in God's mercy! If you did this you would not be afraid of anything.

Telling Others What To Do

Nevertheless, many who call themselves Catholic are afraid to trust in God's mercy. Because of humiliation from being mistreated in childhood they hide their wretchedness. They hide it from everyone, even themselves. As children they were not taught by their parents to turn to God for comfort, and so they were unable to turn to God for comfort when they experienced distress. Consequently, they learned nothing about emotional honesty. Instead, they fell into the trap of intellectualizing their distress by telling others what to do.

When experiencing emotional hurt because of something someone said or did, the hurt bypassed their conscious awareness and passed into their unconscious, and all they could think about consciously was the desperate desire for others to act differently. "You can't do this," or "You can't say that," or "You need to do such and such" all amount to saying, "Change your behavior so I can feel good about myself." In its more primal sense—that is, to a helpless child—it means "Care for me so that I can live. Without your love I am in danger of perishing."

Futile Desires

Without deep spiritual scrutiny or psychotherapy, this desperation—this futile desire to go around proving that someone is wrong—will be carried on into adulthood. Demanding. Critical. Accusatory. Argumentative. Self-willed. These qualities will define such a person's life. It's a life of sad desperation on a continuum whose extreme is terrorism.

Always telling others what to do, you believe that you have done nothing wrong. Yet underneath it all you carry the guilt of being angry at your parents, and it's an anger that has now been driven into your unconscious. Because you fear the guilt you are desperate to call it a "false sense of guilt." It's all because you lack faith, and you fear God's mercy. Instead of admitting your wretchedness to God and calling upon His mercy to be freed of guilt, you try to convince yourself that you haven't sinned. Trying to convince yourself that you haven't sinned, though, is opposed to God's mercy. How can you say, "God have mercy, I have sinned" if you persist in saying, "But I haven't sinned!"? When you are warned, you get angry, and you fall into the futile desire of trying to tell others what to do.

Let me say also that when we are given a warning and

> corrected for doing something wrong, we should not
> be so foolish as to take offense and be angry. There are
> times when we are unconscious of the sins we commit
> because our hearts are fickle, lacking in faith. Futile
> desires becloud our minds.

Think about that. It sounds like something that psychodynamic theory would say, right? Well, it was actually said in a homily written in the second century. We don't know the identity of the author, but part of the homily is still used in the *Liturgy of the Hours*.[1] It was a truth given to Christians who lived well before psychodynamic theory was even thought of—and it's a truth still relevant today.

Holy Desire

Our salvation depends on our renouncing the deep futile *desire to commit sin* that lurks in our hearts because of our fallen nature.[2] If we can renounce that desire to commit sin and battle against it in every moment, then we will be on the way of perfection, motivated by the holy desire to seek God with a pure heart.

Your predicament is like someone who has received the gift of spiritually enlightened truth, and then, because the truth he sees conflicts with the futile desires that becloud his mind, sins by trying to turn off the lights.

35   HEART ATTACK

I tend to struggle with anxiety. I am a very scrupulous person, and although I frequent the Sacraments regularly, I tend to agonize over the state of my soul. So to be presented with your statement that "by continuing in your self-sabotaging behavior you show that you would prefer to send yourself to hell just to prove to someone how much he has hurt you" was just about enough to give me a heart attack. Don't equivocate the truth, but out of charity for those of us with such crosses, you may want to consider softening the corners of your presentation a bit and reassuring us that the mere presence of depression and/or anxiety is not an automatic ticket to hell. I now have twice the anxiety than I did before, a panicked lump in my throat, and no more courage to continue reading, although I am in a state of grace!

From what you say, I don't think your problem is clinical anxiety so much as scruples. The clue to this psychological deduction can be found in your saying that you almost had a heart attack in reading about self-sabotaging behavior. Now, the irony here is that "almost having a heart attack" is itself a manifestation of the very sort of self-sabotaging behavior that so troubled you when you read about it.

Self-sabotaging Behavior

So, why is "almost having a heart attack" a form of self-sabotage? Well, consider your unconscious intent in saying it to me. The implication is that something I have said has offended you. So, if you really were to have a heart attack, then you could turn to me and say, "See? Look what you did to me!" Thus we can see that you derive a satisfaction from "almost having a heart attack"; that is, your pain is intended to give you the satisfaction of hurting me. You carry this dynamic even further—that is, you double your satisfaction—when you conclude that "I now have twice the anxiety than I did before, a panicked lump in my throat, and no more courage to continue reading."

Consequently, the truth of your anxiety reveals itself: *the satisfaction that you throw at me comes back to hit you as a disability.*

Sending Yourself to Hell

This illustrates the psychological meaning of preferring to send yourself to hell just to prove to someone how much you have been hurt: you feel hurt, and then, whether consciously or unconsciously, you sabotage yourself in the hope of hurting the one you believe is responsible for hurting you. All of this returning of hurt for hurt is a form of unconscious anger, and it's called *revenge*. Moreover, revenge is a form of hatred, and hatred is a form of murder; that is, as we are told in 1 John 3:15, everyone who hates his brother is a murderer. Therefore, revenge—that is, unrepentant revenge—will send you not just to a psychological hell of emotional misery and scruples (see Chapter 45) but also to the real hell.

Proving, not Preferring

After reading the shocking truth about preferring to send yourself to hell just to prove to someone how much he has hurt you, some persons worry that I'm saying that all people will go to hell when they self-sabotage, regardless of how they do this or what they do. Well, the answer is "No, that's not what I am saying." Perhaps that goes to show how profound the issue really is. Let me explain.

The focus of my statement properly belongs on the matter of *proving*, not on the matter of *preferring*. In the dynamic I describe, the person in question has not just been hurt by some mistreatment, and is not just feeling frustrated at the unfairness of it all, but he or she also clings to the hope of somehow regaining the affection of the offender. Thus the victim reasons, "If I can make [the offender] realize how much he or she has hurt me, then maybe he or she will feel sorry for me and have pity on me and start being nice to me." Consequently, the victim seeks to *prove* to the offender that the mistreatment has had hurtful effects.

Now, that proof can be expressed in many different ways. For some persons, the proof can be expressed through criticism or nagging. "There you go again. You're always [making me late, getting in my way, insulting me, embarrassing me, and so on]."

Or the proof can take on an accusatory tone. "What's wrong with you? Why do you keep making me look bad before the children?"

Or the proof can become an act of rudeness and insult. "You [expletive] idiot! You almost caused an [expletive] accident!"

Or, for some other persons, the proof can take on a subversive quality, such that the harm is self-inflicted, and the unspoken implication is, "Look at what you made me do to myself!" This self-harm can take on many manifestations, such as alcoholism, eating disorders, drug addiction, smoking, masturbation, academic failure, criminal activity, or whatever. Moreover, as I have seen through my work in health psychology, even some physical illnesses—even a heart attack—can be caused in this way. Regardless of how it manifests, though, it's all self-harm, and it's all a sin because self-harm is a defilement of love. It's all a sin against love, and if it isn't recognized as a sin and repented, it can send a person to hell. It's not that the person *wants* to go to hell but that the person would *prefer* to go to any lengths, even to hell itself, to *prove* something to someone.

The Solution

So, what can you do? Well, you can give up the smug satisfaction of thinking that you are in a state of grace when you unconsciously desire to harm yourself and others. To give up this satisfaction, it will be necessary to accept the fact that the root of anxiety is a lack of trust in God's providence. When you are in a state of anxiety you are preoccupied with a concern for what others think and do, especially for what they think about you and how they can hurt you by rejecting you. But when you trust in God's providence the focus of life shifts away from what others do and turns to the bond of love between you and God.

> Keep in mind that this holy bond of love will never be broken by God, and that God never rejects anyone, but that we can reject God by defiling love with sin.

When you have surrendered your life to this love, there will be no more anxiety, no more depression, no more self-sabotage, and no more desire to send yourself to hell to prove a point to anyone. Love, after all, never misses the point, and so it never needs to prove anything.

36 BLIND TO YOUR OWN ANGER

I saw a TV program the other day where a group of religious and non-religious people were discussing faith and mental health. A psychologist mentioned the harmful effect it can have on some adolescents and in some cases it can be linked to OCD. This I believe is what happened to me although only recently have I become aware of this.

I was brought up a Catholic and at the age of eleven was an ardent and literal believer of all I had been taught and learned from the New Testament and Catholic Truth Society pamphlets. We had yearly retreats at school, usually from Jesuit priests, and I found them marvellous experiences where I felt close to God and absorbed the experience.

Over a year or two I became much stricter in my observance of Christian morals, and as I approached puberty I was determined to lead a "pure" life. I began to realise that I thought God wanted me to become a priest. I attended Mass every day and visited a chapel in my free time to pray.

Unfortunately, at the same time I began to feel that I was not obeying God's laws closely enough and found this feeling was invading every action—if I was eating, I'd believe I needed to fast or that I'd eaten more than I needed to, or if I prayed I hadn't prayed enough. I would be washing

*and think I'd touched my nipple and therefore had sinned.
Going to the toilet was a nightmare because I couldn't carry
out hygiene appropriately without thinking I'd sinned.*

*The consequence of all this was that I became utterly
miserable and friendless; even my family thought I had gone
crazy. I had no feelings of anger towards my parents. I was
lucky to have a very caring family, and I felt no reason to
be angry with them. My behaviour arose from a desire to
please God.*

*As years passed the behaviours gradually ceased, and
I decided that I really couldn't live according to Christian
principles because it affected me so negatively. People speak
of being freed by Jesus' words—I feel they imprison me; I
become paralysed and lose my joie de vivre.*

*I would be very interested in your comments or thoughts
if you have time. I've never really discussed this with anyone
before, but now in my late fifties I am beginning to see it as
unfinished business.*

You may not *feel* any anger towards your parents, and
you may not be able to see a reason to be angry at them,
but, contrary to what most persons tend to believe, anger
is not felt as an emotion; instead, it manifests very subtly
in your actions. Moreover, anger is often unconscious, and
for that reason you can be blind to it. In fact, you can be
so spiritually blind to your anger that you cannot even
interpret your own actions that evince the anger.

Now, in your comment, you reveal your anger quite

plainly, even though you don't see it. When you say that Jesus' words imprison you, you are taking your redemption and throwing it back in His face. With the price of His own Blood Christ freed humanity from slavery to sin, and you claim that He imprisoned you. The truth is, you have imprisoned yourself in your own false beliefs. You have imprisoned yourself in your anger at God.

So what did God do to deserve your anger? Well, nothing. Absolutely nothing. But He has done everything to demonstrate His love for you.

So why are you angry at God? Well, you are really transferring your anger onto God from someone else. And who might that be? The answer should be no surprise to a real psychologist, rather than a TV psychologist: your father.

The Father

Here we get to the truth of your life. If your father had shown you how to love God with a vibrant, living trust, you would not be in your current mess. If your father had taught you the truth about sexuality at the beginning of your adolescence, you would not have feared it. If your father's entire being had been based in real love, you would have seen that love demonstrated, and you would have learned its purity by example. But you didn't learn it by example from a loving father. Instead, you had to learn it intellectually from pamphlets. For you, love is just an idea in your head, not a vibrant warmth in your heart.

Legalism

When love is all in your head and not in your heart, you will fall into legalism. Legalism, after all, is just a politically safe place to do battle with your father. A strict, literal approach to things allows you to overpower authority—symbolically, your father—with logic and reason. You act out your anger through intellectual triumph, and all the while you push out of awareness the inadequacy you feel about yourself because of your father's failures.

But no one who loves God from the depths of his heart, and no one who values holiness more than any satisfaction of the world will fall into dry, intellectual legalism. This sort of obsessive behavior is nothing but an attempt to cover up a profound fear of love.

Parental Hypocrisy

Faith, then, is not harmful to adolescents. Parental hypocrisy is harmful to adolescents. Parents—especially fathers—whose real trust is not in God but in the satisfactions of the world (competitive sports, politics, fundamentally anti-Christian entertainment, lust, and addictions) may have prayers on their lips but their hearts are lukewarm. Parents like this cheat you of faith, and when you are cheated you have good reason to be hurt.

You have good reason to be hurt, but that hurt has fallen into anger, and, as I said before, you are blind to your anger. You have done such a good job of hiding it from others that you have hidden it from yourself to such an extent that you deny it even exists.

Love

Still, deep in your soul, you do want God's love, just as you crave the love of the father who angers you. You will never see this love, however, by denying your anger. Anger—even unconscious anger—makes love impossible. But if only you acknowledge the anger, understand it, and heal the hurt that lies beneath it, then you can forgive your father—and then you will be capable of real love.

Unfinished Business

If you really want to finish your unfinished business, accept the fact that you are spiritually blind and that no effort on your own will enlighten you. You cannot understand the unconscious with logic and reason—you must learn to see it with your heart. And right now your heart is hardened by your anger.

Seek the truth, then, with all your soul. Discuss the

matter with God Himself. Implore Him for mercy and pray that He will open your eyes and your heart to see the truth. Maybe then you will be able to interpret the depths of what you cannot now see: your unconscious anger at your parents.

37 SENDING YOURSELF TO HELL

. . . one thing I did notice was that the tone of "sending your-self to hell" could be perhaps overly severe for many patients suffering from low self-esteem to the point of exacerbating the condition, since they are unable to approach the article in a neutral way. Just a thought.

The greatest problem with the Church today is that people avoid speaking the truth about the faith because they fear offending someone. Christ was killed because He spoke the truth and offended the Pharisees, but do we see a lesson in this for us? Well, if we did, we wouldn't have so many individuals, from popes, bishops, and priests to religious education teachers to parents, all cowering in fear of the Cross itself.

So, what is the truth about low self-esteem?

Denying the Truth

Low self-esteem results when children who are raised in

dysfunctional families deny the truth about their parents. Wounded and traumatized by abuse or neglect, a lack of emotional awareness, hypocrisy, manipulation, and family game playing, children have a clear idea of the truth but are too terrified to admit it to themselves. They circle around it like a moth around a flame, but the terror is overwhelming. "My parents don't love me." Those words are terrible. Just to say the words seems like death itself.

So, to hide the truth, children deny their emotional pain, make excuses for their parents, and then blame themselves. "There must be something wrong with me. That's why everyone treats me so miserably. It's all my fault."

Wanting to be Loved

Deep in their hearts they want to be loved, but they don't have a teacher or mentor explaining the meaning of what they are experiencing. So they take up an impossible task: to make their parents love them. "Maybe if I can let my parents know how miserable I am, then maybe they will love me." But because their parents never taught them how to talk honestly about themselves, they act out their pain, rather than speak it, hoping that someone will notice their wretched behavior and in turn notice how miserable they are feeling.

So the children act out. Some throw themselves into study to hide their pain, but for many others, their grades in school drop. Some smoke cigarettes. Some drink alcohol. Some use marijuana. Some become overweight. Some dress immodestly. Some defile their bodies with tattoos and piercings. Some defile their souls with sexual perversions. Some allow their physical and mental health to degenerate. Some reject the Church. They all scoff at authority. They're all lost in pain, lost in confusion, and lost in an empty desperation for love. They will do anything it takes to make someone notice them. They will even send themselves to hell if only then their parents would say, "I'm sorry. I failed you. Come back to me, and I will do anything it takes to learn how to love."

But rarely do parents say they are sorry—at least from the heart as an expression of true sorrow for their sins.

The Real Hell

So what becomes of the children? Well, if no one tells them the truth about their behavior, their imprudent attempts to send themselves to hell will actually send them to hell—the real hell. And then they will be really lost. Their life-long success at failing will be supremely manifest.

Low self-esteem, therefore, isn't something that should cause us to walk on eggshells for fear of exacerbating it. It's something—like sin itself—that we should speak the truth about, in the hope of healing it, before it's too late.

38 PARALYZED IN A DYSFUNCTIONAL FAMILY

I had a conversion during college. I had 3 years down toward my degree, but my conversion led me seriously to consider the priesthood. Partially because of that, and because of financial considerations, I stopped school and came back home to start trying to pay off my loans so I could try a vocation.

I realize now that there were always some things messed up, but right about the time I came home, my younger brother's life fell apart. Heroin addiction, arrests, threats of suicide, etc. My family was torn apart. I handled the whole situation terribly. My siblings took the tough love approach. My parents enabled him. I originally agreed with the tougher approach as well; I was going to move out, but I was too weak. I questioned myself. My parents' defense of their own position wore on me.

I went back and forth. And in my uncertainty, I just ended up doing nothing. I shut down.

Your writing has helped a great deal; has helped me see many things in a much more clear light, even when what I often see isn't pretty.

But in my uncertainty, I am still doing nothing. I am still not sure what to do.

My brother has been clean a year. But I think mostly because of the medication he was taking. I know you have to start off slow, but my parents still enable him. My mother makes him special meals, my father basically admitted to having given up on trying to get him to help out around the house, etc. He basically just plays video games all day. He also displays some major anger towards religion (Satanic tattoos, etc.). I have almost no relationship with him.

Should I tell him why I have almost no relationship with him? I want so badly to just tell him, "Don't expect me to have a relationship with you when you disrespect our parents with your laziness and ingratitude. Don't expect me to have a relationship with you when you blatantly disrespect Our Lord," etc. Is he too fragile on account of his addiction to say this? Should I just let it go? Is the small amount of improvement he has shown actually quite significant for what he has gone through which I just don't understand?

Also, how (if at all) should one fraternally correct their parents? Is it my place? I don't mean just in relation to the things above, but other stuff too (especially when for so long, you haven't said anything).

In general, I am torn between a feeling that I should be more firm, detached, (almost harsh). Say what's on my mind and how I feel and they can take it as they will.

Another part of me believes it would only make it worse to act like that. "Let it go, and just try to show enthusiasm and joy, and hopefully they can see that and that's the best witness you can provide right now." (I just believe that this is lying somehow, like it's me saying, "Everything is okay.")

But again, my uncertainty leads to me doing nothing. As you mention in your writing: lack leads to desire. I sense so much lack from the past few years. So much inactivity, paralyzed by uncertainty. The desire to undo it all kills me. How I can start anew? I am still looking for a job to try and move out. I feel so paralyzed.

From what you have told me, I think that your thoughts about the priesthood were an unconscious excuse to quit college. In my opinion, this is a manifestation of your particular symptom of procrastination. Moreover, in your symptom you have something very much in common with your brother: your father.

The Consequences of a Failed Father

If you read my writings about the symbolic role of a father, you will see quite clearly two of the many consequences of a failed father; one consequence is addictions and another is procrastination. Thus your father is the cause of your family's dysfunction; he fails to be a leader and a guide, and he fails to stand up to and correct your mother's timidity.

Nevertheless, blaming your father will get no one any-where—at least, nowhere pleasant.

In your conversion you saw the light of your father's fail-ure and were drawn to God the Father as the only hope for guidance in your life. Conversions, though, require hard work—a lifetime of hard work—and you are just at the point of starting that work. Learning to witness the faith—gently, not ruthlessly—will be one aspect of that work.

What to Say to Your Brother

Therefore, you could tell your brother about the truth of your relationship. You could say something such as, "I understand your emotional pain because the cause of your pain is our father. He has been lacking as a father and has failed to provide us with proper guidance. I suffer from the same pain, but it manifests in a different manner: for me it's procrastination, and for you it's addictions. Your addictions and the self-sabotage that go with them are an unconscious way for you to inflict your anger on our father. Your anger, however, will not make our father change, but it will destroy you. Right now you are on a collision course with hell. Until you see the truth of that, there is nothing I can do for you. If I said anything more, I would be wasting my breath. So, until you decide to change, I will keep my distance from you. But I will be there for you if you ever become serious about changing and want my help."

What to Say to Your Father

As for your father, it's unlikely that your saying anything

to him will make him change. Still, you could give him a copy of my writing about the role of a father and say something such as, "This might help you in the difficulties you are facing in our family. Up until now you have been a weak father, and my brother's addictions are the result of his anger at you. The only way for you to help him is for you to radically change your behavior. It's all up to you. But remember that being a real father comes from allowing God's grace to flow through you; so even if you feel afraid you can still do it. There's nothing more for me to say. I've seen the true light; I converted to the Catholic faith, and I will follow that path on my own. But I will be there for you if you ever become serious about changing your life and want my help."

The Spiritual Battle

As for you, grow in faith and learn to witness it. Take up the great spiritual battle against evil, but remember that it's not for you to fight with your own hands; the strength flows through your hands from God, and it doesn't belong to you. Fight all battles with one weapon: your love for God.

39 DANGER TO SOCIETY?

I am a single male, 36 years of age. Both my parents are Roman Catholic, and I was raised Roman Catholic.

In terms of my family background, I have three siblings and my parents divorced when I was in grade school. My father won custody of all four children and has not since remarried. My mother was eventually diagnosed with schizophrenia and is currently living in a group home and receiving, by all accounts, a relatively high standard of care and medical attention.

I was exposed to pornography as a child. I saw a pornographic magazine that my mother left in front of us in plain view on a table. I can recall fixating on several of the photos. One of the pictures involved group sex. I can also recall instances as a grade school student where I searched out pornographic magazines with my friends.

My grade school teachers commented that I was a daydreamer, that I lacked attention/focus and that I rushed through my class work (i.e., often making careless mistakes).

I was a frequent masturbator. I started masturbating somewhere between the ages of 5 and 9. I usually masturbated between 1 to 3 times a day, and I still masturbate on occasion. Most of sexual thoughts/fantasies were about my

219

grade school and high-school teachers (while I was attending school), 'porn starlets' and pornographic film scenes. A central theme to my pornography viewing choices would be 'taboo' subject matter (e.g., incest) and mature/older women.

Several years ago, I engaged in a series of regrettable sexual acts. In all cases I reached each of these individuals ("call girls") via newspaper advertisement/yellow pages.

Around the same time, I was instructed by my employer to see a company-paid psychiatrist and, later, a company-paid psychotherapist. Although I was deemed fit to return to work, I was eventually let go by my employer. Later, on my own initiative, I began to see a psychologist on a weekly basis (an hour a week) for about a year and a half. I spoke to him about various areas of my life including the above noted pattern of behavior.

On repeated occasions, I have smelled (for an extended period of time) my own feces, flatulence, body odor and urine. I have repeatedly defecated in the bathroom sink and while I showered, and I have a tendency of looking into the toilet stall (after I have relieved myself) with some satisfaction.

I continue to have a habit of pulling at my hair and trying to rub out my hair follicle. I pick my nose during business hours. Many nights I find myself unable to fall asleep. Lately, a group of people I know tell me that I seem nervous when I am around them, and this scares me.

I am asking you if I pose a danger to society and if so what I steps I should be taking to put an end to that danger. I am also asking for some guidance as to any steps that I *should be taking to deal with the above noted pattern of behavior.*

To lead you into an understanding of your own question, let me begin with a short explanation of a seemingly unrelated topic.

Through the ages, we have been fascinated with flight. We watch birds fly and, in our own quiet awe, we desire to soar in the sky also. In the past, many men have tried to fly like birds. But, because they understood nothing about aerodynamics, they tried simply to imitate birds. They made frameworks of sticks and string, attached feathers to them, and strapped them onto their arms, hoping to be able to fly. But their hopes, strapped to their ignorance of the real physics involved, crashed to the ground.

Now, your life, too, has been structured around a desire. Your deep desire, however, is not the desire to fly; your desire is the desire to love. Still, your desire has "crashed" because of your ignorance of the psychology involved.

The Destruction of Love

Given your childhood history, you learned nothing about love. Your mother was too caught up in her own inner psychological confusion to be capable of nurturing you with the love of a real mother; moreover, your father most likely had his own flaws that you fail to mention, thus leading to your childhood lack of concentration and your current lack of direction in life. Thus, even though you may have been "raised Catholic," you learned nothing about parental nurturance and guidance, the Catholic faith, or real love.

So there you were, yearning for what was missing. And then you were exposed to pornography.

Pornographic "Gifts"

Like men watching birds fly, you saw in pornography something that aroused your awe. Like men building wings of sticks and feathers, you began to create your own framework for feeling acceptance and "love." And, like men ignorant of aerodynamics, you, being ignorant of God and soul, tried to find love through your body.

In all of your lack of understanding, though, you did know one truth about love: love is a matter of giving. Children know this intuitively when they offer their feces and urine as gifts—the only things they have—to their mother in exchange for her love. This becomes especially apparent during the stage of toilet training when a child pleases a parent by peeing or pooping on demand.

Ultimately, most children grow past this primitive stage of a preoccupation with bodily gifts and learn that real love involves giving something we don't possess; that is, real love involves giving intangible things (such as patience, forbearance, compassion, mercy, and forgiveness) that derive from divine love. In real love we give what we don't really have, yes, but unlike children giving their bodily products, we give away what God gives us. Moreover, through an awareness of real love, we learn to respect our bodies as chaste temples of the Holy Spirit and therefore cease being preoccupied with mere bodily products.

But pornography took you along a perniciously different path. Instead of learning to respect your body as a chaste temple of the Holy Spirit, you made your body into a sex toy. You became preoccupied with feces, urine, and semen as the only "gifts" you could imagine. You especially sought out the love of the "mother" you didn't have; to you, such love seemed taboo, and, despite your desiring it, it terrified you.

So there you are today, lacking any meaningful sense of direction, stuck in a body ignorant of its own soul and indifferent to the Holy Spirit.

Are you a danger to society?

A Danger to Society?

Well, just as you are a danger to your own soul, your lack of love is a danger to the souls of others. In other words, you are a danger to society just as pornography is a danger to society, just as prostitution is a danger to society, just as sexual perversions and activists for sexual perversions are a danger to society, and, in short, just as the devil is a danger to society.

Still, there's a difference between you and the devil. The devil rejects love deliberately and willfully. His place in hell is his own choosing for ever.

At this moment, though, you merely lack the understanding of love. And, at this moment, you have the rest of your life to acknowledge your fear of your childhood pain, to see the effects of that pain in every moment of the present, to feel sorrow for all the damage that the effects of that pain has caused, and to recognize your desire for real love. When you get to that place of spiritual conversion, instead of defiling love with your body, you can, with a chaste body and pure heart, learn to give love to others as God gives His love to you. Then, having renounced lust and having chosen to live a pure life, you will be a benefit to society.

40 PROCRASTINATION

I find myself stuck in many of the unconscious conflicts that you describe, the most striking of which has been outbursts of anger and blaming my parents. My question regards study and self-discipline. I have had a consistent problem of serious procrastination since about the 7th grade (it was also during this grade that I discovered pornography and became addicted to it and that I began to spend many hours on the Internet). This procrastination has led to the near failure of a class in high school and my failing a class last year in college; I also had to drop another class. I feel as though I'm taking a gamble every semester between getting my work done at the last possible minute (quite literally) staying up all night and failing the class.

I've found that if I can at least study with another person around, then I can get some work done, but having someone to study with isn't always possible and the results have been mostly inconsistent.

One issue that I've noticed especially in the past few months is that I lack motivation to get things done. I even feel as though the love of God is not a strong enough motivator in my life due to my own brokenness. When asked by my spiritual director if there was anyone I could be accountable to that would motivate me to get my work done, I responded that I couldn't think of anyone to be accountable to. I feel like I'm aimlessly floating this way and that, doing my work on a whim, if I do it at all.

I feel as though I understand in my mind that I need to enter deeply into the spiritual life and be healed through God's grace of any past hurt that I'm carrying, but I continuously stumble over the same problems, such as procrastination and masturbation. I'm also almost always constantly fatigued (although this probably might be due to sleep deprivation).

How can I discipline myself to study well? What can I do to stop procrastinating? Do you have any advice for studying? What else do you think is going on here?

From your first sentence we both know that anger at your parents is behind your problems, but merely knowing about the anger doesn't do anything to resolve it. Instead, it will be important to understand how and why the anger affects you in everyday events.

Puberty

Let's begin by examining what occurred when you were in 7th grade. This is a time of puberty—when you would have been about 13 years old—that marks the entrance into the body's sexual maturity, and, by extension, into adult social responsibility. From what you have told me,

I surmise that, because of your father's failures, you faced the prospect of puberty with considerable uncertainty. Without the guidance of someone showing you how to face the unknown mysteries of life with confidence in God, you would have been crippled with fear at the prospect of facing the unknown obligations of adulthood.

Moreover, when all the manipulative aspects of sexuality were imposed on you through pornography at this time of adolescent crisis, you had no opportunity to develop a stable identity other than that of a slave to lust and hatred.

The Psychological Meaning of Masturbation

In this context, you used masturbation to provide a form of self-soothing and a feeling of control. Yes, masturbation feels good in the moment; nevertheless, it is a failure of sexual responsibility because it distorts the reproductive function into mere self-serving pleasure. Hence we can see the spiritual danger of masturbation: *it's a non-achievement that provides the illusion of achievement.* At its core is anger at your father (and your mother, as may also be the case) for not comforting and guiding you when, in the face of impending responsibility, you felt vulnerable and insecure.

The Psychological Meaning of Procrastination

Similarly, procrastination can be understood psychologically as a sort of mental paralysis that arises when you face the fear of the unknown. It all results because of a lack in your father's guidance when you most needed it. Thus, with no accountable person around, your journey into mature life became an aimless wandering without a guide—and so it can be said that your every action was not much more than a whim. Therefore, when new tasks appear in front of you now, you freeze psychologically. Behind it all, at its core, is anger at your father for not motivating you when you most needed guidance.

Thus it can be said that procrastination is not just a matter of *not knowing how to do something*, but that it's an emotionally poignant matter of despair about what you do know: it's a matter of your *knowing that you lack confidence in how to do something*, combined with your *knowing unconsciously that your father has failed to prepare you to do anything*, combined with your subtle *knowing that, in your despair, you really are afraid to do it "right now."*

How to Stop Procrastinating

Understanding this, we can now proceed to describe what you need to do to stop procrastinating.

Make the Connection

First, admit to yourself that your father's failures have had real and practical consequences in your daily life and have led especially to your own failures. When you experience a lack of motivation (or a lack of discipline, or distraction when trying to study, etc.) tell yourself, "This is occurring because of how my father failed me." The point here is not to blame your father so as to punish him, but to *take the blame off yourself*. Your difficulties don't mean that there is something defective about you; the real problem is that you have been cheated of something you very much need. Furthermore, this means that with proper guidance you can acquire what is now lacking in you.

To Become A Father to Yourself

Second, resolve to become a "father" to yourself. Instead of staying stuck in blaming your father for what you don't have, and in unconsciously punishing him with your failures, focus on taking personal responsibility to provide for yourself with what until now has been lacking in you. This is easier said than done, so there are three things you can hope in to overcome your despair.

1. Hope in psychological guidance, such as you are now receiving from my writing, and do whatever it takes to learn from it.

2. Hope also in a growing cooperation with your own unconscious, so that your unconscious will be an ally in learning. Realize that your unconscious is not "out to

get you"; it is, in essence, the truth of your life, which, until now, you have largely suppressed because, in not having your father's guidance in how to appreciate truth, you have feared it. Through your psychological work of healing you will find that your unconscious can be a trusted source of enlightenment.

3. Hope also in prayer, which will become more and more meaningful to you as you let go of your anger at your father and come to see God not as a reflection of your father's failures but as He really is: your truest and deepest hope.

Beyond Blame and Into Forgiveness

Third—speaking of letting go of anger at your father— begin to discharge the static buildup of desiring the satisfaction of "hurting your father as he has hurt you." This satisfaction is called *revenge*; it traps you in blame and in psychological blindness such that you fail to see that all your failures have had one secret intent: to hurt your father in your hope of getting justice with your own hands.

Your true success now will depend on giving up the satisfaction of hurting your father. You can do this by trusting that justice belongs to God; this means that your father will have to answer to God for his failures, not to you. This is not a matter of condemning your father, because his destiny depends on whether he has contrition before God for all his failures; it's not your job to "save" your father, so leave his judgment before God in the merciful hands of God. The best you can do for your father is relinquish your anger at him. Having done that, you will be free to pursue real achievement for the love of God. Up until now, in your anger at your father, you have been unconsciously seeking failure so as to punish him; now you can seek your personal achievement in all things, and in doing so you will exalt God the Father. This "discharge" of anger is called *forgiveness* because it is the cessation of your secret hatred for your father and the beginning of genuine love for God.

Summary

In summary, then, when faced with any new task, (a) remind yourself that you fear the unknown and doubt yourself because your father failed to provide you with comfort and motivation; (b) then, in spite of your doubts, bring the pain before God by telling Him how you feel while relying upon the hope of receiving real guidance and comfort from God in a way you have never known before; and (c) call upon His justice while you offer your true successes and achievements from now on to God, for use in His service—and also as a special gift to your father, that someday his eyes, too, might be opened. Above all, cling to the knowledge that with prayer and psychological guidance you now have all the resources you need to succeed in life, despite what your father failed to give you.

41 UNDOING PAST SINS

Several years ago, I met a girl. We were both quite young. Around this time, I started developing a lot of the symptoms you list as being indicative of anger at my father. I procrastinated heavily; habitually and obstinately used pornography; retreated into fantasy worlds at length; etc.

I was raised in a protestant background, and she is Catholic. I had already started reading and becoming interested in the Catholic Church when we met, and I thought it was great to have a good, new Catholic friend.

However, we perverted our relationship quickly. There was a pathological need for acceptance from both of us, I think, but I can only say that authoritatively for myself. I had rage all the time--true wrathful, sinful anger—at her, at my parents, at a traffic light! I had intense fear of abandonment. I lost an appetite for work which previously I enjoyed. I used pornography and escaped into fantasy realms. I slept all the time as another mechanism of escape.

We soon started to to have sexual relations. I engaged in incredibly evil, emotionally manipulative patterns of behavior. I used her dependence on me and tried to manipulate her by harming myself and lashing out in anger. She had manipulative behavior too. Our relationship ended disastrously. The end of our relationship led to my suicide attempt. Now, thankfully, that suicide attempt made me realize just how wretched and wrong I was and has led me to the Catholic Church.

I now am seeing the full effects of my actions. I have entered into psychotherapy to confront all of the ugliness that has tainted my soul. I realize now that my mother was over-bearing and smothering, and my dad, though well-intentioned, did nothing to stop this. I realize that I've engaged in self-defeating behavior out of anger at them. But more importantly, I realize now that when we were having sex, it wasn't that I loved this girl. I just wanted to her to soothe me. I wanted her to want me, and I wanted her to depend on me. I realize that while I was playing victim, I was really preying on the emotions of an emotionally vulnerable young woman. I realize that I've done incredible, lasting damage to her soul!

The other day I sent her a text message. I told her how sorry I was. Then she sent a text back saying that although she wished me well, she wished she had never met me. Her response is the truth, and it forced me to confront it. It would have been better for her soul if she had never met me. She is right to wish that!

I do not feel guilt about my behaviors. I did at the beginning, but I do not think that guilt is the right word to describe it now. I just wish I had never engaged in all this destructive behavior. I know I've done lasting damage to her soul, both because of the sexual perversion I consented to with her and because of the evil, angry, manipulative behavior I used against her.

So now, I can finally ask my question. I know that I cannot "undo" what I did to her soul, but what should I do? All sin requires reparation. I pray for her soul. Is that all that I can do? I do not want her to go to hell because I invoked malice in her heart.

Of course, her decisions are her decisions and only acts of her will can constitute a mortal sin for her, but I did influence her. She was at an emotionally sensitive time in life, and I took advantage of that because of my own unconscious desires. How can I make this better for her?

I am coming into the Church and fully expect to live a life of denial and penance, as required by the Lord. I am in psychotherapy and am confronting all of the blocks I have encountered to this. But what is the profit if I manage to go to heaven or gain merit while this soul to which I have done so much damage still suffers? I no longer feel the desire to punish myself for these actions, but I do feel sorry. I just want them to be undone!

A fundamental element of Christianity is that although love overcomes evil it doesn't just wipe evil away as if it never existed. After humanity fell from grace, God did not just destroy everything with the intention of starting all over again. God knew very well that in order to allow us to be capable of love He had to give us free will, even though that very free will makes us vulnerable to rejecting God's will and falling into sin. So even if God had started over again after the fall, the fall would have happened again. Hence God left creation in its place and redeemed us with His love through a plan that He had in place even before the fall. Through His Word incarnate in His own creation—that is, Jesus Christ—He demonstrated for us how divine love should be lived in daily human life to overpower evil.

Redemptive Grace

Consequently, even though you have committed grave sins and have caused great damage to another person, your wanting that you could undo the mess really disavows the redemptive grace of divine love. In other words, even though you contributed to this girl's fall from her faith, she alone is responsible for accepting the redemption God offers her in working out her salvation.

It's imperative, then, that you focus on your salvation; turn to God asking for mercy for your sins and dedicate yourself to living a holy life from now on. Living a holy life—with all the chastity, modesty, prayers, sacrifices, and renunciation of temptations that such holiness entails—will, for the rest of your life, be your reparation for the sins you have committed, and it will be your protection from any desire to commit new sins.

The Mystical Effects of Good and Evil

Furthermore, keep in mind here that all of our thoughts

and behaviors have a mystical effect on others; the sins we commit feed the powers of evil and extend the realm of darkness in the world, and the chaste, holy love we manifest in our lives radiates healing and serves to overpower evil. Therefore, your decision to live a chase, holy life puts you on the side of God in the great spiritual battle against evil in your own life and in the lives of others.

In the context of that holy life, you can pray that this girl will repent her sins and, like you, turn to God for mercy. Hold her in your heart with all your prayers, but especially remember her by name as an addendum to the Collect of the Leonine Prayers that you should be saying privately after every Mass.

The profit of your going to Heaven is in your own soul, but in the course of your spiritual struggles—with all the anger, lust, and social corruption that you renounce—the holiness that you bring into the world will profit the contrition not just of this girl but also of countless other souls as well.

The Leonine Prayers

- *The Hail Mary (thrice)*

  Hail, Mary, full of grace!
  The Lord is with thee;

blessed art thou amongst women, and blessed is
    the fruit of thy womb, Jesus!
Holy Mary, Mother of God, pray for us sinners
    now and at the hour of our death. Amen.

- *The Hail Holy Queen*

Hail, Holy Queen, mother of mercy;
hail, our life, our sweetness, and our hope!
To thee do we cry,
poor banished children of Eve;
To thee do we send up our sighs,
mourning and weeping in this vale of tears.
Turn then, most gracious Advocate,
thine eyes of mercy towards us:
and after this our exile
show unto us the blessed fruit of thy womb, Jesus.

O clement, O loving,
O sweet Virgin Mary!

V.   Pray for us, O holy Mother of God.
R.   That we may be made worthy of the promises
    of Christ.

- *A Collect*

Let us pray. O God, our refuge and our strength,

look down in mercy on Thy people who cry to Thee, and by the intercession of the glorious and immaculate Virgin Mary, Mother of God, of St. Joseph her Spouse, of Thy blessed Apostles Peter and Paul, and of all the saints, in mercy and goodness hear our prayers for the conversion of sinners, and for the liberty and exultation of our holy Mother the Church. Through the same Christ our Lord.

- *The prayer to Saint Michael the Archangel*

Saint Michael the Archangel,
defend us in battle;
be our protection against the wickedness and snares
      of the devil.
May God rebuke him,
we humbly pray:
and do thou, O Prince of the heavenly host,
by the power of God,
cast into hell Satan
and all the evil spirits
who prowl about the world
seeking the ruin of souls.
Amen.

42 ANGRY TRAD

I started attending the Traditional Latin Mass (also known as the Tridentine Mass or TLM) about 2½ years ago. In my experience attending it amazing things have happened, pain has surfaced and even healed, I "feel" fathered (this is very important to me because my father was absent and apathetic in protecting me from my mother's emotional and sometimes physical abuse). I feel that at the TLM that I come into contact with God and am totally captured by its beauty. . . . The image of God presented in the TLM really inspires me to love God for his own sake, despite the fact that I fail in this miserably. It also provides a refuge against the liturgical chaos in our Novus Ordo church.

I have tried to talk to the priest at my parish and offered to start a Latin Mass Society, and I have offered to get financial assistance for him to learn the TLM and offered to go leaps and bounds (including getting the local FSSP Priests to come and offer the TLM and even train him for free, and offering to train alter servers and recruit people to start a choir that could do Gregorian Chant), and the response that I get is, "That sounds great, but I don't have the time" or "I understand these things have value, but the liberals will rebel so I have to go at a 'baby steps' approach."

My problem is that this has evoked serious anger from me because I feel that while people at the Novus Ordo say they take liturgy seriously, I don't believe that they really do. I feel ignored and mistreated pastorally because while the school has to be reformed and they are going leaps and bounds for that, it appears that it is OK that Our Lord in the Eucharist is mistreated, and I am the crazy one for getting upset about it.

So this evokes terrible anger in me because my wife who does not entirely understand my appreciation for the TLM wants to continue to go to our parish. I find myself so angry about this whole issue and even when I attend the Novus Ordo (priest facing the people, way too many extraordinary ministers of Communion, terrible choir, bad lay readers, etc.) I can't help but get angry and wonder why doesn't anyone do something about this? It is hard to take my mind off it.

I often wonder if there is something deeper to this anger, something more; I feel like I am becoming an "Angry Trad" and I know this is not what God wants. I wonder why this issue makes me so mad. Life is about the salvation of souls right? Not about arguing endlessly over externals in the Liturgy. Why do I feel the need to constantly learn every argument to protect myself in case I am questioned about it? Why do I feel I must fight for this and why do I get so angry about it? I feel that the issue while being about the liturgy is important my overwhelming anger about it points to something much deeper, and I am wondering if you have any insight as to what that might be?

Should I avoid the Novus Ordo to help cope with my

anger? I recognize I probably am mad at my father, but when I think about my father my rage never flares up even though I know intellectually he really has failed me. I never get angry with him beyond just irritation because he is a nice guy so I find it hard to be mad at him, but I suspect this is the root of my anger because he was never around and failed to protect me from my mother. How do I undercover this anger toward my Dad so I can feel the pain, give it to God and take responsibility for it?

The fundamental purpose of prayer, whether private or liturgical, is to grow in love. Real love will be manifested as love of self, love of neighbor, and love of God, all embraced in a dynamic unity. Thus, if you say you love God but hate your neighbor, you're a liar; if you say you love your neighbor but hate yourself, you're a liar; if you say you love God but hate yourself, you're a liar; and if you say you love your neighbor but hate God, you're a liar.

Any anger and hatred, therefore, puts you in a bad place, regardless of whether the anger is about liturgical abuses or not.

Love—or Veiled Hatred?

Now, in regard to liturgy, the Traditional Latin Mass preserves a reverent environment well suited to nurturing love. The language, the music, and the liturgical actions of the priest(s), server(s) and the congregation all combine to focus human action into an act of love.

Still, many men come to the Mass in jeans and sneakers, and women, heads uncovered, are clothed—or unclothed, more often than not—in a display of secular pride.

Now, the Novus Ordo Mass, just like the Traditional Latin Mass, has a potential for reverence. The *Kyrie* can be sung in Greek; the *Gloria, Sanctus*, and *Agnus Dei* can be chanted in Latin; Extraordinary Ministers of Communion can be avoided; and Communion can be received on the tongue while kneeling.

Nevertheless, many persons receive Communion in the hand while standing and without showing any more reverence than children eating candy. This illustrates that the Novus Ordo has as much potential for abuse as it has potential for holiness. Consequently, in many parishes today, the "love" in the Mass is no more love than the "love" experienced by someone having sex with a girlfriend or a boyfriend. Everyone calls it *love* but it's really a hatred for authority that itself is a veiled hatred for God.

Notice that word. Hatred. Most people will cringe when hearing it; they will say, "That's ridiculous! We don't hate God!" Yet they do hate God. Hatred is an expression of anger, anger derives from emotional hurt, and people who want to liberalize the Church were once children who were emotionally hurt by their parents' hypocrisy. It's a long chain of events, but when you follow it out psychologically it takes you to one inevitable conclusion: emotional hurt always provokes an impulse to hatred, and because of that dynamic unity I spoke about earlier, all hatred ends up as hatred of God.

This, now, brings us to your questions.

Fear of Love

You ask how anger at your father manifests in your behavior. Well, even though you do not say very much about it in actuality, you say very much psychologically. "My father was never around and failed to protect me from my mother." In your eyes, therefore, your mother was a danger; she must have been very angry, and you must have suffered from her yelling and screaming and her hostile, irrational behavior. Moreover, by shirking his responsibility to the family, your father cheated you of a confident image of fatherly guidance and protection that could stand up to—and take command over—irrational behavior.

What, then, was the result of all of this? In learning to fear your mother's hatred and to hate your father's cowardice, you learned to fear love.

You learned to fear love through a series of psychological steps. You would have felt hurt by your mother and you would have experienced impulses of anger at her—but, because your father failed to teach you anything about emotional responsibility and how to limit and direct impulses of anger, you learned to fear your own anger. You feared it as if it were an uncontrollable wild beast that could overpower you and devour everything around it.

So, not knowing how to manage anger in a spiritually healthy manner, you stifled your awareness of your anger by stifling your emotional life. You didn't eliminate emotions entirely (because no one can), yet you stifled your feelings sufficiently to convince yourself that what you were feeling was somehow wrong, or in error, or unnecessary, or of no real purpose. You learned to function in the intellectual realm, seeking out reasons and explanations—learning every polemic in the book—to allow you to ward off your emotional hurt. You did what many children do. You hardened your heart sufficiently to the emotional pain of yourself and others to protect yourself from your anger while still allowing you a sense of duty to carry out your responsibilities.

You did this all, not realizing that, in denying your own feelings, you were essentially cheating yourself of the very love your father denied you. Again, notice the words: cheating yourself of love. What does this mean?

Cheating Yourself of Love

Well, reflect on why God gave us free will. If we couldn't

say "No" to God, our saying "Yes" to God would be meaningless. In a similar way, if we cannot acknowledge our capacity to hurt others—indeed, our *desire* to hurt others—when they hurt us, then we cannot express our love for them through a refusal to hurt them. Without an honesty about our hatred for others, any good we do for them is just an act of duty; it's not really an act of love. To love others is to wish them good, especially by refusing to do them the harm that, somewhere in the recesses of our minds, we would like to do to them.

Consequently, to love others you must first know that you *want* to hurt them; then, as an act of love, you can *refuse* to carry out that hurtful impulse.

Thus, maybe now you can understand that, because your mother allowed herself to carry out her anger in actuality, she did not love you. Moreover, your father did not love you because, in fearing his own anger at your mother, he implicitly gave your mother permission to carry out her anger in the family. Your father, therefore, is as guilty of your mother's abuse as she is—and you have been angry all your life at your father because he failed to protect you as he should have done.

Where does that leave you? All this hidden anger at your father leaves you angry at Mass, doesn't it? It leaves you in a place where you get angry at others because they don't do what you think they should do. It leaves you hating others because, in shirking their responsibilities, they demonstrate that they don't love God—but then your hatred for them leaves you hating God too. Your dilemma is that you are surrounded by people who don't know how to love God and that you're one of them, too.

The problem isn't specifically with the Novus Ordo Mass.

The problem is that, because of the way your parents treated you, you fear love—and, because you fear love, you have been suppressing your anger just enough to keep it out of sight but not enough to prevent it from leaking out when you are most vulnerable. In your case, you are most vulnerable when others' lack of respect for your sense of duty causes you to catch a momentary glimpse of the truth that *duty is not love*. Your anger is just a puff of smoke—a magician's trick—that allows you to quickly remove from sight your lack of love for God and replace it with your indignation that others lack love for God.

Removing the Obstacles to Love

What can you do, then? You cannot force yourself to love, because then it would be duty, not love, but you can do whatever it takes to remove the obstacles to real love. Endeavor, therefore, through prayer and personal scrutiny, to look back into your past with honesty to feel the pain you have been suppressing; to identify the family behaviors that caused you to fear love; and to embrace and transform that fear.

This is hard work. It means that once you open up the door to your suppressed emotions you run the risk of letting your anger out as well. This, however, is really not as bad as it may seem.

If you can learn to acknowledge and understand your angry impulses, rather than shut down any process that would reveal them to you, you can then learn to make a conscious effort to refuse to carry out those impulses.

For the love of love you can resist carrying out those impulses.

Instead of allowing your impulses to push you right into sin, you can let those angry impulses be warning signs that you have been emotionally hurt somehow, you can then turn back to examine that hurt honestly, and you can then turn to prayer for assistance. Pray for God to protect you, pray for the repentance of those who have hurt you, and pray for your ability to grow in love because of your trials—and pray especially that you can remain in a place of love regardless of what others do around you.

Still, the difficulty of this work explains also why a priest will balk at opening up his church to liturgical reverence: if he does, the liberals' lack of love will be exposed, and their anger will come gushing forth—and many priests, just like your father, back away in fear, because they lack the courage to face the anger of others, to restrain it, and then to teach others how to love, rather than hate.

Conclusion: Self-deceived

In the end, no matter what prayer and liturgical practices you follow, if they are not leading you to love God with all your heart, all your soul, all your strength, and all your mind, if they are not leading you to forsake the world and its enticements, if they are not leading you to live a chaste and modest lifestyle, and if they are not leading you to reject hatred and treat others with forgiveness and compassion, then, to borrow an expression from Saint James (James 1:26), you are self-deceived.

43 REVENGE FACTOR

My abusive mother left her house to me when she died and it's legally mine, but it will, in reality, always be my mother's house. My neighbors, sweet as they may be, constantly remind me how I'm not doing things like my mother did and maybe I'm doing that on purpose. I don't know. It's not the house I grew up in, however, so there are no childhood or even unpleasant memories associated with this house, other than she died here. She was an immaculate housekeeper and I'm not. When I'm at home, I'm either reading or writing, and keeping house and washing dishes just isn't on my radar screen until it's absolutely necessary. Maybe that's a revenge factor on my part that I wasn't aware of. I just figured it was because reading is a more important activity, for me, anyway. Do you have any comments about this?

The issue about neatness and cleanliness is really a profound issue of love. When you care about a possession, you consequently want to keep it in good condition.

It's the same for creation itself. When we really, really understand that God created this world, we are moved to take good care of it. Environmental abuse—even the act of spitting on the ground or throwing litter on the side-walk—shows us up as hypocrites if we claim with our lips to love God.

Furthermore, it's the same for the body. Anyone who re-ally understands that the body is the temple of the Holy Spirit (see Chapter 47) would want to keep the body well-groomed, modestly dressed, free from addictions, properly nourished, and physically fit.

Think of cleanliness and order, therefore, as aspects of the holy, whereas chaos and filth are aspects of the anti-holy—that is, the demonic. If you respect your environment as an aspect of a holy life, you will be pained to see dirt and disorder anywhere, but if you tolerate dirt and disorder, then something deep in your unconscious is at work: anger and hatred.

Anger and Hatred

Although your mother was a meticulous housekeeper, she probably did her chores out of duty, rather than for the sake of pure love; that is, if she had any love for God she wouldn't have abused you, so we know she certainly wasn't living a holy life. Despite what others thought of her, you know she was a hypocrite, and that angers you. Thus your unconscious desire is to throw her cleanliness back in her face so that you can get the satisfaction of showing her what a fraud she was. But she's dead. So into whose face can you throw the dirt now?

Well, although, the disorder in your house is a manifestation of your anger at your mother, your allowing the dirt to accumulate is an expression of anger at both yourself and God. Because you have to live in it daily, the dirt signifies your hatred of yourself, and because the dirt stains God's creation, it also signifies your anger at God.

You hate yourself because you have no other way to come to terms with the abuse you suffered. As a child you must have tried desperately to find an explanation for your mother's behavior, but, because abuse is always irrational and never makes conscious sense, you came to the same conclusion that every other child comes to: "It's my fault. I'm bad. That's why I'm treated so miserably. I deserve it." So you hate yourself as self-punishment for being "bad."

You are also angry because no one ever stopped your mother from abusing you. All your life you have been blaming God for being absent. But what did God do to deserve your anger? Well, nothing. Absolutely nothing. He has always been present and has done everything to demonstrate His love for you. So why are you angry at God? Well, you are really transferring your anger onto God from someone else. And who might that be? Well, it's your father, the one who never stopped your mother from abusing you. In fact, he was so absent from your life that you don't even mention him in your question.

So you hate God, and you hate yourself, and you hate your father, and you hate your mother. Distracting yourself by reading and writing is just an intellectual way of ignoring the hatred that is always right under your nose. Nothing will ever be resolved this way. It's like sweeping dirt under the carpet and saying to yourself that the room is clean.

For love of your soul, allow yourself to see the dirt—the dirt of your hatred—and then, through prayer, fasting, and forgiveness—and, ultimately, love—do anything it takes to clean up the mess.

44 KEEPING THE PEACE

I have always forgiven, you have no idea for how many things. What I really need is how to love myself enough to stop the feelings that I keep stuffing down in order to not hurt others. It's myself I keep hurting, because I care so much about keeping the peace. I only (at times) try to tell them how I feel, in the hopes that they will understand.

However, (and I begin the paragraph with that because it really is a whole different subject) it is very different to allow those that you don't live with, and especially those who have nothing to do with influencing or raising your children, to make serious mistakes and treat them with patience and kindness than it is to allow someone who does have those direct influences on yourself and those you love to make mistakes that can cause harm.

For example, a person I know recently drank alcohol in his car while driving home from work. This person has youngsters and teenage children at home and is old enough to know better. Even as you treat such a person with patience and kindness, at what point do you stop allowing such behavior? How do you explain it to a teenager? How do you make peace with yourself for allowing it without any consequence?

You say that you want "to love myself enough to stop the feelings that I keep stuffing down in order to *not* hurt others." Well, this means that right now you are pushing your feelings out of awareness—that is, "stuffing" them—to avoid hurting others, and you think that it would be better to have no feelings at all—that is, to "stop" your feelings.

Your feelings, however, are an expression of your reality, so if you "stop" your feelings it's like murdering a part of yourself.

If you really were to love yourself, therefore, you would be able to love your feelings; in psychological terms, "to love your feelings" means that you could understand them rather than just "get rid" of them as if you were having an abortion.

The real way to not hurt others, then, is to learn to love yourself; to do this, endeavor to follow a step-by-step psychological process of emotional honesty. First, acknowledge exactly how you were hurt. Then admit to yourself your feelings of hurt. Then recognize your humanly natural impulses of hatred and revenge that result from feeling hurt. Then make the decision not to act on those impulses, and, despite what you're feeling, to give to others your patience, kindness, compassion, forbearance, mercy—and forgiveness.

In other words, forgiveness is not a matter of ignoring

offensive behavior while keeping your mouth shut. For-giveness is a matter of refusing to hate someone despite your knowing very well that your mind is surging with impulses to get a sweet taste of revenge.

Follow this process of choosing forgiveness over hatred, despite your feelings of hurt, and you will do good to your-self and to others. That's real love.

Offenses Made in Your Presence

Now, in regard to a "whole different subject," you have no control over what someone does when you are not present. Moreover, you have no responsibility for changing the be-havior of another person (with the exception of your own children while they are still minors). But when someone does something in your presence that you find contrary to your moral values, assert healthy boundaries. Speak up and say, "I cannot accept this." Tell the other person why you feel offended; if the other person does not treat you with respect, then leave the situation. Don't leave in a huff, and don't leave with indignation; leave with gentleness and kindness. Just walk away to make your point, but not to sulk in resentment. Your leaving is only temporary, so as to assert a boundary; it shouldn't be an act of anger in an attempt to hurt the other person.

If, in a misguided attempt to "keep the peace," you say nothing, you will give the impression that you condone the offending behavior, and that hurts both of you. It will hurt you because you come across looking like a coward, and maybe even a hypocrite; it will hurt the other person because it deprives that person of a warning that could, perhaps, inspire repentance.

When Children are Involved

When children are involved, then be honest. Tell the children that the offending behavior is wrong, let them know that you cannot change the behavior of another person, admit that you feel frustrated, and tell the children to pray for the enlightenment and repentance of the offender. That way, in your being honest, you have at least given the children reason *not* to believe that they are crazy—or bad—for seeing what almost no one else will admit.

Learning from Mistakes

Finally, how do you make peace with yourself for having betrayed the children by allowing misconduct "without any consequence"? Well, you tell the children *openly and honestly that you made a mistake.* By admitting the truth to them (and you can believe that they already know the truth anyway), you not only make peace with them but you also make peace with yourself because finally you have had the courage to face the truth of your own dishonesty. Then, from the depths of your heart, pray for the wisdom and courage to learn whatever you need to learn from your mistakes so that you will be able to act with greater courage the next time your feelings tell you that you have been offended. And that's real love.

45 SCRUPLES

I am beginning to realize that I need some professional help, and yet I am having a hard time accepting that. I have always tried to figure my problems out by myself, and yet have never been able to do this. I have lived outwardly as a "normal person" while interiorly hiding terrible guilt feelings and mental anguish. I do not dare tell anyone the truth about me. I spend a lot of time helping others, while all the while feeling like a total hypocrite. This problem is not new—looking back, I can see a pattern of real spiritual scruples and false guilt from my childhood; I had a real spiritual dilemma that I did not know how to handle and did not trust the adults in my life.

Eventually I realized I had wasted the best years of my life, and had never loved or been loved. I had health problems and depression and an addiction to pornography. I had spent the majority of my life hiding the anguish inside of me and not being able to turn to anyone. Now I am struggling to practice my Catholic faith again. Yet, I am running into the same old scruple patterns.

Your comments show how psychologically complicated

the matter about scruples can be, and how much of the problem derives from early family experiences.

So let's begin with some background information necessary to understand the origin of scruples.

The Background: Knowing and Not-knowing

Every child is born into a pre-existing social world of language, science, technology, art, literature, and so on. But even more profound than the mystery of the sum total of all this factual information is the mystery of the child's own body. The child finds itself literally at the mercy of biological processes—hunger, vomiting, defecation, urination, bleeding—that it can neither control nor comprehend. Thus the child will feel wretched and will believe—rightly so—that the world "knows" something that he or she does not know. Right from the beginning, then, the child is located in the unknown surrounded by a profound emotional space of "not knowing" and feeling "left out."

This natural experience is difficult enough, but when children are criticized and humiliated by others—especially their families—they can develop the belief that others are deliberately withholding knowledge from them, and this belief can cause the children to burn with anger at their parents in particular and the world in general. Such children can develop an intense desperation to want to figure out everything in advance, before taking the risk of doing anything, so as to avoid further feelings of humiliation.

It's an awkward, uncomfortable, and frustrating place to be—and so we all devote considerable energy to overcoming the feeling of "not knowing."

- We might seek out intellectual knowledge through formal education.

- We might engage in scientific research.

- We might join country clubs, gangs, cults, cliques, or any other social organization that purports to offer some secret "knowledge."

- We might search through myriads of pornographic images hoping for the special privilege of finding pleasure in seeing what is usually kept hidden.

- We might seek out "carnal knowledge" through the body of another person and attempt to locate the psychological agony of our bodily mystery in the pleasure—or pain—of the other.

- We might create our own fantasy worlds—with thoughts and images of eroticism, heroism, revenge, or destruction—in which we can "figure it out" on our own so as to possess the power and recognition we so desperately crave.

Nevertheless, all the "knowledge" that we can find in the world is nothing but a thin veil that hangs over the dark anguish of helplessly "not knowing." Standing before the veil, suspecting our "not knowing," we feel confused, wretched, weak, useless—and angry.

Because it is this anger—and your fear of it along with your hiding it—that fuels the problem of scruples, let's explore how it occurs.

The Unconscious Conflict of Scruples

You might be afraid that everyone who reads this question will know exactly who you are—and yet you are just one of millions, in every parish of every diocese of every country. I've seen this problem with men and women, with the laity, with religious, and with priests. It's all the same thing: "If anyone knew what I was really like, they wouldn't want anything to do with me." Your life is caught up in the misery of desperately hiding your reality.

Consequently, when you are tormented with scruples you are essentially caught in an unconscious conflict, such that even as you are confessing your sins you are secretly trying to hide them.

So, what exactly are you trying to hide? Well, let's find out by considering some practical guidance about scruples and see where that takes us.

Finding the Psychological Motive

It may seem surprising, but you don't have to confess the psychological thoughts and fantasies about which you have scruples. Yes, you must confess actual behaviors, such as using pornography for self-arousal or for masturbation, but the inner fantasies themselves are venial sins that can be healed with inner contrition and a dedicated desire to discover the underlying psychological motive for the thoughts and fantasies.[1] (Nevertheless, speaking about these inner experiences to a priest in confession could also be helpful, provided the priest is psychologically astute and able to provide psychological guidance through spiritual direction that uses psychotherapeutic techniques.)

For example, while you're trying to pray you might find yourself drifting into fantasies—often sexual, but not always—that intrude into your mind. If you notice what's occurring and break out of the fantasy, then you can say, "Why am I thinking about such-and-such right now? What's going on?" Then put your intended prayer "on pause" and begin a different kind of prayer, a prayer of self-examination directed to discovering what you have been experiencing recently and how you feel about it all.

In that examination you might discover some event from the day—or from recent days—that left you feeling helpless or useless or weak in some way. Then make yourself deal with that event by admitting your weakness and helplessness and implore God for the strength to endure the pain and for the guidance to deal with the problem. In other words, the fantasy is a sort of intoxication, a drug-like "hit" that covers up the emotional pain you don't want to accept.

Interpretation, Not Fear

Given the information above, you can learn to listen to and interpret your fantasies, rather than act them out or fear them, and thus you will be guided into real healing for your psychological pain. Feeling true sorrow for your behavior, you can open your mind and your heart to move past your mistakes into purification: to learn, to grow, and to be formed by God, all through a holy attentiveness to the small details of life.

> Note here that someone who pays close attention to details out of *love* for the work at hand acts virtuously, whereas someone who obsesses about details out of *fear* that "something bad might occur if everything is not done perfectly" acts with the characteristics of Obsessive-Compulsive Disorder.

Then, when you have learned to face your not-knowing with humility, and can trust in Christ's mercy and His inexhaustible love for all sinners, you can remain confident that no matter what you do, Christ will never abandon you and that He will ceaselessly call you into repentance and draw you back to His grace.

Well, so far, so good. But there's a catch here, isn't there?

Anger and Self-condemnation

You cannot trust in God, however, if you're angry at Him. "What!?" you ask. "Angry at God? I'm a devout Catholic!"

Well, sit down and listen to a shocking piece of psychology here.

Yes, you are angry at God because you're angry at your parents, especially your father. But, because it's too psychologically terrifying for some persons to be openly angry at someone so close to them as their father, they turn their anger to someone more distant: God the Father.

Now, why would you be angry with your parents? Well, you're angry with them because of their failure to lead you into a proper knowing of the world. You're angry because you were left having to figure out everything for yourself. As a child, you wanted nurturance, guidance, explanations, and emotional and physical protection, but for one reason or another your parents failed you. They may have been absent physically or emotionally, and in that absence they essentially disabled you psychologically and spiritually.

As a result, you feel hurt and irritated at your parents, and you don't trust them. Those feelings lead you to impulses of hatred and anger. But that is not all. Some part of you enjoys your disability because it allows you a means of expressing your hatred and getting revenge on your parents; that is, you throw your disability back in their faces as evidence that they have failed you, and in that very act of "throwing your disability in their faces" you get the satisfaction of hurting them—and in your hurting them is your revenge.

Thus you have stumbled into the odd dynamic of self-condemnation: in hurting yourself, you find a clever way to hurt others.

Self-condemnation and Scruples

In reaching this point of self-condemnation, some individuals will openly reject their faith and leave the Church. This act itself is a form of self-sabotage, and it illustrates the point that many people will send themselves to hell in order to get revenge on others.

Other individuals, however, will not make an open break with their faith. They are angry at their parents, yes, and they are angry at all authority, too, but their anger takes the form of varying levels of conscious resentment mixed with hidden unconscious anger. Consequently, these persons find themselves in the conflict of wanting to serve God while at the same time wanting to hurt others. So when it comes to self-scrutiny and confessing sins, they unconsciously hide the very sins they try to confess.

And there you have it: scruples. *You're overly concerned about things that might be sins in order to hide the real sin of your secret anger at God.*

The Solution: Salvation Depends on Love Not on Human Perfection

In his first letter, Saint John tells us to love not just in word or speech but in deed and truth (1 John 3:18), and he reminds us that in this love we shall *know* that we belong to the truth (1 John 3:19).

> Christ chose ordinary men, not scholars and theologians, to be His Apostles and disciples. Why? To demonstrate that the Church He was establishing would grow through divine grace, not through mere human intelligence.

So keep in mind that your salvation depends on your willingness to grow in love, not on your attainment of human perfection. The "knowing" that comes from love is the only knowledge we really need. When we understand love to be a plain matter of suffering and self-sacrifice for the good of others, we do not need to fret about questions such as "Does God really want me to do this?" or "How do I know this is enough?" or "Is this really a sin?" or "Have I really done anything wrong?"

When you're paralyzed by scruples, then, you are really

stuck in an unconscious belief that God has some preordained plan for you that, through your own efforts, you have to discover and put into practice in order to please God. The truth, however, is that all God wants from any of us is to learn to love Him with a pure heart by maintaining a constant awareness of His presence in all things.

Consequently, when you are praying and distractions interfere with your concentration, say to yourself, "It's OK. I don't have to repeat the prayer until I get it perfect. My intent is love; I don't have to be perfect to love."

When fantasies and "blasphemous" thoughts intrude into your mind, if you try to fight them they will only get more intense, and you will become more anxious. The key here is to understand that God does not hold against us the things we think spontaneously, nor does He expect us to stop all spontaneous thoughts; all He wants from us is to grow in love by recognizing that certain thoughts are offenses to love and to tell ourselves so—and then to draw our awareness back to Him.[2] Therefore, say to yourself, "It's OK. I know these thoughts are an offense to love, but I don't really intend to carry them out in actions. My intent is love; I don't have to be perfect in not having intruding thoughts. So let's return to the prayer."

Learning from Mistakes

When we make the decision to commit ourselves to love,

we, by the very definition of love, set aside all acts of revenge, both in regard to others and in regard to ourselves. This is an absolute decision; when our lives are governed by a commitment to learn and grow from our mistakes, we are freed from self-hatred and therefore freed from being stuck in fear.

The knowing that comes from love is, therefore, an elegant, simple solution to scruples.

But it's not easy. Hatred and revenge are such sweet delicacies in our social culture that hardly anyone wants to let go of them. Yet giving up revenge and committing yourself to a life of pure love is your only choice—other than sending yourself to hell to get your revenge.

God asks of you only that you openly admit your mistakes to Him and then be willing to learn from them. So rejoice, no scruples can hide here; every mistake, from small simple mistakes to large sins, can be overcome by asking God to teach you whatever you need to learn from them to set yourself on the spiritual path of overcoming the temptations and to learn how to not make those same mistakes again. You don't have to worry if the sin really needed to be confessed or if you confessed perfectly enough; just repent, confess, and ask God to show you how to learn from your mistakes—for the sake of learning rather than for the sake of trying to be perfect.

Note that if you keep falling into the same sin over and

over despite repeated confessions, then you are not confessing the real sin of anger at your parents that the pleasure of the fantasies is working unconsciously to obscure. In such a case it will be necessary for you to face the emotional wounds from your childhood that drive you into sin—the same emotional wounds that your scruples are trying to hide.

Moreover, accept all things, no matter how emotionally painful, as coming from God to teach you to grow in your love for Him and to trust in Him. God wants you to be holy, not to bury yourself in blame.

The Final Shocking Point

Thus we reach the final point, a shocking revelation to those who are scrupulous: being scrupulous is itself a sin. Scrupulosity is sin because it denies God's mercy; instead of trusting in God's guidance to remedy your mistakes, you fall into self-hatred and paralyze yourself with the fear of making a mistake.

But you don't have to panic! The solution is simple: admit that you have been making a mistake in being scrupulous and then throw yourself into God's mercy. It's that simple. Christ didn't start His Church with the intention that it should be otherwise.

46   "ANGER" WITHOUT SIN

In the Night Prayer of The Liturgy of the Hours, I wonder about the passage that says to let your anger "be without sin." Then it talks about wrath and not letting the devil work on you. What does that all mean? I thought wrath was sin, so what is "anger without sin"?

The passage to which you refer is found in Night Prayer for Wednesdays, and it comes from Ephesians 4:26–27. Usually translated as "Be angry but do not sin," it can mistakenly and superficially be interpreted as permission to "be as angry as you want because it's not a sin." Such an interpretation, however, overlooks the passage from Matthew 5:22 where Christ warns us, "But I say to you, whoever is angry with his brother will be liable to judgment." Consequently, to avoid being led astray by a superficial reading of the passage, it will be important to understand what Saint Paul really meant in this passage that is embedded in the overall context of rules of daily conduct for Christians practicing a new and holy way of life.

Most likely, in what he wrote, Saint Paul was thinking

of Psalm 4:5 that says, "Tremble, and do not sin." In this verse, the Psalmist reminds us that trembling in fear before God will shield us from committing sin. But to Greek speakers, such as Saint Paul and the persons to whom he wrote, *trembling* also had the connotation of "trembling in indignation at an offense committed against you."

Thus, to emphasize the matter of holy conduct that avoids sin in a social context, rather than speak of avoiding sin as a general mystical principle of awe for God, Saint Paul chose to speak of *anger* rather than *trembling*—and to understand his meaning we need to think psychologically and distinguish "anger" as *a feeling of irritation* (i.e., pseudo-anger) from genuine anger as *a desire for revenge* and therefore a sin.

"Anger" as a Feeling of Irritation

Whenever someone or something obstructs you or hurts you in some way, you will experience an immediate response. This response begins when your brain, perceiving a threat to your safety or well-being—and completely outside your conscious awareness—sends stress hormones surging through your body. Then, as your conscious mind starts to process the situation, you will experience some noticeable emotions, such as irritation and frustration.[1]

Now, so far, this collection of feelings is a self-defensive response to a perceived threat. It's a warning sign, as it were, that you are being threatened and that you need to protect yourself. Traditionally, when someone feels this way, we will say that he or she is feeling "angry." But this feeling isn't a sin because, in psychological language, this is a feeling of *irritation*, not real anger.

Anger as a Desire for Revenge

When you allow your feelings of irritation to go a step beyond mere feelings and progress into the realm of *desire for revenge*, you enter into sin. This revenge is an expression of hatred because it seeks the other's harm rather than the other's good. That's why anger is a sin: it's a desire to cause harm.

Usually, the underlying motive for anger is the hope that in harming the person who has hurt you, then you might make that person stop or change the offending behavior. Nevertheless, even though the motive may seem to be "good," the act of causing harm is still a desire that is opposed to love. Therefore, just as love is not a feeling but an act of the will (i.e., to wish the good of someone [2]), anger, too, is not a feeling but an act of the will (i.e., to wish harm to someone).

As long as the desire for revenge stays in your imagination it is a *venial sin* that can be absolved with perfect contrition; that is, once you recognize the desire, you can renounce it as disordered and wrong while calling upon God to have mercy on you; then you can give the injury over to God's justice knowing that the offender will have to answer to God for the offense committed against you. You can also pray that the offender will ultimately acknowledge and repent the sin that was committed.

Anger becomes *mortal sin* when you actually inflict harm on someone in return for the hurt inflicted on you.

For example, if you were driving a car and another driver did something rude to you, then you would feel irritated and maybe even threatened. If you silently muttered an insult to the other driver, that would be a venial sin, and it could be corrected with heartfelt contrition. If, however, you screamed a curse at the other driver or made an insulting gesture, you would have progressed from an imagined insult to an actual insult, and that would be a mortal sin. Mortal sin requires sacramental confession to be absolved.

Note that revenge can be carried out either as a calm, calculated act or as a impetuous, emotionally-charged act. Traditionally, this latter case has been called "wrath." But either way—whether unconscious, calculated, or impetuous—carrying out this anger is a grave sin.

The Devil's Work

Because revenge is an act of hatred, it stands in opposition to love, and, in standing in opposition to love, it stands opposed to God's will. Notice here that Satan fell from grace because he refused to do God's will; consequently, all desire for revenge opens the door to demonic influence because all desire for revenge refuses to do God's will. Thus, to progress from *"anger" as a feeling* into *anger as a desire for revenge* is to allow the devil to work in you. That is, with an injury simmering in you, the devil only has to turn up the heat of your resentment until it boils over into the flagrant sin of anger. Thus you will have fallen into the diabolic trap of seeking justice with your own hands rather than trusting in God's perfect justice.

Is Anger Ever Justifiable?

When "anger" is really a feeling of irritation, then it is justifiable, because all feelings are justifiable. But anger in its true sense—that is, a desire for revenge—cannot be justifiable as a Christian act. "But I say to you, whoever is angry with his brother will be liable to judgment" (Matthew 5:22). Christ told us to give a blessing to our enemies, not to get even with them. Moreover, Christ never sought revenge on anyone, not even on those who ridiculed and killed Him.

Resist Him, Solid in Your Faith

In Night Prayer for Tuesdays we are reminded, from 1 Peter 5:8–9a, that "the devil is prowling like a roaring lion, looking for someone to devour." Then we are told, "Resist him, solid in your faith."

So what does this tell you about how to prevent your falling into grave sin because of anger? Well, the answer is simple. To resist the desire for revenge is to *remain solid in your faith by doing what Christ told us to do*: bless your enemies rather than curse them.

Therefore, when others obstruct you or hurt you, (1) *acknowledge* the feelings of irritation that tell you that you have been hurt; (2) *admit* that you have the desire to harm those who hurt you; (3) *recognize* the fantasies of revenge going through your mind; (4) *admit* that the desire to harm someone is wrong and renounce it as wrong; (5) and then, rather than seek revenge, turn the justice over to God and pray for the good of the offenders (i.e., for their enlightenment and repentance) that they might experience Christ's mercy rather than doom:

- If the injury was *accidental*, endeavor to put yourself in the place of the others so as see things from their view and then pray that they might acquire better judgment in the future.

- If the injury was *intentional*, pray for the others that they will repent their sins, and then, for your own peace of mind and to resist the temptation to seek justice with your own hands, trust that God will administer perfect justice in the end.

47   MODESTY

I grew up in a "Catholic" family without any sense of personal boundaries. My father would sometimes walk around naked and liked us to watch him urinate. My mother was always trying to make me dress "sexy," right from grade school. I was hated by other kids. I felt miserable and hated myself. I left the Church because my parents were too disgusting, but my life has been a mess with divorce, masturbation, pornography and, well, a mess. Now I'm trying to come back to the faith. What does "the body is the temple of the Holy Spirit" mean? It seems to be something important for me but I never hear anyone talk about it.

In his first letter to the Corinthians, Saint Paul responded to reports of sexual immorality in the church at Corinth. He specifically used the example of prostitution. Saint Paul's preaching about sexual morality (see 1 Corinthians 6:12–20) points to the fact that, whereas most sins are "outside the body"—that is, they are offenses against charity to other persons—sexual sins not only defile love but also they are sins against one's own body. Sexual sins are sins of lust, and lust strips the body of dignity and turns it into an object. Thus Saint Paul reminded the Corinthians that they were "members of Christ"; that is, members of His mystical body. Saint Paul told them that they must know that the body is "a temple of the Holy Spirit." Furthermore, he emphasized that this Spirit, the Spirit they received from God, is within them. Bringing this to conclusion, he stated that "you are not your own. You have been purchased, and at a price. So glorify God in your body" (1 Corinthians 6:19–20).

> This understanding about the Holy Spirit points to the real meaning of the statement we often hear that "God is within." The statement does not mean that we are gods; nor does it mean that God is just a product of human psychology. It really means that God is within us when we receive the Holy Spirit at baptism.

Sadly, most individuals today do not consider their bodies to be temples of the Holy Spirit; instead, they make their bodies into temples of lust. Our modern culture has glamorized the sin of lust, and even Christians have been duped into rejecting their baptismal promises. These promises are to renounce Satan, to turn away from evil and sin, and to turn to Christ in chaste and holy service. Yet many Christians reject these very promises just to seek the acceptance and approval of a world sinking ever deeper into the insanity of self-deception. They watch movies and TV filled with lust. They look at magazines filled with lust. They listen to music filled with lust. And then they say to the world, "We are devout Catholics."

Purity of Soul and Body

The theology of the body tells us that Christianity is not, like some Eastern philosophies, a matter of abstract spiritual knowledge or esoteric enlightenment; instead, Christian life fully involves purity of both soul and body. This explains why genuine Christian mysticism is not about strange out-of-the-body experiences. After all, Christ was born in a body, He suffered and died in His body, and He was resurrected in His body. Furthermore, He left us His Body and Blood—really, truly, and physically—to nourish us during the hard work of our salvation.

The Body as a Temple

But from where, you might wonder, does the idea that the body is a "temple" derive?

It comes from Christ himself. All four Gospels recount the story of "The Cleansing of the Temple" (Matthew 21:12–13; Mark 11:15–17; Luke 19:45–46; John 2:13–17) when Christ drove away the money changers and merchants, proclaiming, "My house shall be a house of prayer, but you have made it a den of thieves." This cleansing was not an act of anger, as is often incorrectly taught; Christ had no intention of causing harm to anyone. Instead He performed an act of purification. When asked for a "sign" He could offer for doing this, Jesus replied, "Destroy this temple and in three days I will raise it up" (John 2:19).

In other words, the Resurrection was a purification of humanity from the stain of sin, and the cleansing of the Temple was a foreshadowing of the Resurrection.

The Body's Role in Our Salvation

Thus, in requiring both spiritual and physical cleanliness in the Temple, and in promising the resurrection of the body as justification for requiring that cleanliness, Christ shows us that our physical bodies play a key role in our salvation. Joined to Christ in the saving grace of Baptism we become part of Him, "members of Christ," the true Temple itself.

At Confirmation, when we receive the Holy Spirit, who dwells in our bodies to teach us prayer, we become "temples" of the Holy Spirit. Then in the Eucharist we receive Christ's real Body and Blood to feed our real bodies and strengthen our spirits.

> In the 1960s the hippie movement seemingly brought a sense of spirituality into the world. But, grounded in its protest of social hypocrisy, it really did no more than incite us to an adoration of pure physiology cut adrift from all moral guidance. It began with the false idea that our spiritual brokenness can be healed with psychedelic drugs, marijuana, mind-numbing music, and "free" sex, and it led to rampant divorce and abortion on demand. In the end it shows that spirituality,

when divorced from religion, is mere psychobabble
that leaves the body in the moral wasteland of cultural
insanity.

The Body Serves Love and Holiness

This all means that we were not created to serve our own
worldly desires—or the "lusts of the flesh," as Saint Paul
calls them. We were not created to seek social acceptance
by using our bodies to incite lust in others. We were created to share in God's love. Thus, in Christ, we are all called
to serve God's will in holiness, and, once accepting that
call, we must have our lives overturned and our "temples"
cleansed in baptism.

Thereafter, we must keep ourselves clean and chaste,
physically and morally. So, too, our hearts, the center of
our body, must be pure: "Blessed are the clean of heart, for
they will see God" (Matthew 5:8). Furthermore, a clean
heart must be clothed with dignity.

Why Modesty?

Why do we wear clothing? The most commonly given
answer is, "To cover our nakedness." But that's the wrong
answer. The correct answer—the Christian answer—is
that we wear clothing to give our bodies dignity. Modest
clothing covers our bodies with dignity. Immodest

clothing, in contrast, reveals the body by making a pretense of covering it.

Our bodies are meant to be chaste and modest temples of the Holy Spirit so that we can relate to others through our hearts with true love. Our bodies are not meant to be covered with the graffiti of tattoos (Leviticus 19:28), or made into works of "art" with piercings, hair dye, gaudy make-up, shaved heads, or hostile punk hair styles. Our bodies are not meant to be defiled by making our reproductive organs into the equipment of a recreational sport. Nor are our bodies meant to be made into instruments of social acceptance, expressions of vanity and pride, and provocations to lust.

Consider here the example of the Blessed Virgin. The Blessed Virgin herself is the model for all feminine modesty and humility. Because of her purity and humility, Mary was chosen to bear Our Lord, and, because of her love for the divinity she carried within her, she maintained a demeanor of modesty throughout her life.

In a similar way, every Christian woman is called to see herself as a vessel of grace. Thus she is called to treat with respectful humility the vessel of her reproductive functioning—which, being given by God, is not something she possesses—and to protect the vessel of her entire body with the cloak of modesty.

Women are often told that if they are not deliber-

ately dressing to provoke lust then they are doing
nothing wrong. But this is a lie. Everyone knows that
contemporary fashion has one purpose: to be sexy.
And sexy means inciting lust. Sexy dress broadcasts
one message, intentional or not: that the wearer has
rejected moral responsibility to the body and enjoys
sexual pleasure as a form of entertainment. A woman
who dresses as "everyone else" does and pretends that
she is morally innocent is deceiving herself.

Modest clothing, for both women and men, should take
the precaution of doing everything possible to avoid inciting lust. It should cover the body with dignity rather than
reveal the body. Consequently, clothing can be immodest
either because it is tight-fitting or because it exposes bare
flesh. For women especially, tight-fitting clothing, shorts,
short skirts, bare shoulders, and low or V-shaped neck-
lines all serve one unspoken purpose: to incite lust. Political correctness is irrelevant; lust is an unspoken dialogue
between a woman's body and a man's imagination.

The Desire of the Other

This whole psychological issue relating to modesty is
desire—or, more specifically, *the desire of the Other.*

As a simple example of how this desire of the Other plays
out in everyday life, consider how a boy might see a girl
eating ice cream and then declare to his parents, "I want

ice cream!" Psychologically, the boy has seen the girl's desire for her ice cream, and this perception of her pleasure arouses the boy's desire for ice cream. "She sure looks like she feels real good about herself! Give me some ice cream so I can feel good about myself too!"

Similarly, when a man sees a woman dressed immodestly, he thinks to himself, "She looks like she really enjoys her body! Well, I'd like to enjoy her body too!"—and that is what lust is all about. The woman has forsaken her supernatural dignity and is inviting everyone who sees her to rape her visually.

Even though contemporary culture has been indoctrinated with the idea that lust—and social nudity, or near nudity—is truthful, liberating, and natural, lust is deception, not truth, because it makes the body in itself seem to have meaning while it mocks the divine truth of the chaste soul.

Therefore, just because certain styles of clothing (or lack of clothing) may be socially accepted does not prevent them from being weapons for wickedness; that is, sins of pride, lust, and all the effects of Satan that we rejected in our baptismal vows when we were bound to the mission of attaining everlasting life—and we received Christ's personal promise that nothing external would ever thwart that mission. The only threat is our own carelessness.

In Romans 6:12–13 we are told that sin must not reign

> over our mortal bodies lest that we obey their desires.
> We are warned not to present the parts of our bodies
> to sin as weapons for wickedness, but to present our-
> selves to God as raised from the dead to life and the
> parts of our bodies to God as weapons for righteous-
> ness.

We can use our bodies as "weapons of righteousness" if only we develop a "modesty of the eye" that does not seek to be "seen" as a sexual object or to "see" others as sexual objects. Then, with pure eyes and hearts, we will feel the tragic sorrow of God's holy creation being defiled by immodesty.

The Roots of Immodesty

All children need a comforting sense of belonging and acceptance. Some children receive this comfort as babies, under their parent's protection, but many children suffer a deep lack: some parents are emotionally or physically distant and rarely provide any comfort and acceptance to their children; and some parents are outright abusive, leaving their children to languish in an environment of criticism and neglect.

Thus it's rare that children are taught to love God with all their hearts and souls and strength and minds and aren't indoctrinated right after baptism with all the impiety of the anti-Christian world around them. Because many parents do not live out in their actions whatever religious faith they profess with their lips, normal family life is more often than not characterized by self-gratification, resentment, defensiveness, manipulation, hidden alliances, and a general lack of healthy communication.

As a result, many children emerge from their families with a lack of personal identity and a profound craving for approval and acceptance from others—and one sure way for insecure and emotionally broken children to satisfy this craving for approval and acceptance is to use their bodies to manipulate others with lust.

Summary

Even though lust has become a cultural religion, Christian bodies are meant for holiness in Christ, and in Christ we are not our own; we belong to Christ, soul and body. Our salvation depends on the Body and Blood of Christ, not on our own bodies or the body of another person.

> Saint Paul said in Galatians 5:19–21 that "the works of the flesh are manifest, which are fornication, uncleanness, **immodesty**, luxury, idolatry, witchcrafts, enmities, contentions, emulations, wraths, quarrels, dissensions, sects, envies, murders, drunkenness, revelings, and such like. Of the which I foretell you, as I have foretold to you, that they who do such things shall not obtain the Kingdom of God." *[Emphasis added.]*

48   TATTOOS

Is it a sin to get a tattoo? Some of them are really bad, but what about flowers and nice things, or religious pictures? My daughter got one on her ankle, and I think it looks cute. I was thinking of getting one too.

In the story of Cain and Abel from the book of Genesis we learn that God warned Cain to discipline his passions, but that Cain, not listening to God, and out of anger and envy, slew his brother Abel. God then put a mark upon Cain so as to indicate to other men that Cain was being punished by the hand of God and that he should not be slain by the hand of man.

No one knows what sort of mark God put on Cain. Some commentators claim that this mark was a tattoo and that it relates to the practice, prevalent in ancient times, of using tattoos for tribal identifications. Nevertheless, even if the mark were a tattoo, it bears a distinction that separates it from any typical tattoo.

A typical tattoo has one fundamental characteristic: it is

placed on the individual *by the hand of man*—that is, it's the work of human hands, whether those hands belong to a man or a woman.

A tattoo, therefore, signifies a social identity. Whether it serves the function of a tribal membership or whether it fulfills your idea of "nice," it points to an identity that you choose for yourself. But notice carefully: you place this identity upon your body. And here, precisely, we come to the place where a tattoo receives it own mark as sinful.

By the Hand of God

God put a mark upon Cain to indicate that Cain belonged to God. Moreover, this belonging was not just a bodily belonging; it was also a belonging of soul. Cain belonged to God body and soul, and the mark pointed to this reality. As such, the mark foreshadowed another reality, a future reality.

The book of Ezekiel (9:4) tells us about the mark of the *Thau* (or *Tau*—the last letter in the Hebrew alphabet) that God Himself would put on the foreheads of those who belong to Him. This *Thau* therefore signifies the mark of the cross which, as a consequence of the redemption worked by Christ, is placed on an individual at baptism to mark his or her identity as a Christian.

Note that this redemption is a gift from God and is totally

unmerited on our part. There's nothing we have to do—or can do—to earn it or be worthy of it. To be redeemed is to be rescued—rescued from sin—simply as an expression of God's love for us. Our redemption, therefore, comes from the hand of God. It comes *only* from the hand of God. Any identity we have, therefore, is meaningless unless it comes from the hand of God, and so the only mark on our body that can ever legitimately identify us is the mark of baptism.

Consequently, any indelible mark that you place upon your body is the work of human hands. It identifies your body—which God intended to be a pure and chaste temple of the Holy Spirit—as belonging to something other than God. Belonging to something other than God is idolatry, and so any tattoo—tribal or "cute"—is ultimately Satanic because it marks your body with the sin of idolatry, and that sin marks your soul with something, well, not very nice.

Penance

The fact that your daughter got a tattoo and that you approved of it points to your failure as a mother in teaching your daughter about bodily modesty. That's a sin that you will have to repent and pay for.

As for your daughter, a tattoo cannot be easily removed by human hands; laser surgery, for example, is painful and expensive. Only the fire of Purgatory can remove a tattoo completely—and the only way for your daughter to have Purgatory do its work is for her to get there through sincere repentance. Therefore, it will first be necessary for her to acknowledge that she committed a sin in getting a tattoo; then it will be necessary for her to confess her sin; and then, for the rest of her life, she will have to keep the tattoo hidden from public view, as penance, no matter what the inconvenience, lest she give scandal to others.

49 DISCOVERING MASTURBATION

My son (age three) has "discovered" masturbation (at this point rubbing a toy on his genitals or rubbing on the floor). Before I became a Catholic (this year), I would have probably said something like "go to your room, honey, if you need to do that...," but now that I know it is just WRONG, I don't want to allow him to do this any more than I would allow him to eat whatever he wants at every meal. At the same time, I don't want to do anything to inhibit a healthy/correct view for the future of his body/sexuality (or make a big deal so he does it for negative attention). I have been first trying to distract him, and if that doesn't work I then tell him (strongly) to stop. He often gets upset, even very angry, and doesn't want to. I often force him to stop by removing him from the room and helping him get involved in something else. This doesn't work well if we are in the car.

How do you recommend I handle this situation? Is it OK to forcefully make him stop? Is discipline like time-out called for?

I pray for his purity and try not to worry (but I do). Priests or friends say don't worry because he can't really sin at this age, but I know he can certainly develop bad habits that could become a pattern of sin later.

Before you can do anything about your son's masturbation, it's important to be clear in your own mind about the reason why masturbation is wrong. If you are not clear about the matter, then you cannot be clear about what to say to your son, and if you are not clear about what you say to him, then trying to make him stop masturbating will be like trying to take a bone away from a dog. He will growl and snarl, and you will be left frustrated and angry.

So let's discover that clarity.

The Meaning of Reproduction

Masturbation is wrong for one simple reason: it defiles the God-given reproductive purpose of our genitals.

God designed the male and female genitals for the sacred purpose of reproduction, thus allowing a man and a woman to conceive a child and thence to raise that child in a holy environment so that the child can grow to love and serve God. A child, therefore, is the parents' gift to God of a holy soul who can help to fill up the ranks of the fallen angels. Consequently, to use the genitals for mere self-gratification is a defilement of God's love.

Now, for an adult who can comprehend the concept of reproduction, a misuse of the genitals for self-gratification would be a grave sin. But a child who has no understanding of reproduction cannot comprehend why masturbation is wrong. To the child, masturbation simply feels good. The fact that masturbation involves the genitals really means nothing to the child. In fact, sexuality means nothing to the child.

Childhood Masturbation is Not a "Sexual" Pleasure

Even though most adults fail to understand this, the psychological truth about childhood masturbation is that, in the child's mind, masturbation has nothing to do with sexuality. Yes, masturbation, by definition, is self-stimulation of the genitals, and the genitals are organs of sexual reproduction. That part is true.

To a child, however, masturbation is just a form of self-soothing. In its essence, it is no different from thumb sucking; both behaviors derive pleasure from bodily stimulation. Masturbation is different from thumb sucking, though, in that it utilizes private, sacred parts of the body. A thumb does not need to be protected from public view, and so a thumb is not surrounded with a veil of secrecy. Although the genitals are usually kept private and hidden from view because of their sanctity, to those children who do not understand the reason for this sanctity an element of secrecy—and shame—surrounds the genitals.

Therefore, when a child discovers masturbation as a source of soothing pleasure, the child enters into a psychological state of exploring the unknown and the forbidden.

The Unknown and the Forbidden

Imagine how any child feels when surrounded by a vast and mysterious world. In the midst of rules and traditions that adults take for granted, the child will feel ignorant and helpless and will be driven by an urge to acquire a sense of power and efficacy to compensate for a shameful sense of "not knowing."

> For example, imagine what occurs when a child is confronted with a "Do Not Enter" sign on a door. To a child driven by the urge to acquire a sense of knowledge and power, the words "Do Not Enter" will reverberate with enticement. "If they don't want me going in there, it must be something special. I wonder what it is?" To a child, then, "forbidden" usually means "something to be desired and explored because someone else surely must be enjoying it."

This leads us to an odd psychological irony: *to tell your child that he is doing something "bad" only increases his desire for it.*

So what can you do when you find him masturbating? Telling him that masturbation is bad, just because you know that masturbation is bad, won't help him one bit. Telling him it's bad will only make it more compelling.

But before moving on to what you can do, let's first consider some clinical issues.

Clinical Considerations

Given that masturbation is a form of self-soothing, you should be alert for any abnormal psychological reasons that could cause your son to need to soothe himself. Here are some clinical issues for inquiry.

- Investigate the possibility that someone could be sexually abusing your son.

- Is your son in daycare? If he is, then it would be helpful to determine if he masturbates in that setting and what the teacher does about it. For example, you could be working at cross purposes with a liberal teacher who condones, or even encourages, his behavior.

- You might also try to determine if he learned this behavior from other children, whether siblings or neighbors, especially older children who were themselves sexually abused or who were taught to masturbate by sexual indoctrination programs in school.

- Are there any current underlying conflicts between you and your husband that your son could be unconsciously acting out? A child's abnormal behavior can be a reflection of parental distress.

- Is your husband actively involved with the family? If not, your son's behavior could be a symbolic response to his need for attention from his father.

• What were the circumstances of your son's conception? Was he cursed with a conception outside of marriage? Was his conception a holy matter of your desiring to have a baby, or was the conception the result of mere lustful pleasure, thus cursing him with the burden of being an "accident"? How did you feel about your son as you carried him in the womb? Were you experiencing any emotional turmoil about other matters during the time of your pregnancy? How did you feel about your son in the initial months of his life? Was he "difficult" in such a way that you secretly resented him? Any of these issues could be an unconscious reason for anxiety that your son is trying to alleviate with masturbation.

Therefore, even though it might seem that masturbation is something a child just "discovers," it can really be a symptom of a deeper, emotional problem that might now need to be addressed openly—with some outside professional help, if necessary.

What You Can Do

At this point, there are two topics to consider. One topic concerns what can be done now to correct the behavior of your son who has probably not been taught, right from his birth, to live in respect for the holy. The second topic concerns the ways parents can raise their children, right from birth, to respect the holy so as to avoid the need for any drastic correction later in life.

Correcting Unholy Behavior

Below are several interrelated behavioral techniques that you can use to help your son stop masturbating, whether or not there may be clinical issues as well.

Naming. Give a name to the masturbation that your son can understand at the level of his own language skills. Calling it "that" (as in "Don't do *that!*") only makes the whole subject seem mysterious. You might therefore refer to his behavior as "playing with the private parts of your body."

Affirming. Affirm his reality. Let him know that, in regard to his personal experience, he is not inferior in knowledge to you; that is, he knows that masturbating feels good, and you know it too. So acknowledge it openly: "Playing with the private parts of your body feels good; I understand that."

Encouraging. Encourage him to identify with adult behavior. But be careful here. If you shame him by saying, "Stop that! That's bad!" you will only drive his behavior into secrecy. Instead, calmly say, "Adults who love God respect the private parts of their bodies as holy and do not play with their bodies like toys. You can learn to love God like an adult, too."

Teaching. Teach your son that his body is a temple of the Holy Spirit. Explain to him, constantly—and in increasingly mature terms as he grows—how he can care for his body as an instrument of divine will. Demonstrate to him, through your own example, how all aspects of caring for the body—eating, grooming, playing, and resting—are ways to sanctify the body. Explain to him that the desire for divine love is more important than any other desire. Show him how to satisfy bodily needs by subordinating bodily desires to the supreme desire for holiness.

Nurturing. Do what many parents—even those who call themselves devout Catholics—fail miserably in doing: nurture your child's desire for the holy. Realize that because of his drive to understand the world (including his body) he already has the desire to feel good. Now teach him that there is something more powerful and more mysterious than feeling good with masturbation. Teach him about the love of God. For example, when you find him masturbating, rather than stifle his curiosity with shame of the forbidden, take his hands, join them together in front of him, and say, "Let me show you something really special. This is how we pray to God, who is a powerful Father to all of us and who protects us when we feel scared and who teaches us everything we need to know about the world." Then recite the Our Father with him.

Permitting. If your son persists in masturbating even after you pray with him, then, instead of getting into a battle of wills with him, simply give him permission to play with himself.

> "Giving permission" is a temporary psychological method that utilizes paradox to bypass resistance; that is, in giving permission, you actually reduce the mystery of masturbation and the disobedient desire for it. It's neither a declaration that "masturbating is OK" nor an attempt to condone sin. The goal here is to stop a behavior without causing long-lasting emotional scars from a shameful, guilt-producing battle of wills.

This giving of permission can take one of two possible responses depending on the circumstances.

1. You might say, "If you want to play with your body, you have my permission. But go over into the corner by yourself (a variation of *time out*—see Chapter 16), and, when you are finished, then we can *resume* [doing whatever activity he was enjoying with you previous to the masturbation]."

2. Or, you might say, "If you want to play with your body, you have my permission. But if you stop, then we can [do something together that he really enjoys]." Then ignore him until he responds positively.

The point here is that your son will have to decide to stop masturbating of his own will in order to resume participating in enjoyable activity with you and to receive your attention. The key to making this work is *repetitive consistency*; that is, employing the same technique, in every circumstance, over and over.

For information about how to raise a child to revere the Holy right from birth, see Chapter 19.

50   LUST AND MARRIAGE

On the subject of the purpose of marriage (procreation), how does it affect a married couple whose children have grown and the wife is no longer of child-bearing age? Is sex between the couple a sin? I am a Catholic and my husband is a non-practicing Muslim. This would make it a bit tricky explaining to him why sex is not allowed anymore, as he is not bound by the Catholic faith. But even if both of us were Catholic or Christian, do we need to refrain from sex under pain of sin?

Many individuals fail to understand the essence of the Christian faith because they think about life issues in practical, worldly terms. Hence they concern themselves more with outward behaviors—and to what extent they can get away with them—than they concern themselves with working out their salvation with fear and trembling (see Philippians 2:12b) by directing every aspect of their inner motivation to protecting their souls from spiritual doom.

The answer to your question, therefore, does not require

some statement about sexual intercourse *per se*; instead, it requires us to examine a deeper issue, the issue of lust.

Lust

We know that lust is a sin because it is one of the Seven Deadly Sins: pride, wrath, envy, lust, greed, gluttony, and sloth. Lust is a sin precisely because it makes a person into a sexual object; that is, it sees another person in terms of whatever pleasure that person can bring to you. Whereas love wishes good to someone,[1] lust seeks your self-gratification through the use of someone. You can use a person in actuality or in imaginative fantasy, but, either way, lust, being a defilement of love, amounts to hatred for the good—and that amounts to an obstruction of that person's salvation.

Knowing this much about lust, let's ask a question: *How is it possible to have intercourse without making it into an act of lust?* Well, let's find out.

The Possibility of Protection Against Lust

When a man and a woman engage in intercourse within Holy Matrimony and with an openness to procreation,[2] (that is, with the desire to conceive a child) it is *possible* for them to engage in a supreme surrender of the physical to the spiritual. This awareness of the possibility of procreation, along with a profound spiritual surrender, keeps God as the focus of their ecstasy, and this profound focus on God banishes lust from the experience.

But notice that *possibility* is one thing and *actuality* is another thing. For example, Christ told us to love God with all our heart, with all our soul, and with all our mind (see Matthew 22:34–40). Many Christians know this intellectually, but how many of those who call themselves Christian actually do this? How many of those who call themselves Christian actually maintain a constant awareness of the presence of God and pray constantly with their whole heart and their whole soul? More often than not, prayer is just a duty rather than love from the heart. Consequently, with constant prayer lacking, sexuality in marriage becomes a form of lust, rather than a mystical expression of spiritual bonding—especially when the man demands it as an act of marital "service."

So, in seeking an answer to the question, "How is it possible to have sexual intercourse without making it into an act of lust?" ask yourself yet another question: *Is my deepest desire the purification of my whole heart and whole soul through overcoming concupiscence, or do I seek merely the satisfaction of bodily pleasures?*

Love and Purification

The opposite of hatred (and lust) is love, yet before we can enter into the pure love within the Kingdom of Heaven we must be purified of all that is not genuine love.[3] Therefore, endeavor to make your mortal life a life of spiritual refinement, directed to doing everything you can to grow in love and to avoiding anything that contradicts love. This is important because after you die you will have to pay for everything you have ever done that has contradicted love, and there will be no excuses.

No Excuses

At the moment of your death, you will find yourself standing before Christ in the light of divine truth. Every act of your life will be accounted for. Truth will be absolute. There can be no excuses and no deception.

> A man in treatment for depression, and prone to sexual fantasies and affairs, had a dream.
>
> He was walking through vast, empty fields. Suddenly, a great wall loomed up before him; it had the appearance of shimmering, crystalline light.
>
> He approached a door. On the ground was a metal bucket filled with tiny transparent crystals, like sand, but stained and discolored, and with a stench worse than rotting fish. He knocked on the door.
>
> A voice from the other side answered. "You may not enter. Go away." After a pause, it continued. "The price of entry is tears of love, cried out in prayer. Look down at the bucket by your feet. That is what your life has

amounted to; that is all you have to offer: a bucket of
rotten orgasms." And he woke up.

When you stand in the light of that divine truth, will
your baptismal promises be a shield for you or will they be
hanging from you uselessly in tatters?

Esau sold his birthright for a serving of stew (see
Genesis 25: 29–34), and many Christians today are
just as willing to sell their birthright—their baptismal
birthright—for a bucket of rotten orgasms.

In this regard, keep in mind that right now the salvation of
your soul is your responsibility. You will be held accountable to the answers to those questions you asked yourself
above.

Even if your husband is not Catholic, you, as a Catholic,
still have the obligation to live a holy life and witness the
Catholic faith, for the sake of your own soul, no matter
what the cost. You have the obligation to not let your husband tempt you into sin, because, if you do, you will have
to answer to Christ Himself, and there will be no excuses.

Yes, you may be afraid of the cost of choosing the holy
path, but the cost you pay now to protect yourself from
lust will be hardly anything compared to the cost you will
have to pay later.

Note carefully that a willingness to risk the doom of

your soul for the sake of temporal pleasure is in itself an act of concupiscence.

51 ANGRY BAPTIST

I have been married to a Baptist for 10 years. I began the marriage very blind and lost, but have come to know and love the Catholic faith over the course of those years. My husband was severely physically abused by his father as a child. He is critical, quick-tempered and seems to always be looking for a reason to be angry and frustrated. We have 5 daughters and I worry about what this will do to them emotionally. He is not present, but is addicted to hunting and working outdoors when he is not at work.

I look at this situation as my cross in life. I modeled the lives of St. Monica & St. Rita, trying to be a good example to him, to love him and serve him, doing anything he asks of me, besides sinning. We are like single people, he lives his life and my girls and I live our lives. He has much resentment for the Catholic Church and is not open to anything it has to offer. He refuses natural family planning, and so we do not have a sexual relationship, which has been a blessing to me because he does not understand anything about that area of life, so it is a relief not to be an object for his affection so to speak. However, I think by agreeing to live like brother and sister he is trying to punish me for not using ABC or supporting him when he talked about sterilizing himself.

My question is, I do not believe that I am helping him at all. He has not changed in the slightest and sometimes I just believe that I am feeding the fear-monster inside of him by catering to him and living a facade that he is perfect. He is a narcissist, so it is like he has so many psychological problems that he doesn't think he has any. Whenever I have gently tried to talk to him about his behavior, he immediately starts talking about his rights and how he works so hard for his family and he is SO good to us that I should not complain. Then if he does admit to any fault whatsoever, it somehow came about by something that I do wrong.

I was depressed for 7 years of our marriage and just felt so torn about leaving or staying. 3 years ago, I went to a priest for the anointing of the sick before a c-section. My eyes were gradually opened to God, his Providence, Love and goodness of how every life is a gift. I was so blind before this, I realize that every breath I take is an opportunity to thank my Lord. I know that God deserves so much. I guess I am confused as to what you do in a situation so hopeless. I love my husband and want him to obtain heaven but I just want to make sure that just praying for him is enough.

I can recognize three issues here, two of which you ask about; so let's begin with your questions.

How the Children are Affected

Your husband's general behavior will affect your daughters

in the way any "missing" father affects his children's psychological and spiritual growth. (I have described these effects in Chapter 5, "The Father," so I won't repeat that information here.)

Moreover, your husband's specific resentment for the Catholic Church will also affect your daughters' spiritual growth. In order to develop a living, heartfelt faith, rather than a dry intellectual and legalistic "faith," children need to witness both the mother and the father living that faith from the heart. When the father rejects the faith of the mother, the children suffer a profound loss of guidance and protection and are cheated of a necessary spiritual example.

Nevertheless, all is not lost if the mother can carry the weight of the father by being a spiritual example to the children, and if she can also make it clear to the children that she is taking on the role of a father deliberately but reluctantly; hence, it will be critical that the mother do three things:

1. Clearly and honesty, but without anger or blame, explain to the children the truth of the father's spiritual failure;

2. Engage the children in praying for the father's healing from his childhood trauma and for his repentance for the sins he has committed because of his unhealed wounds;

3. Demonstrate by her teaching and by her personal example that she relies totally on her faith to carry her burden in the family.

Note that a related circumstance, but different from yours, often results in spiritual tragedy for the children. When the father is not openly hostile to the Catholic faith but is either a lukewarm Catholic or hypocritical in his behavior, the children will be compliant to the mother in their early years, but, once leaving home (e.g., going to university), their unconscious anger at their father can often erupt as anger at God, and they will abandon the faith.

Temptation and Perseverance

You say that you do not believe that you are helping your husband, and you wonder if "just praying for him is enough." I agree that your marriage is your "cross" in life. Your first task, just as you well know, is to pray for your husband's enlightenment and repentance. Moreover, besides prayer, it will also be important for you to be an unfaltering example of Catholic faith to him. Demonstrate to him that no matter what happens and that no matter what he does you will not be pushed into committing sin and will not relinquish your trust in God's providence and protection.

So pray constantly and live in humility—that is, in quiet confidence—like a star in the midst of a twisted and depraved generation (see Philippians 2:14–15). The pain of being surrounded by sin will break your heart, and that soreness in your heart—those spiritual tears—will be the water that keeps your prayer green and fruitful. This sadness is not the personal sadness of depression; it's the spiritual sadness of the Cross itself.

But your "cross" is not just the burden of a difficult marriage. Your cross—the Cross itself—is also a profound spiritual protection against evil. Although Satan will tempt you to believe that your prayers are useless and that you have failed in your faith, through the power of the Cross itself resist this temptation and persevere to the end, even to the end of your husband's life—or your life. It's possible that your husband might repent, if he repents at all, only at his last breath, even if he outlives you. Even if he doesn't repent, your prayers will not be wasted, because they will be applied to someone who can benefit from them. You simply won't know. So persevere to the end. And let the Cross protect you as you demonstrate by your personal example that you rely totally on your faith to carry your burden in the family.

Marriage to a Non-Catholic

Thus, speaking of the burden you carry in your family, we come to the third issue to consider, the issue you didn't mention in your question. You were married at a time when you were blind and lost, so you needn't be hard on yourself now for marrying a non-Catholic. You're paying the price, and you seem to understand why you are paying the price, and you seem to be doing it willingly, in good faith. That is all that matters.

Still, the matter of a Catholic marrying a non-Catholic is a matter of grave consequences. The lessons of your experience have great importance for Catholics in general because your marriage to a non-Catholic has made your life a living tragedy. Therefore, I say this to any Catholic tempted to marry a non-Catholic: *Don't do it. For you and for your children, don't do it—because if you do, it will condemn your children to a life of moral confusion.*

Now, it's true that marriage to a Catholic won't guarantee a peaceful marriage. But there is no point in someone putting a stumbling block in his or her own path—and the path of future children—before even getting started.

I have had a nightmare marriage. My husband has been condescending in non-stop ways. I have been henpecked and could do nothing right. He has disciplined me in front of the children. I feel he is oversexed and does not understand the word "No" in bed. I woke up the other night feeling like I was being raped. He thinks it is my Catholic duty, under pain of mortal sin. He is always telling me I need to do my duty. He is never guilty of wrongdoing. I am always to blame. I just don't know what to do.

Actually, when a man demands sexual contact like this from his wife, he is the one committing mortal sin.

Now, that statement might shock many people, but that's only because they don't understand the entire concept of marital obligations as described in the Bible.

Saint Paul describes the relationship of a wife and a husband as a reflection of the relationship of the Church to Christ—and this relationship demands mutual respect and honor. He told husbands and wives to be subordinate to one another out of reverence to Christ (see Ephesians 5:21). Moreover, when Saint Paul says that wives should be subordinate to their husbands, he meant that wives have a noble and holy duty to their husbands in the same way as the Church has a noble and holy duty to serve Christ. Consequently, a wife does not owe obedience to her husband as a slave, out of law and duty, must be obedient to a master; her obedience is a matter of her respecting her husband in his responsibility as a chaste and pure spiritual leader of a holy family.

Hence Saint Paul also says that husbands must love their wives even as Christ loved the Church (see Ephesians 5:25). Thus a husband has an obligation to treat his wife without bitterness (see Colossians 3:19), to sanctify his wife, to cleanse her, and to present her to Christ without blemish (see Ephesians 5:26–27).

Consequently, if the husband blames and humiliates his wife, or if he reduces physical intimacy to lust, or if he is emotionally absent from the family, or if he shirks his responsibility as a father, then he is not nourishing and cherishing his family according to his Christian duty (see Ephesians 5:29). So, as was said previously, he is committing mortal sin.

Therefore, when a husband fails in his Christian duty to live with his wife "in understanding, showing honor" to her (1 Peter 3:7), his vows of Holy Matrimony become a spiritual failure, and he has no claim on his wife's "duty" to him because her real duty is to serve Christ as a chaste soul without blemish.

> In a marriage where the wife is humiliated like a prostitute, the physical intimacy of the spouses is not a sign and pledge of spiritual communion, it's a defilement of spiritual communion.

Christ does not treat the Church like a prostitute. Satan, however, does treat his followers as prostitutes. In fact, the world is filled with the devil's prostitutes. A husband who violates his wife's dignity by treating her like a prostitute in effect excommunicates himself from the Church and severs himself from God because he is in effect raping Christ Himself.

If, after you explain these things to your husband, he continues to place his desire for bodily pleasure above the welfare of his soul, the welfare of your children's souls, and the welfare of your soul, then he has openly declared his renunciation of his baptismal vows. His state of spiritual blindness and mortal sin give you full justification to distance yourself from him physically, to protect your own soul.

53 BPD SPOUSE

I have long suspected my husband suffers from BPD. He can be sweet and loving at times, but all I have to do is disagree with him about something and a mask of rage and hatred comes over him. He then viciously attacks and devalues me, and afterward never shows any remorse for the wounding he caused me. My husband is unable to care about my feelings. If I try to tell him, "You really hurt my feelings," all I do is open myself to another attack, which may come in the form of verbal insults, hateful glares, or as passive-aggressiveness.

Sometimes when I have greatly offended my husband—especially if I try to set a boundary with him—he will openly burn with anger and hatred against me for weeks or even months at a time. After many years of marriage I am feeling very worn down and exhausted with the constant put downs and hostility I endure. No matter how hard I try to be the perfect wife, raise the perfect family, cook the perfect meals, he treats me with scorn and contempt. Although there are rare times he is affectionate and kind, it is more common for him to tell me that I am useless to him, a burden, that we are in no way equals, and that I should grovel at his feet for everything he gives me. Recently I tried to tell him that due to his scornful treatment of me I no longer felt comfortable with marital relations, and he became so enraged that he tried to kick me out of the house, telling me that he would not pay for me to live here if he got nothing in return.

I believe I should also mention that my husband has many addictions, including cigarettes, marijuana, alcohol, television, and pornography. He takes very little interest in our children but spends the majority of his time watching TV and becoming intoxicated.

I cannot endure any more of the rage and abuse, and I do not want the children to be raised in a home with these ugly addictions and behavior present. Yet I do not believe in divorce. Also, I feel certain in my heart that my husband is a good man deep down, under all the layers of ugly rage and hatred. Is there anything I can do to help this situation? I am seeking God with all my heart, trying to live a holy life, and praying constantly. I also try my best not to be afraid of my husband and to speak the truth in love. But I don't know what else I should do. I just can't take the rage anymore.

Thank you on behalf of all the spouses of BPD individuals out there. I know there are many of us suffering and confused.

Before addressing any of the issues about your husband, it's important to understand the core dynamic of Borderline Personality Disorder (BPD). BPD is based in the rage of being—or feeling—unnoticed and emotionally abandoned in infancy. That rage then takes over a person's whole being, and all of his or her actions—consciously or unconsciously—become directed throughout life to inflicting hurtful revenge on others for any perceived neglect of his or her emotional and physical needs.

Consequently, notice carefully that even though BPD rage may be inflicted on others, it is really "aimed" psychologically at the source of the original wounds: the BPD individual's parents. This, then, points to the most important concept of coping with a spouse who has BPD symptoms: the melodrama and the rage is not about you.

It's Not About You

Although many persons can be legitimately diagnosed with BPD, many more persons have BPD symptoms without meeting all the psychological criteria for a diagnosis of BPD. Nevertheless, all of these persons, diagnosed or not, have the same tendency to react to emotional hurt with a melodramatic rage that the hurt does not justify. In fact, no hurt justifies anger, but the individual with BPD symptoms constantly stirs up the anger so as to stew in a resentment that punishes others and at the same time demonstrates unconsciously that he or she is a despicable person who really deserves the cruelty and neglect experienced in childhood. (That internal self-loathing is the psychological reason for the alcoholism, marijuana use, smoking, and pornography that possess your husband.) It's truly a pathetic state of mind, and so, when you are on the receiving end of the rage, the only way to preserve your psychological and spiritual sanity is to remember that the melodrama and the rage is not about you.

Keep in mind here that even if you ever do something that hurts anyone, you can repent your mistake, tell that person that you're sorry, and ask God in His mercy to teach you to not make the same mistake again. But that won't be enough for an individual with BPD symptoms. Forgiveness will be thrown to the wind, and old resentments will blow up into melodrama.

So, when this happens, to protect yourself from getting worn down and exhausted, remember that you don't have to try to be perfect. Your husband's rage is not about you or any imperfection in what you have done; his rage is about his unconscious belief that he is imperfect. This belief is a psychological defense that was created in childhood to protect himself from the irrational abuse that was inflicted on him. (See Appendix II.) Moreover, you don't have to blame yourself and believe that you are a failure when your husband attacks you; instead, tell yourself that yes, the abuse hurts, but "It's not about me."

This leads us to the work of setting healthy boundaries.

Boundaries

You say that your husband is a good man deep down, and that's in accord with Catholic theology. The Church has always taught that God creates all of us good, and that through our free will we can choose to accept the redemption given to us in Christ if only we repent our offenses against love and return to God in chaste purity. But if we refuse to repent our sins, whether through spiritual blindness or willful disobedience, then we are in the place of doing bad things in defilement of our essential goodness.

Right now your husband is stained with multiple mortal sins—lust, wrath, and pride especially—and the only thing that can help him is his own repentance. You can help him the most by your understanding that individuals with BPD symptoms want someone to stand up to them rather than run from their rage; they want someone to refuse to be pushed away by the hostility and to have the courage to face the BPD rage with compassion, patience, and love. Your having good boundaries will be essential in this regard.

It's also important to keep in mind that individuals with BPD symptoms are very sensitive to rejection, so anything you say to them that has an accusatory tone will provoke intense shame, such that they will stew in resentment and, sooner or later, explode in rage.

Consequently, consider the following points when you set boundaries to protect yourself.

- *Express yourself in the passive tense.* Rather than say, "You hurt my feelings," say, "I'm feeling very hurt right now."

- *Be careful not to tell your husband what to do.* Set boundaries by stating what you will do under specific circumstances. For example, instead of saying, "Stop cussing!" say, "If I hear cussing, I'm going to leave the room."

- *Be willing to teach.* When your husband speaks to you with hostility, smile and say calmly, "I'm not going to listen to anything said with rudeness, but if you speak to me kindly I will be glad to listen to you. So go ahead, try saying it again, but with gentleness." (If your husband reacts with anger, then calmly repeat the same statement, as many times as necessary, without getting caught up in fear of his anger.)

For more information about boundaries, see Chapter 21.

Sexuality in Marriage

Besides your establishing firm and healthy boundaries, your attitude to sexuality will also affect the sanctity of your marriage. Keep in mind here that the matter of sexuality in a marriage applies to any marriage, not just to a marriage in which one spouse is an individual with BPD symptoms.

So, regardless of what any man might try to claim, a husband has no right to treat his wife like a prostitute. Saint Paul tells us that a husband's obligation is to sanctify his wife so that she might be "holy and without blemish" (see Ephesians 5: 26–27). Once lust enters a marriage the husband and wife are both on a path to doom.

In such a case, the wife has a difficult choice to make. Should she take a stand for holiness, or should she capitulate to her husband's demands, thereby condoning sin, so as to make things easier for herself, even though it may lead to the spiritual doom of both her and her husband? Although many women through the ages, such as Saint Maria Goretti, have gone so far as to choose the path of martyrdom, it's a choice a woman must make according to the depth of her love for God and for her soul.

For more information about Borderline Personality Disorder, see Appendix II.

54   OLD LOVE

I'm married over 20 years, have several great kids and a wonderful wife. Here's the deal: For the past 27 years I have not been able to stop thinking about my high school girlfriend. We were young, ignorant, sexually active. For me it was an excessive love. When she dropped me at 18, I spiraled into severe depression, anxiety, sexual addiction, and drug and alcohol abuse for some 5 years. When I married, I was an emotional wreck but covered up pretty well. Over the years, I have improved slowly in fits and falls but consistently so that today I make it through my day. I am a faithful Catholic and have tried to be during my married life.

Now, I was a very sensitive, idealistic, narcissistic adolescent, and being rejected by my girlfriend (my world, my love!) and the pathetic aftermath remains for me a trauma that seems to affect or define my every waking moment. I feel like I will take this unnatural "love" for this woman (that I do not even know) to the grave. This loss is overwhelming, and I feel like all I can do is just try to accept it. I've heard of pining for someone for a few years but never this many unless the person was a stalker type, which I was not, so I have difficulty placing it all. I have not spoken with anyone

*about it because it seems to me to be a pathetic excuse for a
deep trauma. But it has affected me that way. Have you seen
something like this before?*

I see it all the time. But anyone who is Christian should
know that love for God is more important than anyone
or anything in your life—including your own life. Sadly,
most Christians—and most Catholics even—don't know
this.

So let's consider what we are told in Luke 14:26. Christ
said that if anyone comes to Him without hating his father and mother, wife and children, brothers and sisters,
and even his own life, he cannot be His disciple.

Now, *hate* as used here does not mean "to wish harm to."
Instead it means "to remove your emotional dependence
on." Therefore, all of us, whether married or unmarried,
who claim to follow Christ must remove our emotional
dependence on any person.

That's why Holy Matrimony is not based in romance.
Romance is a secular medieval literary concept that seeks
emotional fulfillment in another person to compensate for
the emptiness that results from a lack of religious faith.
But if you know—and believe—that God loves you, then
you don't need to look for other persons to accept you. Instead of trying desperately to fill yourself with fantasies of
romance, you can know the love of Christ that surpasses

all knowledge, so that you may be "filled with all the fullness of God" (see Ephesians 3:19).

So if Holy Matrimony is not based in romance, then what is it all about? Well, imagine two small weights, lying on a table, and joined together by a length of string. Notice that the string joins the weights, but it does not draw them together. Now, however, if you grasp the string in the middle and lift it up, then the two weights, drawn upward with the string, will swing together.

That's Holy Matrimony. In this sacrament, a man and a woman are *drawn together* when they are mutually *lifted up* by God's love through the sacramental presence of Christ. Holy Matrimony, therefore, is an act of service to God whereby the man and the woman are drawn together to bring children into the world for one purpose: to lead those children to God by teaching them to love God in the context of the love for God shared by both the mother and the father.

Intimacy

Now don't get me wrong here about intimacy between a husband and wife. Even though they must not be dependent on each other, and even though they must not seek to draw themselves together, a holy marriage requires emotional intimacy, physical intimacy, and sexual intimacy between the man and the woman.

Emotional intimacy enhances all human relationships, and so it must be present in Holy Matrimony as well, as a concrete expression of one's mystical intimacy with God. This intimacy is the basis for honest communication and for mutual cooperation.

Physical intimacy serves to strengthen the bond between the husband and wife in their service to God. Still, contrary to popular opinion, physical intimacy involves far more than, and does not even have to include, genital arousal and satisfaction. Hugging, holding hands, a compassionate caress, or a kiss on the cheek are all physically intimate behaviors that can be free of lust.

Sexual intimacy is necessary for conceiving children, but if sexuality is stripped of its essential procreative nature and made into a recreational sport, it degenerates into lust and a demonic flirtation with spiritual death that defiles Holy Matrimony.

> In the book of Tobit we learn that Sarah had been married seven times, but that as each husband approached Sarah on the wedding night, he was killed by a demon. Guided by the archangel Raphael, Tobit married Sarah, and because he and Sarah prayed together and renounced lust, God's mercy protected Tobit from the demon (see Tobit 6:14–8:18).

Thus it can be said that the sexual relationship with your old girlfriend has opened the door to a demonic obsession that has been defiling your marriage all these years.

True Christianity

Considering all this, then, your attachment for your old girlfriend is just a romantic illusion that you are keeping alive because you are afraid to renounce lust as Tobit and Sarah did. You fear the consequences of loving God with all your heart, all your soul, all your strength, and all your mind. In essence, you fear dying to the world.

That *dying to the world* is what it takes to set out on the mystic path to true Christianity. You simply cannot get to God if you cling to anything in this world—whether it be another person, a social identity, a substance (such as alcohol or drugs or cigarettes or food), or wealth and riches. Christ said that in various ways throughout His ministry. Nevertheless, most Christians refuse to believe it—and then their lives, the lives of their spouses, and the lives of their children wobble on the brink of doom.

55 THE YEARNING FOR UNION

So then, let's say that we are not seeking to be loved, but rather to love. And let's say that we understand that to love means to give love, that it is an action verb—that to love means to promote the well-being of another, to extend oneself for the good of another. And let's say that after all the mistakes in interpreting love, possibly over several decades, we understand that we cannot heal our broken selves through another—not through their body, their head, their spirit, etc. And let's say that we understand and are now willing to accept the context of a loving male/female relationship; i.e. within the Lord's context. And we can say it's a given to want this—after all, the Lord created woman from man so that man would not be alone. She is of him. She wants a "him" and he wants a "her"—partners to share whatever. Obtaining it and maintaining it within the Lord's context is our challenge. And so let's say we are ready for that, in the right way, that our will is His will. We cannot expect perfection, for only Christ was that, but we can still seek it. We can aspire to love perfectly. What then are the odds that we will find, and recognize, another who is at the same point, or at least of the same will, so that we engage in a healthy relationship? And if we don't, then what becomes of the yearning to generate and nurture a union that is more than the sum of two individuals?

W<small>ell</small>, you say it all very eloquently. And when we get to those final questions, what then? That's where we simply have to remain "within the Lord's context," as you say, and trust in God.

Christianity has nothing to do with odds or fortune or luck. Nor does Christianity have anything to do with happiness. The word *happiness* derives from the word *hap*, which means "chance," so happiness means "good fortune" or "good luck." But nothing in God's creation occurs by chance; everything is in accord with God's will. Therefore, Christianity is all about total dependence on God. *Seek first His Kingdom and His righteousness, and all these things shall be yours as well* (see Matthew 6:31–33). So, if there is "another who is at the same point, or at least of the same will," then God will arrange the meeting—and if such a meeting is not in God's plan, then we should accept that fact, without grumbling or complaining.

Holy Matrimony, after all, is not for everyone.

A Gift from God

Christ's disciples said to Him, "If that is the case with a man and his wife, it is better not to marry." He

> answered that not all can accept this word, but only those to whom it is granted. Some are incapable of marriage, He explained, because they were born so, some because they were made so by others, and some because they have renounced marriage for the sake of the Kingdom of Heaven. Whoever can accept this, He said, ought to accept it (see Matthew 19:10–12).

This tells us that Holy Matrimony is a gift from God. Although some persons do not receive that gift, and although some persons pass it by for the sake of the Kingdom of Heaven, anyone who can accept the gift must also accept the strict conditions under which it is given. Christ's own words show us, therefore, that Holy Matrimony is not a civil right or a way to avoid feelings of loneliness or a way to achieve happiness.

To Love Perfectly

Although marriage is not for everyone, to "love perfectly," is for everyone because that is what Christianity is all about.

> My love so delights the soul that it destroys every other joy which can be expressed by man here below. The taste of Me extinguishes every other taste; My light blinds all who behold it. . . .

> — as told to Saint Catherine of Genoa [1]

Sadly, our secular culture does its best to extinguish real love. Lost in its humanistic emptiness, contemporary culture has made idols of romance and lust as the gods of happiness. Even those who think they are Christian fall into the deception of the seductive allure of cultural insanity. And oh, the many cases of insomnia, anxiety, and depression that result from all this empty yearning!

But if you are truly willing to be Christian and to surrender yourself to the great love for Christ, then you have found at last the deep "yearning to generate and nurture a union that is more than the sum of two individuals." When any soul enters into union with Christ the two become more than two "individuals," for the soul literally enters into union with God Himself. There is no greater desire than to desire this perfect love.

> If, then, I am no longer
> seen or found on the common,
> you will say that I am lost;
> that, stricken by love,
> I lost myself, and was found.

> — Saint John of the Cross[2]

56 WHY MARRIAGE?

I am quite comfortable without marriage. What do I need a husband for? I can still have children with my partner.

I *am quite comfortable,* you say. Nevertheless, you really don't know what you are saying, So now listen to what you are saying unconsciously.

When the gang of thugs came to arrest Jesus in the garden, he declared to them, "I AM," and they fell to the ground in reverence and fear (see John 18:5–6). Thus by saying "I AM" Jesus defines Himself as divine, according to the name God gave for Himself to Moses (see Exodus 3:14). But Judas didn't bring the thugs to Christ in order to have them worship Him; his motive was betrayal, and he brought the thugs to have Jesus arrested. Thus in his kiss of betrayal Judas essentially refused the name of Christ's divinity by reducing its I AM to a descriptive statement: "You are." *You are a body to be seized and bound.* And so Jesus declared again, this time descriptively: "I told you that I AM" (see John 18:8)—that is, *I am the one you seek, the one pointed out to you by my betrayer.*

In accepting the betrayal, Jesus raised its descriptive element back to the level of divine description, as He does throughout John's Gospel: "I am the one you seek because *I am* the way, *I am* the truth, *I am* the light. . . ." All the implicit meanings of the I AM from Exodus are made explicit in Christ.

Our proper response to the I AM is worship, for in worship we accept and adore divinity. That's why in our baptismal vows we answer "I DO" to the questions about rejecting Satan and sin. With each "I DO" we turn away from the sins of the flesh and the world. With each "I DO" we turn toward the spirit. With each "I DO" we cease treating each other as mere objects of lust. With each "I DO" we sacrifice the comforts of the body in order to revere the spirit. It's also why, in the ceremony of Holy Matrimony, our acceptance of the sacrament becomes a mystical "I DO."

Which brings us to your *I am*. "I am comfortable," you declare. You refuse the "I DO" of Holy Matrimony—and divinity with it—to bind yourself to the emptiness of a descriptive statement. With your declaration you reject sanctification by the Holy Spirit, and so you remain in the nothingness of a mere body—a body to be used for recreational stimulation, a body to produce a baby deprived of a matrimonial blessing, a body to be seized and bound by sin, a body to defile the Body of Christ. And sadly, in all of this, you betray Christ as much as Judas did.

57 DESPERATE FOR A CHILD

Today someone told me about a woman who has recently had a baby. She is living in hell—her partner is a womanizer, and he drinks. The person who told me about this said that he would not wish for anybody to live such a life. I replied: "All the sinfulness and hell she lives in can not outweigh the fact that she is blessed with a child. All the holiness and life in perfection is worth nothing compared to the gift of having her own child. Even if the child and the mother both suffer to hell and back." I told him also: "You see, I don't suffer anything like that, but my empty life, filled with religion, is pitiful misery, compared to what she has been given—despite her suffering." If you bring a child into this world, you love God more than if you don't. Children are the gift from God and are not born to their parents solely, but are given this life to praise God and to partake in this earthly drama, no matter how tragic existence may be.

I agree that children should be treasured as gifts from God. And I know, from my clinical work, that many parents treat their "gifts" with such indifference and ingratitude that the children are deprived of blessings and grow up filled with bitterness and anger, even to the point of hating God. A fine way of praising God that is! But this is not the point of your message.

I also know that those persons who were not raised by their parents to love and to fear God can, through the hard work of spiritual healing, resolve their anger and bitterness and learn to love God. But this is not the point of your message either.

I also know that a woman whose "partner" is a womanizer can recognize her sins, repent them, and learn to love God and therein teach her children to love God. But this is not the point of your message either.

Anyone can tell, from what you say, that you are desperate to have a child. Even with all the magnificent resources of the Catholic Church—even with the Eucharist itself— you feel miserable because you do not have a child. That's sad, because it misses the point about Christianity. And this is the point of your message.

Taking the vows of Holy Matrimony and bearing children to raise them to love and to fear God is one way to praise God. But it's not the only way.

We praise God primarily by recognizing that, despite any pain or suffering we ever experience, we are ultimately God's creation and that God calls us continually into holiness and away from our sins.

Furthermore, we praise God by living out this holiness as an example to others, so that they might see us and, desiring to share in our great peace and joy, they might be saved from slavery to their sins as well.

Now, if instead of showing others a beautiful inner peace you show them how miserable you are because you can't have what you think you want, you aren't living your faith. In fact, you are showing others that you lack faith. If you had real faith you would accept everything that God gives you or does not give you. You would accept it all gratefully, and you would accept it with the understanding that it is given to you precisely for the sake of your spiritual purification, to polish out from your soul all the various stains left in you by your past emotional injuries.

Therefore, it is important to accept the fact that God knows exactly what you need and that He will give you what you need and will lead you where He knows you need to go. If you resist, you will be miserable. And what pitiful misery it is, to be miserable even in the presence of all God's gifts. But if you cooperate, you will be plunged into the fullness of the gift of divine love.

58 CAREER OR FAMILY?

I'm a convert, and since my Confirmation eight years ago I've gone back and forth between strictly following Church teaching and barely going to Mass.

I recently started seeing a psychotherapist three times per week and have been making progress. I'm trying hard and I do want to heal more than anything. I'm finally coming to terms with the severe physical abuse, sexual abuse, emotional abuse, and neglect I suffered during my childhood. My parents, the abusers, were fanatical born again Christians, and much of the abuse I suffered, although not all, was in the name of their religion. They were also drug and alcohol abusers. Because of all this, I have a hard time believing in God, or at least a loving one. When I can believe in God, I can only feel fear and resentment. This makes me sad because I want to have God in my life. I just feel He wants to punish me.

One of the things I'm struggling with, as far as the Church is concerned, is birth control and family size. Sometimes, I want to be a good Catholic, even though I don't really feel it; it's more of an intellectual decision. Other times I don't want religion at all or find New Age type thinking appealing. My husband (also Catholic) and I have three children all under age six, and I believe that given the psychological issues I'm trying to deal with I can't handle more. Sometimes, because of the anxiety I suffer and the mixed up emotions I experience, I can barely handle my life as it is. I always wanted a big family (I felt so alone as a child), and had I not begun this process of psychotherapy I probably just would've had more children for the wrong reasons (mainly fear of being alone). Now I'm starting to see that I need to work on myself first. But at the same time I feel guilty for not being open to life. Also, we use the withdrawal method, as opposed to NFP, to prevent pregnancy, and I feel much guilt for this.

My real question is: I'm very, very interested in psychology. I want to heal and eventually I want to help others heal. I was studying to be a psychotherapist in college, but I couldn't face my own problems so I changed my major to math. I've been a stay-at-home mom since my first son was born, but I want to go back to school (not immediately, but in the next couple of years) and slowly (one class a semester) to work on my Masters so I can eventually become a psychotherapist. But this would most likely mean no more kids. This causes a lot of fear for me that I'm letting God down (the same God I can barely believe exists). I feel like I'm being selfish by wanting to go back to school. I know I get my rigid religious beliefs from my parents, but I'm so confused.

I know my question seems vague. I guess what I'm asking is, is it okay for me to stop at three children and pursue a career?

Your question about children and career *seems* vague

because the matter of your faith, which underlies this question, *is* vague. Moreover, your faith is vague because your parents' faith is even more vague.

Even though your parents claimed to be "born again," it's clear from their behavior that they had no clue as to what Christianity really is. Sexual abuse, physical abuse, emotional abuse, neglect, and drug and alcohol abuse are all grave sins; they are evil, and, being aspects of the demonic, they are all fundamentally opposed to Christianity.

Childhood Abuse Begets More Abuse

Parents who abuse their children are themselves suffering from profound emotional pain, but, rather than seek to face up to and heal that pain, they express their frustration at having been psychologically damaged—by their own parents—by lashing out in anger to hurt and damage the world around them. Their own children are convenient targets of this frustration because children are helpless and pose no threat in return.

Therefore, it's important for you to understand that when your parents abused you, they were simply taking out their frustration on a convenient target, inflicting hurt on you for their own personal satisfaction. This irrational abuse derives from your parents' failure to love you, and it has nothing to do with your being punished by God. Nor does it mean that you should be thinking, "God hates me!"

God's Providence is Marred by Sin

Now, bad things often occur in the lives of innocent people, but God never does anything to hurt us. If He allows difficulties to afflict us, it is to heal us and lead us to holiness. Every trial that we experience can lead us to spiritual purification and growth if only we bear the trial with patient endurance and trust in God. And this gets us to what Christianity is all about.

God created us through love, so that we might be able to share in His love. He gave us free will so that we would be capable of love. But with the capacity to love comes also the capacity to reject love, and this capacity to reject love—that is, to hate—is called sin. Therefore, all of us, just like your parents, naturally respond to being hurt by wanting to inflict injury in return. This tendency to make ourselves feel good at the expense of others—and sometimes, even at the expense of ourselves, through self-destructive behavior—is the essence of sin.

Our Rescue from Sin

We have no way to pull ourselves out of our natural tendency to sin. But God, in His love for us, sent His Son, our Lord Jesus Christ, to redeem us from our slavery to sin. Through His Incarnation as a man, He took our sins into His own Sacred Heart and, without any hate, showed us how to love Him as He loved us, even as we hated Him.

Christianity calls us away from sin. It calls us to repent our capacity to hate others and to repent our capacity to hate ourselves. It calls us to invite Christ into our hearts so that we can love Him and love ourselves and love others, as He loves us. It calls us, through our very being, as it is transformed in Christ, to call others to repent their sins so that they, too, can be transformed in Christ.

Notice, here, that your parents did none of this. There was nothing of love in their actions. They didn't love you; instead, they poured out their hatred for themselves and for their parents onto you. So be careful, therefore, not to think that your parents' behavior was representative of the true Church.

If you wish to belong to the true Church, then, recognize that your parents' behavior was sinful. Understand this from the depth of your heart, but accept it without hate.

You might wonder, though, why God allowed the abuse to afflict you. Well, maybe God was waiting for someone in the family—that is, you—to get the courage to say, "I'm sick of this intergenerational abuse! I will be the one to put an end to it. I vow that I won't pass it on to my children."

To fulfill that vow, call upon God's grace to give meaning to your suffering and seek now to forgive your parents for what they did to you; that is, purge from your heart any desire to throw their failures in their faces so as to make them repent what they did to you [1] and leave the justice to God. All sins will be accounted for, but only God can look into each heart to determine its guilt and the price it will have to pay for its offenses to God. Resolve, therefore, to make love the emotional basis of your life—and from thereon pass on love, rather than abuse and hate, to those around you. Hence, if your parents are still alive, pray and make sacrifices that they might repent their sins and that they might surrender their hearts to Christ in loving service to Him so as to experience His mercy. If your parents have already died, for the sake of charity you can assume that their souls are in Purgatory, and you can pray for their souls to assist their purgation; if they did not die in a state of repentance, and if they therefore are in hell rather than Purgatory, your prayers will be applied to another soul in Purgatory who needs them. Prayer is never wasted; such is God's infinite mercy.

So, having considered your problems with your parents, let's now consider your responsibility to your children.

Raising Children by Example

You know, from your own parents' behavior, how not to raise children. But you don't know yet that in the true Church there is only one reason to have a child: to bring a new soul into the world so that it can love God through a life of Christian purity. Such a holy life requires sincere reverence for all the fruits of the Holy Spirit—charity, joy, peace, patience, longanimity (forbearance), goodness, benignity (kindness), mildness, fidelity, modesty, continence, and chastity—and all the sacraments of the Church. Furthermore, the only way for children to acquire this reverence is to learn it by example from their parents. Therefore, to be responsible to your children, you, of necessity, must live a chaste holy life.

In regard to marital sexuality, then, it is important to understand that all sexual activity must be open to procreation, so if you absolutely don't want any more children then refrain from all sexual activity. Surprises can always occur. Moreover, the burden of being conceived as an "accident of lust" deprives a child of the blessing of a holy conception; without this blessing, a child can be crippled with pervasive doubt and self-hatred throughout life.

Repairing the Damage

So what do you do if you already have children, and you and your husband haven't lived holy lives, and your children themselves aren't living holy lives?

Well, in such a case, your fitting "career" now is to repair the damage already done to your children. It will be important for you to be a teacher and "therapist" to bring your children to conversion and into the Church. Dedicate yourself, like Saint Monica and Saint Rita, to the full-time task of living a holy life yourself, of being a humble, sincere example to your children of total love for and trust in God, and of praying constantly and making sacrifices for your children's repentance and conversion.

When you have fulfilled your role as a mother, and all your children have grown to love God through lives of Christian purity, then you might think of a secular career for yourself.

Illusions About Sexuality

In your case, however, it would be a disaster, both for yourself and for your clients, if you became a psychotherapist without having first overcome your illusions about sexuality.

You have been duped by an anti-Christian culture that has been working subversively to destroy traditional Christian family values and to glamorize the sin of lust. Feminine modesty has been defiled by stripping the female body of its holy dignity and reducing it, often with violent overtones, to a soulless sex object. Even though it may seem on the surface that socially progressive values have put women on the fast track to career success, the truth is that women are increasingly enslaving themselves to lust and its demonic effects.

You have been duped by our culture into believing that the Catholic Church is wrong about sexuality and sin (see Appendix I) and that sexual pleasure is necessary for your "happiness". You have been duped into believing that you can use your own body to heal your emotional despair. You have been duped into defiling love.

Therefore, without knowing what love really is, you cannot teach your clients to love—and you will be held responsible by Christ for leading them astray, because not teaching others to love is a scandalous defilement of love.

APPENDICES

APPENDIX I:
CATHOLIC COMPASSION

She stood in silence, smoldering in anger at the smug self-assuredness of her accusers. She knew in her heart why she had committed such an act. Surrounded with hypocrites, she was angry with the world, and she was angry with God. She was fed up with the misery she had to endure and wanted some excitement, some satisfaction, some sense of *something* for herself.

Still, she felt a strange curiosity about that man squatting on the ground in front of her. "What is he going to do?" she wondered. She cast quick glances at him, yet she never caught him looking at her. She waited for what seemed like an eternity. People were shaking their heads and walking away, muttering to themselves. She looked at him. He didn't look at her. He just scratched in the dust with his finger. Then, with a mysterious calmness, he looked up and asked her a question. She shrugged and shook her head, almost whispering, "No. No one sir."

For the first time she felt him looking at her—not just *at* her, but *into* her. His next words stunned and confused her. "Neither do I condemn you." Her heart quivered as it tried to comprehend what was happening.

Yes, what was happening? Call it *compassion*. But note something carefully. He had something else to say: "*Go, and from now on do not sin anymore*." Many persons who retell this story neglect these final words. They try to make it seem that compassion amounts to a broad-minded acceptance of anything. But that misses the point.

Jesus came to us to save us from our sins. His mission was not to condone sin and pretend it didn't exist. His mission was to show us how much we do sin, how much our sin hurts us, how much it hurts others, and how much we will lose if we persist in it. He knew that all sin will be accounted for in His perfect justice, but he wanted us to know that we have an opportunity to repent our sins and call upon His mercy. Thus His mission was a mission of compassion: to call us away from sin and into holiness, and to cause our hearts to quiver in awe at the idea of it all.

Moreover, as this story of *A Woman Caught in Adultery* (John 8:1–11) makes clear, sexuality and sin are closely entangled. A holy life depends on sexual purity. A holy life calls us to chastity.

Chastity

Sin feels good. Period. Sin gives us raw physical pleasure.

It can be intense and intoxicating. But sin is not bad because someone in authority, for some arbitrary, arrogant or mysterious reason, says so. Nor is sin bad because it feels good. Sin is bad because sin leads you away from the goal of holiness and into the empty pleasures of merely feeling good. Sin is bad because sin misses the point of life.

God is the point of life, and, in regard to sexuality, He gave us genitals so that we could bring new life into the world. Note that we aren't creators; God is the Creator and we are *procreators*—that is, we stand in the place of the Creator. Our genitals therefore serve the purpose of *procreation*.[1] They serve love by bringing children into the world who will learn to love Love—God Himself—to become love themselves.

Despite its intensity of feeling, sin defiles love. Sin is the hatred of love. Sin makes pleasure its own end, and so it ends in failure.

Still, sin feels good—and that points to the ultimate spiritual battle. Despite the throbbing intensity of sin's attraction, we have to struggle against its pleasures and struggle to remind ourselves that, despite all the allure our society gives it, sin is the hatred of love. The battle against sin can be fought only with love, and chastity is one powerful weapon in our hands.

> *Chastity is not the repression of sexuality, it is the purifying transformation of desire into love.*

As the full human response to divine love, chastity encompasses all the psychological, social, and physical consequences of accepting that the body is the temple of the Holy Spirit (see 1 Corinthians 6:19). In chastity we renounce lust, dress modestly, set aside our illusions about the "self", and distance ourselves from—or, in scriptural language, die to—the corrupt social world in which we all live, to prepare ourselves for holy service in the Kingdom of Heaven.

> When every child is born, it is in danger of being devoured by the devil. Children conceived in lust are all that more vulnerable to demonic influence throughout their lives. If parents do not take their procreative responsibility seriously, they will be raising demon fodder, not children of God.

Chastity is not just an attitude toward human sexuality, it is the full acceptance of the human responsibility to the holy lifestyle that Christ preached—and lived in His body—and that contemporary society, in all its psychobabble about happiness and self-fulfillment, tries its best to subvert.

Chastity, then, is a way of life—*the* way of life, the only lifestyle, the only "orientation"—for anyone who would follow Christ and claim to be Christian. And woe to the soul that spurns chastity. Love is chaste, and to spurn chastity is to spurn love. If you spurn love, you will find that in the end you are left with nothing but everlasting broken emptiness. To spurn chastity is to spurn Christ Himself, who, in His real and physical suffering on the Cross—truly present to us in the broken bread of the Eucharist—offers the only means to heal our human brokenness.

> There is but one price at which souls are bought, and that is suffering united to My suffering on the cross. Pure love understands these words; carnal love will never understand them.
>
> — as told to Saint Faustina [2]

Chastity is also a choice, a choice of love. Moreover, just as chastity is a choice, the rejection of chastity is also a choice, a choice of hatred.[3] Those who ridicule the Church for its teachings about chastity, saying, for example, that the Church has a phobia about sexuality, are those who themselves have a phobia: the fear of choosing to live a holy life with all the suffering, all the sacrifices, and all the love a holy life entails.

Still, we have an obligation—an obligation that ensues from having chosen to follow Christ in the way of the Cross—to not hate those who hate chastity, to not fear those who fear suffering, to not reject those who reject holiness itself. Even if they close their ears to our words, we have a compassionate obligation to pray that they might someday, before they die, make the choice to listen to, rather than reject, the Holy Spirit. And why should we pray for them rather than hate them? Because the Cross is the supreme reminder of the Christian refusal to hate.

Responsibility

It was almost the end of his shift. He was off at noon that day; a game was on TV early that afternoon, and he wanted to get home as soon as possible. He saw the bag on the floor. There were several men standing by a distant window talking on their mobile phones.

"It's a nice bag. It must belong to one of them," he told himself, as he walked by.

Later, as he was watching the game, he saw the news item: the bomb had killed and injured dozens of tourists.

When he was called before his boss, he stammered, trying to justify his actions.

"What do you mean, you didn't think it was anything serious?" His boss glared at him. "We have procedures to follow! You're fired! Get out of my sight!"

It's a horrific story. But what if this were a bishop or a priest or a religious education teacher or a parent who, having willfully disregarded the true faith just to serve his personal desires, had to stand before Christ in final judgment to discover that his shirking of responsibility was, in Christ's eyes, an act of hate? What if this were you?

Depart from Me, you accursed, into the eternal fire prepared for the devil and his angels (see Matthew 25:41).

Serving the Self

Because chastity is a matter of respect for our bodies, we must be responsible caretakers of our bodily sexuality. Saint Paul said (1 Corinthians 6:12–20) that a lack of respect for sexual and reproductive functions are offenses against one's own body, the temple of the Holy Spirit. Psychologically, these offenses are acts of narcissism[4] and narcissism, by definition, is a psychological defense, a defense that uses self-gratification to "protect" us from making the choice to live a holy life of loving sacrifice for the sake of others.

Self-gratification is therefore a rupture with the divine because it offends real love: it places one's self above love of God, Who made heaven and earth—including our bodies. The offense of self-gratification makes the temple into a brothel, so to speak.

Any activity that reduces the sexuality of the body to something no more than a form of entertainment is narcissism because it seeks to *make yourself seen* through your desire for another person. When you look at another person with desire, you do not see a soul enrobed in chaste beauty; you see only the exuberant fantasy that your aching throb of loneliness might be alleviated through someone's body. Narcissism focuses *your* satisfaction onto *your* pleasure in having *your* body fondled. Narcissism makes *your* pleasure in playing with the body of another person—turning God's temple into *your* toy—into *your* satisfaction.

All of this amounts to placing self-gratification above love of God, doesn't it? So where does all this *self-gratification placed above love of God* lead us? Well, let's find out.

Disobeying God

In order to understand how friends, teachers, "therapists," the entertainment industry—and even priests—can lead you away from God, under the guise of "being compassionate," consider how the serpent tempted Eve to disobey God (see Genesis 3:1–6).

- First, he led her to doubt God by making Him seem irrational: "Did God *really* tell you not to eat from *any* of the trees in the garden?"

- Then he led her to doubt that God was being honest with her: "You certainly will not die!"

- Consequently, Eve saw that the fruit was good for food and looked really *nice*. It was natural, so it had to be good for her, she thought. So, persuaded by disobedience itself, she disobeyed God's command and satisfied her desire.

Moreover, we continue to be tempted in the same way today by those who try to convince us to doubt the moral teachings of the Catholic Church and ultimately disobey God's commands. Today, we are induced to look with desire at behaviors that separate us from a holy life, saying to ourselves, "How can there be anything wrong with something that seems so nice?"

Thus we are in grave danger of being drawn away from God by seemingly "well-meaning" persons who—as odd as it sounds to say it—lack compassion for us. They lack compassion for us because they seek only their own self-gratification.

Same-sex Attraction

The *need for compassion* and the *danger of being led away from God* find a particularly poignant merger in regard to feelings of same-sex attraction (SSA). These feelings can occur in children because of dysfunctional family dynamics that affect a child unconsciously.[5]

For example, a girl whose mother jumps to conclusions, is emotionally cold or distant, and does not listen with tender compassion to her daughter, and whose father does not demonstrate an authority of competent justice tempered with considerateness, can be attracted to the emotional openness of another girl's personality. Likewise, a boy whose mother tends to be angry, critical, and demanding, and whose father does not demonstrate an authority of emotional understanding, confidence and protection, can be attracted to feelings of acceptance and protection from another boy. In these cases, the fantasies of attraction are not natural expressions of the girl's or boy's *being*; instead, the fantasies point to the psychological truth of what is *missing* in the family structure.

> *Having same-sex attraction fantasies, therefore, does not mean that a person is homosexual.*

Consequently, children need competent, emotionally-sensitive psychological explanations of their feelings of same-sex attraction. But if children do not trust their parents to understand their confusing and embarrassing feelings, the children will be afraid to go to their parents for guidance. Thus, lacking any psychological resources, the children will be driven into shameful isolation and will eventually end up in the hands of sexual predators and political activists who, instead of offering psychological truth, will direct the children into a political agenda with its purpose of undermining the Catholic faith. When this occurs, conditions are ripe for a subversive crisis of identity.

Identity

Halloween. Mardi Gras. Masquerades. Our cultures are full of ways we pretend that we can change our identities by changing our outward appearances.

In times past, a person's hat really did identify his or her profession. And even today we wear secular uniforms (*uni-* means "one" and *form* means "shape" or "outward appearance")—as well as religious habits and liturgical vestments—which give one common appearance to all who perform a particular function.

Most of us, however, understand full well that a uniform, in itself, does not mean anything. Unless you have been trained to perform a job, no matter what uniform you put on you won't be able to perform that job.

Nevertheless, there is one uniform which does define us absolutely and which can never be changed. This is the uniform of the body, and it genetically defines our gender, according to reproductive function.

Reproductive sexuality is purely a function of biology. The problems with *sexual identity* begin in the unconscious. Notice how children tend to believe that what is *seen* is *real*. If a child sees a man wearing a Santa Claus costume, the child will think, "That *is* Santa Claus." In the same way that a child attributes *reality* to *appearance*, individuals will unconsciously confuse sexual functioning with the costumes which create a sexual appearance.

But the truth is that no matter what clothes you wear, no matter what kind of play you enjoy, no matter whom you choose as playmates, no matter how you act—no matter, even, how you might change your body surgically—you can never change your genetic God-given reproductive reality.

So why, then, would anyone develop a desire to change a reality made by God? Well, even if you accept the reality of a non-gendered immortal soul, the basic facts of bodily life—reproduction and death—are still painful realities. These realities don't *mean* anything; that is, they do not carry any mysterious secrets about life—they are just facts of life and death. A fantasy of changing your personal reality by changing your gender derives from a misguided belief that your sexuality contains some mysterious, meaningful secret that will release you from the hard facts of social emptiness and death. But social emptiness and death are the result of separation from God, and no human effort can restore the soul's union with God that is lacking in all of us. Only the divine grace of real love can lead a soul back to God.

Consequently, if you fail to recognize the inherent fraud of all social identity and cling to the belief that sexuality has any meaning apart from reproduction, you cling to nothing more than an impossibility: the unconscious attempt to escape responsibility to genetic reproductive reality and, ultimately, to escape responsibility to God Himself.

It would be far better—and wiser—to find your identity in something that never changes, something that never dies, and something that can never be taken from you as long as you don't give it away yourself.

> As Saint Peter said (1 Peter 1:24–25), all flesh is like grass, and all its glory is like the flower of the field;

the grass withers, and the flower wilts, but the word
of the Lord remains forever.

Obedience to False Authority

Two guards lead you into a cold, harshly lit concrete room.
The room is empty except for a man kneeling on the bare
concrete, blindfolded, with his hands bound behind him.
You recognize him as one of the terrorists who have been
undermining your work.

A military officer enters. He quietly removes the pistol
from his holster. Holding it by the barrel, he hands it to
you, glancing at the man kneeling on the floor.

"Here. Take this. Put it to his head and pull the trig-
ger."

You feel stunned, your mind momentarily paralyzed by
the incongruity of the events.

"Go ahead, take it," the officer says. "You have my permission."

What would you do? You will likely say now that you
would refuse. Fair enough. That's what you say *now*. But if
you are like most people, in those particular circumstances
there is a good chance that—unless you have the same
living depth of faith that allowed the Christian martyrs to
not betray their faith—you would kill the man.

Now, that's a shocking statement. But consider two important social-psychological scientists from the 1960s and

1970s who investigated obedience to authority.

Stanley Milgram found that ordinary adults would be quite willing to inflict horrifying electrical shocks on other persons when told to do so by an authority figure.[6] Moreover, Philip Zimbardo, in the Stanford Prison Experiment,[7] found that when ordinary, "nice" students played roles of prisoners and guards, the situation quickly degenerated into demeaning inhumanity to such an extent that the experiment had to be stopped. Years later, Zimbardo wrote, ". . . ordinary people, even good ones, can be seduced, recruited, initiated into behaving in evil ways under the sway of powerful systemic and situational forces."[8]

So think carefully. Raised Catholic, you now hear teachers and priests—as well as television, social media, movies, music, video games, and magazines—telling you, "Go ahead. If it feels good, do it. You have our permission."

Yes, they give you their permission to do anything that makes you feel good, even if it contradicts the tradition and wisdom of the Church—and they even insinuate that there must be something wrong with you if you do not comply with them. You are being duped.

Duped

Those who don't understand the reality of the great spiritual battle against evil are being duped by an anti-Christian society into believing that lust and hatred have the power to redeem our emotional emptiness.

You are being duped especially by the entertainment industry, an industry that for decades has been working subversively to destroy Christian family values and to make the illusion of erotic romanticism the sustaining hope of life in an increasingly atheistic culture; Christian faith has been depicted as contemptible hypocrisy; humility has been mocked as cowardice; hatred, revenge and violence have been extolled as virtues; power, strength, and cunning have been glamorized; foul language has become customary; women have been induced to forsake feminine modesty and dignity and to imitate masculine arrogance and aggression; and immodesty, nudity, fornication, and adultery have become routine behaviors.

Yes, you are being duped and brainwashed by the "progressive" liberal agenda of the entertainment industry into believing that *sin* is just a myth, that religion is foolish, and that lust and violence are necessary for our "happiness". It has all been going on openly right under your own nose, and you haven't even noticed it. As a result, instead of taking personal responsibility to detach yourself from subversive social illusions, you willingly consume them without awareness of the poison within them. Sin enslaves you even as you are told that sin does not exist.

So what is your responsibility here? Well, you're not

responsible for others *trying* to dupe you, but you are responsible for learning the truth and *resisting* the subversive attempts of others to dupe you.

To Die in All Things

In its early years, the Church struggled against the opposition of the Roman government, which drew its identity and strength from pagan religious practices. Thus, when Saint Paul founded churches, he had to remind the converts not to get caught up in the prevailing cultural norms. For example, to the Ephesians he wrote that they should no longer live as the pagans did—with their minds empty and their understanding darkened. Pagans are estranged from a life in God because of their ignorance and their resistance; without remorse they have abandoned themselves to lust and the indulgence of every sort of lewd conduct (see Ephesians 4:17–19).

Then Saint Paul went on to remind the Ephesians that lewd conduct and lust were opposed to Christian conduct. He paused in reflection, perhaps thinking about those individuals in the community who had been preaching untruths and leading the Christians astray—just as it is being done even today. Therefore he added, almost sarcastically, that he was *supposing* that when they learned about Christ, He had been preached to them and taught to them "in accord with the truth that is in Jesus" (Ephesians 4:21) rather than in accord with prevailing cultural ideas about lust and the indulgence of every sort of lewd conduct.

What, then, is this "truth that is in Jesus"? Well, it is the truth that we must lay aside our former way of life and the old self which deteriorates through illusion and desire, and acquire a fresh, spiritual way of thinking. "You must put on that new man created in God's image, whose justice and holiness are born of truth" (Ephesians 4:22–24). Or, stated in its most elegant simplicity, you must die to—that is, renounce—the human identification with sin in order to have life in all things divine.

> Whoever knows how to die in all things will have life
> in all things.
>
> — Saint John of the Cross[9]

The Proof

The proof of all this is in Christ Himself: "Love one another as I love you" (John 15:12). Did He desire the death of His enemies? No. Did He use us for His sexual pleasure to find "happiness"? No. Instead He suffered for us, as an act of compassion and mercy. In His Passion He showed us what love is: to wish the good of others.[10]

Even in today's confused and broken world love continues to manifest itself by calling us away from sin into holiness. The false "love" touted by contemporary society does not call us into anything but sin; it tempts us to abandon holiness for the sake of lust. But as long as you are concerned about what you can get from life you will be dissatisfied. Everything material—food, entertainment, drugs, masturbation, pornography, erotic pleasure in another person—passes quickly only to leave us overpowered by cravings for more.

Real love calls us into acts of sacrifice and giving—not the giving of material things that bribe others to like us, but the giving of qualities such as patience, kindness, understanding, mercy, and forgiveness. These are compassionate qualities whose purpose is the salvation of other souls.

The Call

You were dictated to and reasoned with. You feel emotionally misunderstood and lonely. You crave affection. You feel confused. Then you discover those who seem different. They're free thinkers. They embrace the unusual. They call to you, "Come, be like us. We won't reject you."

You want to be understood. You want to feel appreciated. You want to belong. But STOP. Think. Christ was misunderstood. Christ was rejected. Yet He never *sought* the approval of others. He *brought* truth. Many did not want it. Still, He called them—and He still calls us—to chaste purity in the Kingdom of Heaven. Anyone who wants it can attain it, because blessed are the compassionate.

Appendix II:
BORDERLINE PERSONALITY DISORDER

Psychoanalytic writers tend to focus on identity—or, to be more precise, the lack of a stable identity—as the core of Borderline Personality Disorder (BPD). But *identity* and *personality* are social illusions, and the real core of BPD is rage. Rage is a raw and primitive form of anger as a response to the fear of intellectual, physical, or emotional abandonment.

BPD therefore is not some shameful illness that a person is born with. BPD is really just a collection of psychological defenses—all related in some way to rage—that children acquire in childhood as a way to protect themselves from the emotional trauma they experience in their families. In psychiatric terminology, these defenses are referred to as the *symptoms* of a psychiatric disorder.

BPD Symptoms

Borderline Personality Disorder applies as a descriptive term to a person whose behavior is characterized by:

- Frantic efforts to avoid real or imagined abandonment

- Unstable relationships
- Unstable self-image or sense of self
- Impulsivity (usually involving sexuality, alcohol, drugs, or food)
- Suicidal attempts, threats, or self-mutilating behavior
- Periods of emotional volatility and instability of mood
- Chronic feelings of emptiness
- Self-mutilation and self-sabotage
- Frequent arguments, constant anger,[1] recurrent physical fights

These symptoms tend to develop from early childhood experiences of chronic emotional abuse, sexual abuse, physical abuse, or a combination of various forms of abuse and trauma. That is, when children are not raised in an environment of loving guidance and protection, but are instead mistreated and manipulated, they will be crippled psychologically and spiritually with a smoldering inner sense of self-loathing, mistrust of others, and rage.

The clinical diagnosis of *Borderline Personality Disorder* requires several specific criteria, but many persons can experience some BPD symptoms apart from any clinical diagnosis. Regardless of whether or not the symptoms meet the criteria for a clinical diagnosis of BPD, the treatment is the same: learn to understand that the symptoms derive from childhood emotional injuries, and then learn to respond to injuries in the present without falling into rage.

The Rage from Feeling Abandoned

If you have problems with borderline symptomatology,

and if you look closely, you will see that all of your interpersonal difficulties in both the past and the present were—and are—based in feelings of rage as a result of the trauma of being unnoticed and emotionally abandoned. Abandoned, traumatized, and helpless. You will find that your whole being is given over, consciously or unconsciously, to inflicting hurtful revenge on the world around you for neglecting your emotional and physical needs and leaving you helpless.

In essence, this rage is a sort of knee-jerk attempt to "get back at" the person who injured you. Even masochistic self-mutilation can have a component of this revenge. In cutting their forearms, for example, individuals let out their rage in slow, "controlled" doses that don't kill them. Seeing their blood, they see themselves showing their wound—their life's blood—to the "Other" who, they know, has disavowed the value of their life.

So, too, attempts at suicide are attempts at revenge. "I'll show them! Maybe when I'm dead they will realize how miserably they've treated me!"

Suicide can also have the component of a desire to *silence the rage* by killing it. Sexual activity, alcohol, and drugs can also be used to "silence" the rage by numbing it. But none of these attempts to distract your attention from your rage can ever be successful. What is rage, after all, but a frightened infant crying because he or she has been abandoned? Ignoring the infant and walking away won't silence the crying. The only way to soothe the infant is to pick it up and find out what it needs in the midst of its fear—precisely what your parents didn't bother to do.

It's a difficult thing to admit that your parents did not love you. Most likely, though, they *didn't* love you because they *couldn't* love because they were *afraid of love* because their parents didn't love them. They did to you what was done to them. So, if your childhood was filled with insecurity, hostility, self-loathing, and disobedience, then you have the truth right under your nose: your parents didn't love you. All you have to do is see it.

Sadly, some persons prefer to destroy themselves by suicide or by slow self-sabotage rather than admit that they hate[2] their parents for not loving them.

The Rage Continues: Pushing Away

When you were a child, your father abandoned you emotionally, if not also physically. Maybe he was alcoholic; maybe he was emotionally distant; maybe he was weak and timid; maybe he was abusive; maybe he abandoned the entire family. Maybe your mother was harsh and critical and, not knowing how to accept a child in real love, abandoned you emotionally as well. Essentially, your parents pushed you away with their lack of love, and they gave you the implied message, "You don't matter." So, to cope with that pain, you protected yourself by pushing your parents away.

You found your revenge on them by becoming emotionally closed off; you hid your true feelings from them, and you acted out in disobedience to hurt them.

But now, as you are older, the rage continues. When others offend you, then you become enraged and you push them away, just as you pushed your parents away. Everyone who offends you, you push away. But you don't push them away by cutting ties with them, you push them away by making them reject you because you are so desperate to be accepted.

> The dynamic of *pushing away* actually begins as a benign defense in childhood when, confronted with your parents' general lack of real love, you say, if only silently to yourself in frustration, "Stop!" All you want is for the mistreatment to stop and for your parents to accept you. But then this initial protective act grows into an aggressive act. You slowly transition from passively trying to stop the pain to actively getting revenge by pushing away anyone who offends you.

Sooner or later, then, you will look around and feel completely alone. "Look!" you say to yourself. "I'm all alone! God doesn't care about me. God hates me. Even God has abandoned me!"

But God hasn't abandoned you. Your parents abandoned you, and now you push away everyone—even God—in rage. And you find yourself all alone.

"It's Your Fault!"

When children have to cope with dysfunctional parents—especially when the mother is domineering and the father is absent physically or emotionally—they learn to suppress their own needs and capitulate to the demands of the parents. Essentially, the children learn that hiding their true thoughts and feelings is the surest way to survive.

Eventually, the children will carry this emotional hiding right into adulthood, where it will cause them frustrating difficulties in interpersonal relationships. Always holding back their true thoughts and feelings, they will constantly feel misunderstood. And then something odd—that is, something unconscious—occurs. Blind to their own defenses, and unable to see their role in the communication difficulties, they will blame others for everything. "It's your fault!" They will always be at odds with others because, in blaming someone, they fail to see that they are unconsciously speaking the angry words—"It's your fault!"—they feared so deeply to say to their own parents.

> This hiding and blaming can manifest in two particularly destructive forms of desire. First, it can manifest as a desire to control circumstances to avoid being "blindsided" (that is, taken by surprise), which will amplify the defensive tendency to hide true thoughts and feelings; thus you can give others the impression that you are manipulative, calculating, or untrustworthy. Second, it can manifest as a desire to control others

("You need to do [this or that]!"), which will likely be followed by outbursts of mutual anger.

Moreover, this hiding and blaming doesn't stop in the social world. It even interferes with spiritual growth. After all, how can you love God when every difficulty in life is seen as God's fault? "It's your fault!" How can there ever be healing when those words of blame are constantly on your lips?

> This dynamic explains why BPD clients are so dreaded not only by friends and spouses but also by many psychotherapists. If the psychotherapists have not done their own psychological scrutiny to immunize themselves from getting caught in the unconscious of their clients, those unwary psychotherapists will find that no matter how hard they work, no matter how much of an effort they make, it takes only one difficult BPD client for them to believe they are miserable failures.

The Trap of Seeking the Acceptance of Others

Infants and very young children are by nature helpless and entirely dependent on their parents' care and protection. Because parental rejection can threaten the children's survival, children develop a fear of rejection and an intuitive desire for parental acceptance.

In spiritually healthy families, parents attend closely to their children's needs and teach their growing children the skills necessary to survive independently. Ultimately, the children will progress from an all-encompassing desire for their parents' acceptance to the development of their own personal interests and desires, and they will be well prepared to enter society as autonomous and confident individuals.

In dysfunctional families, though, constant blame and criticism by the parents will keep the children in such a state of fear that the children will suppress their own interests in order to maintain a vigilant focus on the necessity of having the acceptance of their parents.

Consequently, throughout life this anxious focus on getting acceptance from others will define the nature of a person's *locus of control* (from the Latin *locus*, place) as being external. *Locus of control* refers to the psychological "place" in which a person puts responsibility for the outcomes of various life situations. Persons with an **external locus of control** attribute outcomes not so much to personal actions as to the actions of other people—or luck.

Thus when you have an external locus of control you essentially live in a perpetual feeling of frustration, always blown about by the whims of the world around you. When you're caught up in this state of mind, it seems as if your life is being stolen from you. You can never rest, and you can never get enough from life to feel satisfied. There is no room for your own interests and desires because everyone always seems to get in your way, or let you down, or ignore you, or reject you, and you always end up angry—and it all goes back to the childhood pain of not getting the acceptance of your parents.

> If you are always focused on external things, you will always have a bottomless reservoir of resentment for your rage to feed upon.

In contrast, persons with an *internal locus of control* perceive that they can personally exert command over the outcome of any situation because their motivation is always internal; that is, focused on their personal desires and sense of self. With such a state of mind, you will not be thwarted by obstruction from external events, and you will keep your focus on the objective you are seeking. Even if you encounter a situation that is truly impossible (such as changing the behavior of another person, or of preventing a natural or social tragedy) you will still have command over your reactions to that situation.

Therefore, emotional healing from the painful rejections experienced in childhood depends on your shifting your mental focus *away* from what other persons do and *toward* a curiosity about your own inner experiences and what you can do to take command of those experiences. This process requires dedicated effort, but it can be done. Then, when it is done, you will recover a deep respect for your own personal interests and desires, and you will experience the peace of mind of being free from the rage of a wounded child.

Healing the Rage

Some persons will insist that because your original wounds occurred in your early infancy, before you could communicate with language (that is, in a *pre-verbal* psychological state), the psychotherapist must take on the actions of a caring, supportive parent until you can experience pre-verbal healing, and then you can progress to a higher, cognitive level of treatment. Well, that idea misses the point that you are *now* an adult with adult language skills, and that the point of the treatment is to give adult linguistic expression to a trauma that overwhelmed you as an infant precisely because the trauma could not then be contained symbolically in language. Thus it will be important that you now "tell your story" about your childhood pain.

Learning to speak about the pre-verbal pain and terror does several things. It provides a sense of *safety*, through an acceptance of your thoughts and feelings as non-threatening; it *desensitizes* you to the troubling aspects of your memories of the traumatic experience; and it integrates positive *growth* into your lifestyle. Thus you can draw wisdom from pain and tragedy.

☑ To heal this rage, it will be necessary to recognize that it affects you to the core of your very being—that is, to recognize how every childhood wound from your parents' lack of real love continues to live in every emotional hurt inflicted on you in the present. It takes good, honest scrutiny to do this, along with gentle patience, to learn this emotional sensitivity.

☑ It will also be necessary *in every moment* to notice how impulses to rage follow right on the heels of feelings of insult, abandonment, and helplessness.

☑ Finally, it will be necessary to make the conscious decision to push past your impulses of hostility and revenge and respond to all of your feelings in every moment without succumbing to the pernicious lure of anger.

Let's continue now to some specific guidance on how to carry out the preceding points.

The Emotional Triggers that Precede Anger

In order to avoid falling into anger as soon as you feel hurt by someone, learn to scrutinize carefully each event that upsets you. Ask yourself in the moment these questions: *What are your emotions about that event? How have you felt hurt?* Feel the hurt. Feel the pain of your helplessness— but feel it without getting angry. Notice that hurt always precedes anger because anger is a hostile *reaction* to feeling hurt.

A common way to block out unpleasant and frightening emotions, especially emotions of helplessness, is with anger, allowing free rein to impulses of hatred and revenge. When you get angry you don't really allow yourself to feel your inner vulnerability and hurt. All you can think about in the moment is your desire to get revenge, to defend your pride, to do something— anything—to create the feeling that you have power and importance. In essence, your outbursts of rage paradoxically hide your inner feelings of vulnerability, so you never recognize the hurt you're feeling that triggers your hostile reaction. All the bitterness and hostility is a big puff of smoke, an emotional fraud. It hardens your heart toward others so that you can seal off your own emotional pain.

The Emotional Bridge

Next, follow each example of hurt back into its roots in the past to all those times and circumstances in childhood when you felt the same way. Carefully scrutinize your childhood and examine your memories of painful events to discover what you were really feeling then, as a child.

Through your psychological and spiritual scrutiny you will come to understand that all the unpleasant and frightening emotions which you have been pushing out of awareness all your life have been secret, unconscious causes for all the problems and conflicts you have been experiencing all your life.

Remember, your impulsive reactions to present injuries are an unconscious reaction to the original emotions and fantasies you experienced, but suppressed,[3] in childhood. This is what is meant when someone is said to have *overreacted*: the person reacted to something said or done in the present that unleashed a hidden store of emotions from the past.

The Remedy

Having understood the previous two steps, now resolve to deal with future events according to the thoughts and emotions specific to that event. Do something constructive and creative about each event, something emotionally honest and not based in the desire to hurt others as you have been hurt. That is, choose something different from the insanity of modern culture's Satanic Rule of hatred and revenge: "Do to others what they do to you." Endeavor to express your thoughts and feelings to others without blaming or criticizing them. Endeavor to recognize the emotional hurt that underlies all your anger, and then come to terms with that hurt in a responsible manner (see Chapter 20) rather than just get angry.

> Saint Peter, in one of his letters, tells us to be of one mind, sympathetic, loving toward one another, compassionate, humble. Do not return evil for evil, or insult for insult, he says, but, on the contrary, a blessing. . . . (see 1 Peter 3:8–9a).

Keep in mind here that the part of you that falls into that characteristic BPD rage has the emotional maturity of a two year old child. When you feel frightened, it's as if you become two years old again; you become a terrified and angry child, and an angry victim, and all rationality and trust in God flies out the window. You will attack anything and anyone, friend or foe, to protect yourself in the moment.

It will be important, then, that the *adult part* of you be able to listen to the *frightened child part* of you, as a wise adult would listen to a child: with patience and kindness.

Be gentle while the child cries and screams. Give the child permission to cry. Then be firm in guidance. "You're crying because you feel unloved, right? Well, to be loved it is necessary to show love to others. So let your tears speak; understand what occurred—and then find a way for everyone to be treated with respect."

In the realm of pure psychology, constantly making that decision to love, rather than to hate, can be very difficult. Religion, however, offers an elegant solution: Christian love.

Love: The Imitation of Christ

Christ endured intense suffering for our sake and He promised never to abandon us. And He left us His sacraments to console us and strengthen us.

Thus, whenever you feel hurt or insulted by anyone, put it in perspective. Compared to the embrace of divine love, all human insult is irrelevant. All human insult is irrelevant because the desire to receive human love is irrelevant. All human love is subject to lapses, failures, and even betrayals. Yes, all children need the love of a mother and a father, yet even parental love is subject to failures, and no other human love can replace failed parental love. Only God's love can bring healing because God's love is perfect and never fails.

With Christ, there's nothing to fear. If only we are willing to say, "Jesus, I trust in You!"—and mean it from the depths of out hearts—we will never have to fear abandonment by others.

You will be at peace, then, if you surrender your pride to Christ. Accept the fact that without Christ you are helpless and alone. Stop expecting to receive love from others and instead focus on giving to others the love that you receive only from Christ.

> The spiritual realm has an axiom: You cannot hate others and pray for them at the same time.
>
> However, it's not quite that simple. Praying for someone who has hurt you will not make your feelings of irritation dissolve immediately; prayer simply allows you to "sit with" your emotional pain and feelings of helplessness while putting them into the hands of God so that those persons who hurt you can be dealt with

according to God's perfect justice. [4]

The Mystical Price of Love

Yet there is a price to all this. Just as Christ suffered for us, to redeem us from sin, so we, in accepting His loving embrace, are obligated to embrace our own suffering for the sake of others. We are called, therefore, not only to set aside all desire to avenge our injuries (because this desire serves only to hide our wretchedness by defending our pride) but also to do so in the hope that our refusal to fall blindly into anger will be a source of healing for others.

> You say you want to be loved? Well, keep in mind that if you curse others, there will come a time when you will be cursed. If you hate others, there will come a time when you will be hated. And if you love others, well, there will come a time when you will be loved.

This price, then, explains why so many "Christians" fail at being Christian. No matter how much they say, "Jesus, I trust in You!" they really don't trust in Him at all because they fear what they will have to pay in order to trust Him: everything they have. That is, they will have to pay the price of *giving up* their basic and cherished belief that they are *entitled* to being loved by others.

They fear the price because deep in their hearts they cling to the sweet taste of their own rage with a secret, unconscious trust they have known like a good friend all their lives. They commit sin out of the pride of getting revenge for not being loved. They know that they are committing sin, but in the moment it tastes good. In their own fear, they create excuses to tell themselves that they really had no choice because they are such weak persons. Yet it's all an unconscious fraud to avoid the mystical price of love.

The Hard Work of Christian Prayer

It takes hard work to be a real Christian. The Catholic mystics have said this for ages. The only path to real love is through prayer and sacrifice in total surrender to Christ. Therefore, learn to pray by sitting quietly before God with all your emotional pain. Feel the pain—but feel it without anger. Admit that you cannot make others act as you would like them to act. Admit that you cannot save the world from itself. Admit your helplessness before God. Admit that without God you are nothing. Feel the nothingness and accept it. Accept that only in your helplessness and nothingness will you ever receive a mission from God to do anything meaningful. *You are not alone in your suffering.* God is with you in your weakness to help you repair your life—and it takes humility to admit this.

> To be taken with love for a soul, God does not look on
> its greatness, but on the greatness of its humility.
>
> — Saint John of the Cross[5]

If you are willing to learn this type of prayerful humility, you will then understand that God's love is always enough. But beware: the unspoken motto of BPD is "It's never enough."

When Someone You Know is BPD

The communication patterns of individuals with BPD symptoms tend to have the quality of "insanity"; that is, they can be dramatically impulsive and irrational. Being "nice" (e.g., appeasing, capitulating to demands, trying to avoid conflict) in response to such communication will not cure it. Instead, it will be essential that you use strong but sensitive boundaries (see Chapter 21) to contain the rage.

If the person is in a BPD rage, or is just blatantly rude, then use forceful and succinct containment of the unwanted behavior.

- *Contain the insanity.* When someone rants in BPD rage, more often than not facts are distorted, and trying to defend yourself against unjust or unfair accusations will be futile. So calmly but firmly say, "That was inappropriate and unnecessary. Knock it off!" or "Cut out the hostility! That's a sad lack of charity!"

If the person is in a relatively calm state of mind, then speak confidently yet politely to address the unwanted behavior.

- *Apart from containing the insanity, be careful not to tell anyone what to do.* State what *you* will do under specific circumstances. For example, instead of saying, "Stop cussing!" say, "If I hear cussing then I'm going to [*leave the room, or hang up the phone, etc.*]."

- *Be willing to teach.* When someone speaks to you with hostility, smile and say calmly, "I'm not going to listen to anything said with rudeness, but if you speak to me kindly then I will be glad to listen to you. So go ahead, try saying it again, but with gentleness."

- *Resist the temptation to respond to accusatory e-mail, text, or telephone messages.* Responding to such messages puts you in the impossible place of trying to reason with insanity. The only sane recourse is to ignore all such messages.

APPENDIX III:
HEALING THE LACK OF A FATHER

So what can you do if your own father's lack has left you lacking? What can you do if, despite your best attempts on your own, you still feel doubtful, insecure, fearful, and interiorly embarrassed for not living a holy life?

Well, regardless of the lack of your own father, you can be led through Christ to the utter fullness of life in God the Father. To do this, though, you must set aside your unconscious anger at your father and take full personal responsibility to remedy what is lacking in you.

"But wait," you say, "I have no issues with my father. We got along well together. My mother was the cruel one." In that case, don't be deceived by sentimentality. Yes, you have to resolve much anger at your mother—yet, in addition to that, you will find considerable unconscious anger at your father: for his being too physically ill, too mentally ill, or just too weak or cowardly to stop your mother's abuse.

Therefore, acknowledge what was "stolen" from you as a child; feel the pain of that loss and bring it all to Christ;

acknowledge that your father's behavior was wrong and yet put justice in God's hands so as to give up hate for your father; and then turn to Christ in full confidence to lead you to the resources you need to teach you what you never learned as a child.

Putting It Into Practice

Pay attention to times when you get stuck, when you feel blocked, when you lose confidence, when you get impatient, when you doubt yourself, etc. At those times, tell yourself something like the following:

"OK. I'm feeling [stuck, unable to concentrate, indecisive, whatever]. This is happening because of what my father failed to do for me. He failed to [love me, provide guidance to me, give me encouragement, teach me confidence, whatever].

"But now I know that my difficulties are resulting from his failures. In the past, I would have blamed myself. I would have said that I was bad or that I was defective. Now that I know that I am feeling this way because of what my father failed to do for me, I no longer have to blame myself. I have skills, I have talents—they just never got developed properly under my father's guidance.

"So now that I know that I'm not at fault, I will go about learning how to develop my skills and talents. I will take personal responsibility for myself.

"Moreover, I'm not alone. I have God to help me. God loves me and cares for me. Together—God and myself—we can change my life and provide for me what my father never did.

"In all of this, I won't blame my father because blaming him is like hating him, and blame only keeps me in the place of a victim. Blame makes me angry, and anger at him makes me feel guilty, and guilt cripples me. I will be honest with myself about what my father failed to do, and that's not blaming him—it's just about getting to the truth. The truth will set me free, and so I will be free to join with God to fulfill my talents."

Summary

To do this, you must really "die" to yourself. Sever all of your vain attachments to the world and all of your illusory social identifications that only hide your inner insecurity and wretchedness. Take up the task of inner scrutiny through true spiritual purgation.

None of this is easy. It doesn't happen just by thinking about it. It requires mental and physical discipline. It takes hard work. It takes courage. And, if your father was lacking, then you lack courage, don't you? Therefore, the only way to learn to trust in God is to strip away everything we use to hide from Him so that, left with nothing of our own making—with no arrogance, no pride, no hatred, and no bitterness for what others have done to us—we have no choice but to acknowledge our wounds, feel the pain, bring it all to Christ, and depend on Him alone.

APPENDIX IV:
GRATITUDE

A good way to facilitate a constant dynamic awareness of the presence of God in your life is to develop a mystical emotional engagement with your environment, along with a sense of gratitude for what God has given you, so as to maintain a constant focus on what you have been given, rather than dwell upon feelings of deprivation. Here are some suggestions.

In the morning, as you wake up, make the *Sign of the Cross* and give thanks to God for being alive, for being able to breath, and for being able to pray. As you stand up and walk, give thanks to God for allowing you to move, to stand up, and to walk.

Then let your imagination encompass all that is in your house and give thanks to, and bless, it all. (For example, say softly, or just think the words, "Thank you for being here and for all you do; may our Lord Jesus Christ bless you and protect you in the name of the Father and of the Son and of the Holy Spirit.") If you have house plants or pets, or if other persons live in the house, hold in your heart blessings for their physical or spiritual growth and for protection from evil.

Whenever you prepare to leave your home, say the prayer to the *Venerable Cross* (see below). Then give a blessing to all that is in the house, and finally go before the Crucifix and place yourself consciously in God's protection. "O God, protect me from all the filth and corruption in the world. Send a cohort of holy angels to protect me from evil. I believe, I adore, I hope, and I love, and I ask that my prayers and sacrifices might bring to contrition some of those who now do not believe, do not adore, do not hope, and do not love."

When you prepare to drive your car, make the *Sign of the Cross* and give the car a blessing. Then say the prayer to *Saint Michael the Archangel* (see below) for protection.

Throughout the day, be mindful of God's presence and ask for guidance in everything you are about to do. Say a prayer, such as, "O God, I am so alone; help me to do this."

Whenever you have to face an unknown situation, say to yourself, "Trust in God; I don't need to worry about this now. God will let me know what I need to do when I need to do it."

Throughout the day, give a blessing to everything you eat or drink, even if you are taking only a sip of water. Make the *Sign of the Cross* and say, "Bless us, O Lord, and these

Thy gifts which we are about to receive from Thy bounty, through Christ our Lord." Be grateful for everything that nourishes you, for without even the most lowly of God's gifts you would perish.

Also, silently give thanks for and give a blessing to everything you use during the day. Be aware of what you are using while you are using it and don't use anything casually; be aware of its place in all that God has provided for you. For example, even as you throw something into the garbage, silently give it a blessing and thank it for the service it has provided. In doing this, you will learn to experience all things around you as dynamic participants in God's creation, rather than as mere objects to manipulate.

At noon and at 6:00 in the evening, stop what you are doing and pray the *Angelus* (see below). It can be helpful to set alarms on your cell phone or other device to remind you of these hours.

Whenever you return home, go before the Crucifix and give thanks for your safe return. Then let your imagination encompass all that is in your house give a greeting and a blessing to it all.

At the end of every day, just before going to bed, give thanks to God for all the help, guidance, and protection you have received during the day.

As you lie in bed preparing to sleep, say, over and over

until you fall asleep, "Into Your hands, O Lord, I commend my spirit" and, whenever you wake up during the night, resume saying the prayer until you fall asleep again.

PRAYER TO THE VENERABLE CROSS

Use this prayer for personal protection against evil.
It is not a formal exorcism.

LET God arise and let His enemies be scattered, and let them that hate Him flee from before His face. As smoke vanishes, so let them vanish; as wax melts before the fire, so let the demons perish from the presence of them that love God and who sign themselves with the sign of the Cross and say in gladness: Rejoice, most venerable and life-giving Cross of the Lord, for Thou drive away the demons by the power of our Lord Jesus Christ Who was crucified on Thee, Who went down to hell and trampled on the power of the devil, and gave us Thee, His venerable Cross, for the driving away of every adversary. O most venerable and life-giving Cross of the Lord, help me together with our most pure Lady, the Mother of God and Ever-Virgin Mary, and with all the saints, unto the ages. Amen.

Adapted from a traditional Russian Orthodox prayer.

The Cross will protect you when you stop wearing it
around your neck like a piece of jewelry
and start carrying it in your heart.

Prayer to Saint Michael

Saint Michael the Archangel, defend us in battle; be our protection against the wickedness and snares of the devil. May God rebuke him, we humbly pray: and do thou, O Prince of the heavenly host, by the power of God, cast into hell Satan and all the evil spirits who prowl about the world seeking the ruin of souls.

The Angelus

The Angel of the Lord declared unto Mary.
And she conceived by the Holy Spirit.

Hail, Mary, full of grace! The Lord is with thee. Blessed art thou amongst women, and blessed is the fruit of thy womb, Jesus! Holy Mary, Mother of God, pray for us sinners now and at the hour of our death. Amen.

Behold the handmaid of the Lord.
Be it done unto me according to Thy word.

Hail Mary . . .

And the Word was made flesh.
And dwelt amongst us.

Hail Mary . . .

V.   Pray for us, O Holy Mother of God,

R.   That we may be made worthy of the promises of Christ.

Let us pray—Pour forth, we beseech Thee, O Lord, Thy grace into our hearts; that we, to whom the Incarnation of Christ Thy Son was made known by the message of an angel, may, by His Passion and Cross, be brought to the glory of His Resurrection, through the same Christ our Lord. Amen.

APPENDIX V:
DELIVERANCE PRAYER

To strengthen your resolve to fight temptations, make use of this prayer for deliverance and repeat it as often as necessary.

In the name of our Lord Jesus Christ, I renounce the false beliefs [specify] and the unhealthy behaviors [specify] to which I am prone and the hold they have over me; and I affirm the true beliefs [specify] and the healthy behaviors [specify] which I intend to carry out.

In the name of our Lord Jesus Christ, I renounce the spirit of [addictions, anger, anxiety, boredom, deadened emotional awareness, demoralization, doubt, eroticism, fear, frustration, gluttony, guilt, hatred, illness, intestinal distress, loneliness, lust, mania, oppression, pornography, pride, revenge, reward craving, self-blame, self-loathing, self-punishment, sensuality, weariness, victimization, violence, etc.] and the hold it has over me.

And I ask our Lord Jesus to send it to the foot of

the Cross.

This process is not a matter of "getting rid" of the temptations but of fighting them with love—that is, with your love for God.

Keep in mind also that when a temptation is renounced and warded off it can return again even stronger if you have not made dedicated effort to alter the lifestyle that has drawn you into temptation in the first place. Endeavor, therefore, to maintain a holy lifestyle of chastity, humility, modesty, constant prayer, and detachment from the corrupt social world. Then, with little to feed upon, temptations will lose their hold on you.

APPENDIX VI:
A LOVE LETTER

I love you. I have always loved you. I was present in love when you were conceived, even though your parents did not see Me. I was present in love when you were born, even though your mother did not see Me. I was present in love when you cried, even though you did not see Me.

Throughout your life, even in the moments of your hatred and anger, and yes, even in the blindness of your despair, I loved you, knowing that you did not see Me because you so rarely saw your parents acknowledge your deep and precious needs. Yet I could not stop them from being what they were, because I loved them too. I could not force them to love, because love must be pure, like a child's love. I could not stop them from hurting you, but I protected you to the extent that you were able to accept My protection.

In that same love I call you to Me now. Turn away from sin and come to Me. I wait for you. I wait with love. And only you, you alone, have the power to prevent your coming to Me.

I know your pain, and in knowing it as I know My own Heart, I send My blessings as your LORD—and friend—*Jesus.*

APPENDIX VII:
LACK OF TRUST IN GOD

I'll just put this bluntly: I have a problem trusting God. I just can't trust God's providence. I see God as always angry with me, and the failures in my job and lack of progress seem to be punishment for my great sins. I haven't been diagnosed, but I fit many symptoms of borderline personality disorder, anxiety disorder—envy, jealousy, pride, suspicious of others, secretive, all of that.

I'm a Catholic convert, but born and raised Protestant. Converted three years ago when I was 29. I attend weekly Mass, sometimes daily Mass, go to confession semi-regularly.

Recently, I've been getting more pressure at work, and all I'm doing now is failing.

I'm having emotional breakdowns, and I just blame God and get angry at Him because He claims He takes care of us (like the birds of the sky) but I'm at a crisis point with no help in sight. The success of others makes me insecure and envious. I don't desire great success, just enough for my station in life and vocation. I'm just tired of the constant failed expectations, disappointments, and false hope.

Recently I've been having suicidal thoughts, just thoughts, not actual will to carry it out. I wonder how my body would look splattered on the ground, or if I shoot myself how the blood spray pattern would look. Maybe I'm being overly dramatic and catastrophic.

I just don't know how to cope anymore. God who I thought would take care of me is just standing by watching me suffer with great anxiety and fear. He told us not to worry. Well, it's not like I want to worry. It just happens.

I pray the chaplet of Divine Mercy and Rosary every day.

But there's no way out of this. I just don't have the energy anymore to gather together the little bit of hope left in God... only to be disappointed...again and again and again.

How do I trust God? I know I'm supposed to, but I can't.

Although you will be surprised to hear it, the truth is not only that God has not been punishing you, but that you have been punishing yourself. Throughout your childhood you experienced complex emotional pain, but, just like a multitude of others who are afflicted with the same problem, you find it terrifying to admit that your parents could have mistreated you. Consequently, you have been unconsciously trying to protect your parents from responsibility for their failures, and you do that by labeling yourself as the failure. It's as if you have put a curse on yourself to shield your parents from any accusation of their wrongdoing.

This is actually a common psychological problem in some cultures—for example, Asian cultures—where it is unthinkable to say anything negative about one's parents. It's also a common problem in the Catholic Church regardless of culture, simply because the Scriptural admonition to "honor your father and your mother" is commonly misinterpreted and distorted into the idea that parents can do no wrong and that a child owes them total allegiance no matter what they do.

But when parents are domineering or controlling they cheat their children of the healthy autonomy and individuality necessary for the children to work out their salvation, and the effects, as you have so clearly described in regard to your story, amount to a pernicious curse of repeated self-sabotage and failure. Even though you don't want it, it just "happens" because it's all unconscious.

The False Beliefs Behind the Curse

Behind the curse is a fundamental unconscious false belief that you are defective. This belief usually gets expressed consciously as "God hates me." Underneath this belief, though, several other beliefs work a secret havoc. "I'm not worthy." "I don't matter." "I don't deserve to succeed." "I have no right to be independent." "I will die without my parents." "My obligation is to serve my parents." "My parents need me."

These are all false beliefs, and they work like poison against you.

They can, however, be overcome.

The process of refuting negative beliefs can be done in psychotherapy, and it can also be done on your own through study, meditation, and prayer. Regardless of how it's done, though, one key element in the process must be carefully acknowledged: you must feel the pain now, as an adult, of the mistreatment inflicted on you in childhood. It's not sufficient to "know" intellectually what was inflicted on you; you must feel the pain into the depths of your heart. Myriads of tears must be shed; let them speak.

Let your tears speak openly of the pain. Bring the pain before God through prayer.

Without Blame and Anger

Yet be careful to not fall into blaming your parents; that is, state the facts of what *good* they did for you, as well as what *harm* they did to you, and what they *failed to do* for you—but always remember that you must take responsibility for remedying the deficiencies within you. You must take responsibility for paying the price of remedying those deficiencies. You must take responsibility for doing the hard work of the healing. Moreover, it must all be done without blame and anger.

Furthermore, be careful to not fall into blaming God. God has been giving you all the graces you need to heal from the pain of your childhood, but, despite all of the Masses you have attended and all the prayers you have said half-heartedly and out of duty, you have been throwing those graces onto the ground, spitting on them, and trampling them into the dirt. All that ingratitude was all done to avoid the terror of admitting that, throughout your childhood, your parents did not love you in the true sense of Christian love for a child. To avoid that terror you put a curse on yourself: you convinced yourself that you had to serve your parents at all costs—and, sure enough, the cost has been *you*.

NOTES

CHAPTER 3
MARRIAGE

1. See Aristotle, *Rhetoric* ii, 4. Saint Thomas Aquinas, in his *Summa Theologica* I–II, 26, 4, used this same definition of love, acknowledging that it came from the writings of the ancient Greek philosopher Aristotle.

2. See Jacques Lacan, *The Four Fundamental Concepts of Psychoanalysis*, trans. Alan Sheridan (New York: W. W. Norton, 1981), p. 133:

"In persuading the other that he has that which may complement us, we assure ourselves of being able to continue to misunderstand precisely what we lack."

CHAPTER 4
DIVORCE

1. Richmond, R. L. (1997). The fourth pleasing idea. *American Psychologist, 52,* 1244.

CHAPTER 5
THE FATHER

1. If the father doesn't do his job, but if the mother has any faith, the child may turn to God the Father for protection. Sadly, if both parents are failures, then the child will not have any knowledge of God the Father, and so there will be great suffering throughout his or her life unless a conversion experience leads to an encounter with God's love and protection.

2. Schnitzer PG, Ewigman BG. Child deaths resulting from inflicted injuries: household risk factors and perpetrator characteristics. *Pediatrics.* 2005 Nov; 116(5), 687–93:

"Young children who reside in households with unrelated adults are at an exceptionally high risk for inflicted-injury death. Most perpetrators are male, and most are residents of the decedent child's household at the time of injury."

CHAPTER 6
ANGER

1. For more explanation of this psychological fact that anger is a desire and not a feeling, see Chapter 46.

2. For more information about coping with anger, see my book *Anger and Forgiveness* (4th edition).

CHAPTER 7

DOMESTIC VIOLENCE

1. American Psychiatric Association: *Diagnostic and Statistical Manual of Mental Disorders*, Fourth Edition. Washington, DC: American Psychiatric Association, 1994.

2. The concept of *locus of control* (from the Latin *locus*, place) refers to the psychological "place" in which a person puts responsibility for the outcomes of various life situations. Persons with an *internal locus of control* perceive that they can personally affect the outcome of a situation, whereas persons with an *external locus of control* attribute outcomes not so much to personal actions as to the actions of other people—or luck.

See Rotter, J. B. (1966). Generalized expectancies for internal versus external control of reinforcement. *Psychological Monographs, 80*, 1–28.

3. If one person is injured by another, we could say that the two persons are "pushed apart" by the injury, and so, if they are to become friendly again, this gap between them must be repaired—they must be reconciled. *Reconciliation* comes from the Latin words *re-* "again," and *conciliare* "to bring together," so reconciliation means "to bring together—or to make friendly—again."

The act of reconciliation involves two parts: *forgiveness*, which occurs when the offended person stops wishing for harm to come to the offender, and r*epentance*, which occurs when the offender expresses sorrow for the offense.

Chapter 10
LUST AND VIOLENCE

1. See http://nauticom.net/www/chuckm/whmte.htm for an image of Walt Kelly's 1971 Pogo cartoon.

Chapter 12
DISOBEDIENCE

1. Experiences of resentment are human and normal; you can't get through a day without encountering resentment about something. You fall into sin, though, when you use the psychological defense of *denial* to hide this resentment from yourself. Denying your resentment only pushes it into the unconscious, and clinging to unconscious resentment is what *carrying resentment* means.

Chapter 14
PHYSICAL AFFECTION

1. See, for example, Harlow, H. F., and Zimmerman, R. R. (1959) Affectional responses in the infant monkey. *Science*, 130, 421–432.

2. Speaking truth about the harmful effects of someone's behavior is not a form of judgment that is forbidden to us; it's simply a matter of stating the facts. To protect ourselves in life we must always make judgments about

whether things are safe or unsafe, true or untrue, sound or unsound, and so on.

Spiritual judgment regarding a person's salvation or doom, however, is forbidden to us and belongs only to Christ. This judgment will occur after death when the person stands before Christ and has to face a complete accounting for the facts of his or her life.

CHAPTER 15
EDUCATING CHILDREN

1. The mandate of Christianity is *love*; the greatest commandment is to love God with all your heart, all your soul, all your strength, and all your mind.

CHAPTER 19
GROWTH

1. Consider the following passages from Scripture:

> Do nothing out of selfishness or out of vainglory; rather, humbly regard others as more important than yourselves, each looking out not for his own interests, but everyone for those of others. (See Philippians 2:3–4)

> Finally, all of you, be of one mind, sympathetic, loving toward one another, compassionate, humble. Do not return evil for evil, or insult for insult; but, on the con-

trary, a blessing, because to this you were called, that you might inherit a blessing. (See 1 Peter 3:8–9)
Brothers, even if a person is caught in some transgression, you who are spiritual should correct that one in a gentle spirit, looking to yourself, so that you also may not be tempted. Bear one another's burdens, and so you will fulfill the law of Christ. (See Galatians 6:1–2)

I, then, a prisoner for the Lord, urge you to live in a manner worthy of the call you have received, with all humility and gentleness, with patience, bearing with one another through love, striving to preserve the unity of the spirit through the bond of peace. (See Ephesians 4:1–3)

All bitterness, fury, anger, shouting, and reviling must be removed from you, along with all malice. Be kind to one another, compassionate, forgiving one another as God has forgiven you in Christ. (See Ephesians 4:31–32)

All of these passages point to the core Christian ideal of setting aside pride, competition, criticism, sarcasm, manipulation, and so on, for the sake of mutual cooperation in the task of living the Christian faith.

CHAPTER 21
BOUNDARIES

1. See Ezekiel 33:7–9. This passage concerns the re-

sponsibility of warning others of their sins when inspired by God to do so. God told Ezekiel that, when He warns someone that he shall die because of his sins, "and you do not speak out" to dissuade the wicked man from his way, not only would he (that is, the wicked man) die for his guilt, but also God would hold Ezekiel responsible for the wicked man's death. "But if you warn the wicked man, trying to turn him from his way," God told Ezekiel, "and he refuses to turn from his way, he shall die for his guilt, but you shall save yourself." This shows that responsibility is in giving a warning, not in making the offender change his or her behavior.

2. Note, however, that laws are hierarchical. If state law contradicts federal law, federal law has precedence over state law. Similarly, if federal law contradicts divine law, divine law has precedence over federal law.

3. See Chapter 48.

CHAPTER 25
WHEN CHILDREN FALL

1. In Galatians 5:22–23 Saint Paul names nine fruits of the Holy Spirit: love, joy, peace, patience, kindness, generosity, faithfulness, gentleness, and self-control. Later Church tradition, however, lists twelve fruits of the Holy Spirit: charity, joy, peace, patience, kindness, goodness, generosity, gentleness, faithfulness, modesty, self-control,

and chastity (for more information, see the *Catechism of the Catholic Church*, §1832).

Chapter 27
Cultural Subversion

1. During WWII, President Roosevelt privately said to Treasury Secretary Henry Morgenthau, Jr., and a Catholic appointee, Leo Crowley, "You know this is a Protestant country, and the Catholics and Jews are here under sufferance." See *The Conquerors: Roosevelt, Truman and the Destruction of Hitler's Germany 1941–1945* (Simon & Schuster) by Michael Beschloss.

2. St. Catherine & Don Cattaneo Marabotto. *The Spiritual Doctrine of Saint Catherine of Genoa* (Rockford, IL: TAN Books and Publishers, 1989). See "The Life and Doctrine of St. Catherine of Genoa," Chapter XX.

3. In the Prologue to *The Ascent of Mount Carmel*, Saint John of the Cross wrote that "we are not writing on moral and pleasing topics addressed to the kind of spiritual people who like to approach God along sweet and satisfying paths. We are presenting a substantial and solid doctrine for all those who desire to reach . . . nakedness of spirit."

That's a strong statement, and yet it was spoken in all humility by a man who knew deep in his heart, from personal experience, that God calls us all, purely out of love for us, to a healing sanctity. We are all called to be saints, because saints are made, not born. And saints are made when wretched, broken hearts open themselves to divine love and, being willing to pay the price of holiness, dedicate themselves, through sacrifice, obedience, and prayer, to the service of others.

See *The Collected Works of St. John of the Cross*, trans. K. Kavanaugh and O. Rodriguez (Washington, DC: ICS Publications, 1991).

4. See *The Imitation of Christ*, trans. William Creasy (Notre Dame, IN: Ave Maria Press, 1989), 1.11.

5. For example, see Matt Baglio, *The Rite: The Making of a Modern Exorcist* (New York: Doubleday, 2009). The bibliography therein also references many other books pertaining to exorcism.

Chapter 28
too busy?

1. From an excerpt of Saint Francis de Sales' *The Introduction to the Devout Life*. This excerpt can be found in the *Liturgy of the Hours*; see the Office of Readings for 24 January.

2. The prayer is short and simple: "Lord Jesus Christ, Son of God, have mercy on me." Repeat this prayer silently, as a sort of ongoing background task, while performing all other activities. It will actually increase your concentra-

tion and focus in doing your work.

3. *The Collected Works of St. John of the Cross*, op. cit., "The Living Flame of Love," ch. 2, no. 27 (p. 667).

Chapter 31
botched

1. *The Spiritual Doctrine of Saint Catherine of Genoa*, op. cit., "Spiritual Dialog," First Part, Chapter XII.

Chapter 33
anger at parents

1. Pornography derives from the desire to defile another person. To most persons today it may seem that pornography is simply about sensual pleasure, but when the human body is made into a biological toy, it is stripped of all human dignity, and this defilement is an act of hatred and aggression. The hostility may be unconscious or it may be openly violent, but, either way, it has its basis in resentment.

The resentment goes back to the parents. Deep down, under all the apparent excitement, and despite the attraction to what is *seen*, lurks the dark urge to hurt and insult—to "get back at"—what is *behind the scenes*: a mother who devoured, rejected, or abandoned, rather than nurtured, or a father who failed to guide and protect.

CHAPTER 34
UNCONSCIOUS ANGER

1. See the Office of Readings for the Saturday of the thirty-second week in ordinary time, in the *Liturgy of the Hours*.

2. In Canto I of Book I (Hell) of Dante's *Divine Comedy*, Dante finds himself lost in a dark woods (symbolizing the spiritual blindness of a heart hardened by sin). He tries to escape by climbing up a beautiful mountain, but he is driven back to the woods by three animals, a leopard (symbolizing lust), a lion (symbolizing violence) and a wolf (symbolizing malice). Back in the woods he meets the shade of Virgil, an ancient Roman poet, who proposes to guide Dante down through Hell to get to Purgatory and ultimately Paradise.

> "The Mountain, which on the mystical level is the image of the Soul's Ascent to God, is thus on the moral level the image of Repentance, by which the sinner returns to God. It can be ascended directly from the 'right road' but not from the Dark Wood because there the soul's cherished sins have become, as it were, externalized, and appear to it like demons or 'beasts' with a will and power of their own, blocking all progress. Once lost in the Dark Wood, a man can only escape by so descending into himself that he sees his sin, not as an external obstacle, but as the will to chaos and death within him (Hell). Only when he has 'died to sin' can he

repent and purge it. Mount Purgatory and the Mountain of Canto I are, therefore, really one and the same
mountain as seen on the far side, and on this side, of
the 'death unto sin.'"

[From Dorothy Sayers' commentary on Canto I of
Cantica I: Hell (*L'Inferno*) in Dante's *The Divine Com-
edy*, trans. Dorothy Sayers (Baltimore, MD: Penguin
Books, 1949).]

The "will to chaos and death" within us that Sayers describes is the futile desire to commit sin that characterizes
our fallen nature. The psychological implication of this is
that in order to attain holiness we must all descend into
the inner hell of a "desire to commit sin" that lurks in the
unconscious of us all and that will lead us to our doom unless we encounter it and pass beyond it with a courageous
holy desire for purification.

Chapter 45
SCRUPLES

1.   If you dwell upon a spontaneous fantasy for the sake
of pleasure or satisfaction, then it becomes a conscious act
of your will, and you are culpable for the sin of dwelling on
the fantasy.

So what does it mean to "dwell upon" a fantasy? Well,
if you pay only enough attention to the fantasy to understand something about the emotional pain from your
childhood that is driving the fantasy, then you are engag-

ing in *therapeutic healing,* and that's not a sin. But if you pay attention to the fantasy just to derive pleasure from it, then you are *dwelling upon the pleasure deriving from the disorder of the fantasy* and in that dwelling upon pleasure of a disorder you are committing a grave sin that needs to be confessed.

Note also that if you keep falling into the same sin over and over despite repeated confessions, then you are not confessing the real sin of anger at your parents (or anger at God) that the pleasure of the fantasies is working unconsciously to obscure. In such a case it will be necessary for you to face the emotional pain from your childhood that drives you into sin—the same emotional pain that your scruples are trying to hide.

2. See note 1 of this chapter.

Chapter 46
Anger Without Sin

1. Here are some examples of similar emotions: aggravated, annoyed, bothered, cross, displeased, distressed, exasperated, frustrated, goaded, grumpy, impatient, offended, overwrought, peeved, provoked, shaky, strained, tense, troubled, uncomfortable, upset, or vexed.

2. St. Thomas Aquinas, *Summa Theologica.* I-II, 26, 4.

Chapter 50
LUST AND MARRIAGE

1. See note 1 of Chapter 3.

2. Note the word "openness" in the phrase *openness to procreation*. This is not to say that every sexual act *must* produce a child. It means that the fundamental meaning of sexuality is in its procreative function—rather than as something done for fun or sport or entertainment or to soothe feelings of loneliness. To cast away the fundamental meaning of sexuality (as in masturbation, oral sex, anal sex, artificial birth control—or any act of sex done just for pleasure and stained with lust) is to fall into sin.

The *Catechism of the Catholic Church* expresses it this way in very strong language: ". . . every action which . . . proposes, whether as an end or as a means, to render procreation impossible is intrinsically evil" (§2370).

3. Keep in mind this analogy: *fire does not burn itself*. If two candle flames are put together, neither flame will hurt or damage the other. Therefore, only that which is not fire is burned by fire.

Thus, in the spiritual realm, the fire of God's love does not harm those who love God, but God's love does "burn" and torment whatever is not love.

Hence the fire of Purgatory is God's love purifying and burning out of repentant souls every worldly attachment that is not love, until those souls become pure in love and so are prepared to encounter God's love in heaven without being burned or harmed by it.

In contrast, God's love is a torment for unrepentant souls stained with mortal sin, and so they flee to hell, which is a "place" as far from God's love as possible. Still, even hell is not excluded from God's love, and so the tormenting fire of hell is really God's love that burns and torments those souls who are "not love" because in this life they have chosen lifestyles defiant of love, thereby refusing the opportunity to become love.

CHAPTER 55
THE YEARNING FOR UNION

1. *The Spiritual Doctrine of Saint Catherine of Genoa*, op. cit., Part III, Chapter VII.

2. *The Collected Works of St. John of the Cross*, op. cit., "The Spiritual Canticle," stanza 29 of the poem.

CHAPTER 58
CAREER OR FAMILY?

1. There are a multitude of unconscious ways to keep alive your resentments: argumentativeness, competitiveness, disobedience, protest, offenses to chastity, immodest clothing, smoking, eating disorders, marijuana use, alcohol abuse, tattoos, body piercing and disfigurement, shoplifting, gambling, risky thrill seeking, time-wasting

video games, occupational failure, and on and on. All of these self-defeating behaviors make a mockery of love and have in common one unconscious intent: to throw your failure back into your parent's faces as evidence of their failure to live a life of genuine love and mercy.

APPENDIX I
CATHOLIC COMPASSION

1. See note 2 of Chapter 50.

2. Saint Maria Faustina Kowalska. *Diary* (Stockbridge, MA: Association of Marian Helpers, 2003), ¶324.

3. The spiritually negative emotion of hate does not necessarily mean a passionate loathing; it can just as well be a quiet, secret desire for harm to come upon someone or something. Hate can be a subtle thing, therefore, and it often is experienced more unconsciously than consciously. Consequently, it will often be very easy to deny that you *feel* any hatred for anyone at all simply because hate, being a desire, can manifest without any feelings.

Most often, this hatred will be unconsciously directed at your parents because of their failures in love; that is, in their failures to understand your emotional experiences and to guide you rather than control and manipulate you to serve their desires. Whether your dysfunction be extreme—such as suicide, drug addiction, alcoholism, and personality disorders—or more subtle—such as perfectionism, chronic procrastination, a lack of success in a career, or even a rejection of Church teaching—it has the unconscious intent of hurting your parents by hurting yourself.

4. *Narcissism* refers to the desire to make oneself be seen and noticed; its operations are concerned entirely with the self and its satisfactions, such that all motivation begins with the self and returns to the self.

> See Jacques Lacan, "The Partial Drive and its Circuit" and "From Love to the Libido." In *The Four Fundamental Concepts of Psychoanalysis.* (New York: W. W. Norton, 1981, pp. 194–195):
>
> ". . . The root of the scopic drive [i.e., the motivation to see and be seen—RLR] is to be found entirely in the subject, in the fact that the subject sees himself. . . . in his sexual member. . . . Whereas making oneself seen is indicated by an arrow that really comes back towards the subject, making oneself heard goes towards the other."

In contrast to the self-centered orientation of narcissism, Christ, *makes Himself heard* by compassionately calling us out of ourselves, to listen to Him, and to follow Him. He is the good shepherd; the sheep hear His voice as He calls them by name and leads them. The sheep follow Him because they recognize His voice (see John 10:4).

5. Those who do not understand the concepts of the un-

conscious—such as unconscious desire and unconscious anger—fear the unconscious, and so they eagerly take up the politically-correct ideology that we are "born with" our desires. Thus they refuse to take responsibility for their own psychological behavior.

6. Early in the 1960s, Stanley Milgram, a professor of social psychology at Yale University, conducted experiments about obedience to authority.

For example, see Milgram, S. Behavioral study of obedience. *Journal of Abnormal and Social Psychology*, 67 (1963): 371–378.

Milgram's experiments revealed a dark side of human nature: many persons were quite willing to obey an authority figure even if such obedience meant overriding their conscience and consequently inflicting severe pain on someone, even to the point of risking that person's serious physical injury or death. Moreover, even though the experiments were a deception (that is, the "electric shocks" that the subjects administered to the victims were not real, and the "victims" were actually part of the experiment, only pretending to feel pain), many of the subjects suffered considerable disillusionment and trauma to discover that they had the capacity within themselves—in obedience to authority and peer pressure—to inflict such agonizing torment on another person.

This should be a spiritual wake-up call to anyone who asserts that we can be good stewards of the Christian faith just by following our consciences about morality. Only a conscience firmly grounded in Catholic tradition has any hope of resisting the fraud and lies of social pressure.

7. P. Zimbardo. *The Lucifer Effect*. (New York: Random House, 2007).

8. Ibid., p. 443.

9. *The Collected Works of St. John of the Cross*, op. cit., "The Sayings of Light and Love," number 160 (p. 97).

10. See note 1 of Chapter 3.

APPENDIX II
BORDERLINE PERSONALITY DISORDER

1. For more information about coping with anger, see my book *Anger and Forgiveness* (4th edition).

2. The emotion of *hate* does not necessarily mean a passionate loathing; it can just as well be a quiet, secret desire for harm to come upon someone or something. Hate can be a subtle thing, therefore, and it often is experienced more unconsciously than consciously. Consequently, it will often be very easy to deny that you feel any hatred for anyone at all. Nevertheless, whether your dysfunction be extreme—such as suicide, drug addiction, alcoholism, and personality disorders—or more subtle—such as perfectionism, chronic procrastination, or a lack of success in a career—it all has an unconscious intent of hating and

hurting your parents (especially your father in regard to his lack of guidance, protection, or emotional involvement) by hating and hurting yourself. And, because this intent is unconscious, it can be maintained right into adulthood—even after your parents have died!

3. Many persons fear that in admitting that their parents hurt them it will condemn the parents to hell. Well, it's true that everyone, even your parents, will eventually have to stand before Christ in judgment (see Note 4 below), but if, by the time of their death, your parents have repented their sins they can receive Christ's mercy. No child, though, is responsible for a parent's salvation, and no child can protect a parent from God's justice.

4. We have all encountered individuals who commit offenses and seem to "get away with it." Although the irritation that we feel is justified, we can also be drawn into the desire to take matters into our own hands and get revenge. If we remember, however, that every crime—every sin—every offense against love—that a person commits is an offense against God that will be accounted for during his or her judgment at death, then we can understand that no one can evade God's perfect justice. All sins will be paid for. If the sins are not repented, they will be paid for in hell, but if the sins are repented they will be paid for in Purgatory, thus demonstrating that mercy is a fundamental part of God's justice. To trust in God's justice, then, is to set aside our anger for the injuries inflicted on us and to let God administer His own justice according to His

will.

5. *The Collected Works of St. John of the Cross,* op. cit., "The Sayings of Light and Love," number 103 (p. 92).

Appendix iv

deliverance

1. Some examples of negative/false beliefs:
     I don't matter.
     I have no right to succeed.
     I am worthless.
     I am bad.
     I am disgusting.
     I cannot figure this out on my own.
     I am ugly and no one will ever love me.
     Without my father's [or mother's] love I am
        doomed.
     I'll never change. I'm stuck.
     It's hopeless. Give it up.
     God hates me.

INDEX

ABOUT THE AUTHOR

Raymond Lloyd Richmond, Ph.D. earned his doctorate in clinical psychology and is licensed as a psychologist (PSY 13274) in the state of California. He completed a Post-doctoral Fellowship in Health Psychology.

Previous to his doctoral degree, he earned an M.A. in religious studies, an M.S.E. in counseling, and an M.S. in clinical psychology.

During the course of his education he received specialized training in Lacanian psychoanalysis, psycho-dynamic psychotherapy, cognitive-behavioral therapy, and hypnosis.

His clinical experience encompasses crisis intervention; treatment for childhood emotional, physical, and sexual abuse; trauma and PTSD evaluation and treatment; and treatment of psychotic, mood, and anxiety disorders.

Made in the USA
Middletown, DE
20 October 2023

41113721R00265